SOCIAL AND POLITICAL DYNAMICS OF THE INFORMAL ECONOMY IN AFRICAN CITIES

Nairobi and Harare

Kinuthia Macharia

University Press of America, Inc.
Lanham • New York • Oxford

Copyright © 1997 by
University Press of America,® Inc.
4720 Boston Way
Lanham, Maryland 20706

12 Hid's Copse Rd.
Cummor Hill, Oxford OX2 9JJ

Library of Congress Cataloging-in-Publication Data

Macharia, Kinuthia.
Social and political dynamics of the informal economy in African
cities : Nairobi and Harare / Kinuthia Macharia.
p. cm.
Includes bibliographical references and index.
1. Informal sector (Economics)--Africa--Case studies. I. Title.
HD2346.A55M33   1997 330.96--dc21 97-13284 CIP

ISBN 0-7618-0840-X (cloth: alk. ppr.)
ISBN 0-7618-0841-8 (pbk: alk. ppr.)

In loving memory of Mzee Nganga Macharia, my father-in-law, who departed us early this year.

Table of Contents

i

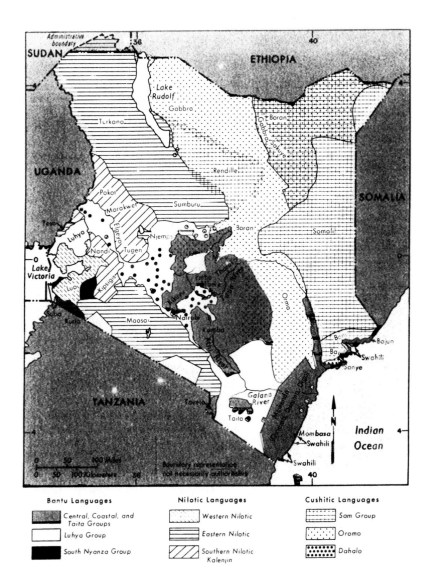

Map 1 Kenya: Ethnic distribution

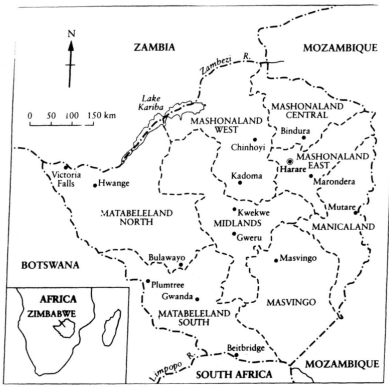

Map 2 Zimbabwe

Acknowledgments

I am indebted to many people, friends, members of my family and scholars who have contributed to the process leading to the production of this book.

The original ideas and the research were formulated at the University of California, Berkeley. Profs. Manuel Castells, Claude Fischer, Neil Smelser and the late Carl Rosberg were very helpful during the research and the writing of the doctoral dissertation that I have revised to become part of this book. The first three have continued to support my work and advise me whenever I have called them.

I am grateful to the United States Information Agency for the Fulbright Fellowship that supported my graduate studies and paid for the return trip to Kenya to conduct the original research. Other support came from the International Development Research Center, the Institute of International Studies in Berkeley and from the Institute of French Research in Africa (Nairobi office). The latter supported my research in Harare as well as a visit to the Republic of South Africa.

Colleagues in two institutions, Harvard University and now at American University have been supportive and constant reminders that "this book should be out." Graduate students at both institutions have been very helpful in suggestions as well as preparing the manuscript for the final production. I am grateful to Francesco Duina at Harvard University, to Jennifer Rothchild at American University, who did last minute proofreading and to Evita Bynum, also at American University, who has been my main support and architect especially in editing and formatting the manuscript. She has been instrumental in seeing this project through. Helen Hudson at UPA has been responsive whenever I had a quick question.

I am especially appreciative of my wife, Njeri, who has been very supportive and encouraging throughout the years that this book has moved from a simple idea to its present form. My children, Wanjiku and Macharia, have been a source of inspiration. My parents and family members have all been steadily supportive. Thank you all!

I should finally thank those engaged in the urban informal economy both in Nairobi and Harare who were willing to spend their valuable time answering my questions as I "intruded" into their business life.

All those who assisted in the study are absolved from blame or responsibility for any of its shortcomings. The views expressed are my own and not necessarily shared by supporting institutions, colleagues or friends.

Introduction

This book offers an explanation for the development and growth of the urban informal economy in African cities in the 1980s and the 1990s. During this period, the formal economy has been performing poorly in most African nations, partly due to the high foreign debts incurred in the 1970s, corrupt governments, bad weather (especially drought), civil wars and high population growth, among others. Increasing population growth in most countries has been unsupported by the skewed and unequal distribution of resources leading to wide gaps between the minority rich and the majority poor. The informal economy is not a solution to the poor economic performance or the rising poverty in the African nations. It should be seen as part of the solution. Its important contribution to the economic welfare of many urban and rural Africans is emphasized in this book because at least 40 percent of most African urban dwellers today are actively engaged in the informal economy. How does it operate and what are the social and political dynamics that continue to support the informal economy? Historically this economy has had to play "the cat and mouse game" to avoid official harassment. The evolvement of a government policy that eventually tolerates and somehow *supports* this economy is one concern of this book. The social support and the creation of a social capital through different forms of social networks have been the backbone and the mortar that have made the engine of the urban informal economy keep on running even when the going was tough. The role of the social networks and the State (which I argue is also informal) forms a good part of the discussion in this book. The contribution of the informal economy, especially the *Jua Kali* entrepreneurial activities in Kenya and small enterprise development in general, toward positive economic development for all is discussed and elaborated with the idea of combining the theory and the practice.

Although Africa is the least urbanized region in the world, with about 75 percent of its people still living in the rural areas, Africa has been experiencing the most rapid urbanization process. From 1980-1987, Africa's urban population grew at an annual rate of 6.9 percent that was the highest recorded anywhere in the world (World Bank 1988). A later (UNDP/World Bank 1992) study put the annual urban growth in Africa at 5.7 percent, which was still the highest except for the People's Republic of China which had an annual urban growth of 11 percent. The Latin America region had an annual urban growth of 3.2 percent. Urbanization in Africa increased rapidly beginning in the mid-1960s, a few years after most of the countries became independent from many years of colonial rule. Cities in Africa, especially in Kenya and Zimbabwe, were developed to suit colonial needs. The infrastructure in the African sections of the city was poor, the formal economy was not developed to suit the African and the informal economy was restricted. After independence, Africans in the formerly restricted countries could now migrate freely in the urban areas, most of them going to the capital cities where they had hopes of getting employment. The trend of rural-urban migration since the mid-1960s has continued to date, making Africa the most rapidly urbanizing region in the world. African cities are not the largest compared with some Latin American cities like Mexico City and São Paulo, each with about twenty million inhabitants. Fewer African cities like Cairo, Lagos and Kinshasa have more than five million inhabitants. While the cities may not be as large as in other regions, the rapid growth of some cities has caused a strain in the provision of many services—availability of employment, housing, sanitation—leading to environmental hazards, poor transportation and increasing urban violence and crime (as had been the case in Nairobi in the mid-1990s). Thus, the increasing rural-urban migration and natural population increase have contributed to over-urbanization in some African cities.

I use the term over-urbanization to refer to the excessive migration of the rural people into the urban areas. "Excessive" suggests that for the available amenities in a given urban setting, too many people are competing for them, and there is therefore not enough for all. In a city where there are inadequate houses for all and especially for the majority low income groups, few jobs to ensure steady incomes, clean water to reach all those living in the city, adequate transport and communication systems, that city is over-urbanized. Nairobi with about 2.5 million people and falling short of amply supplying all the amenities mentioned here is currently over-urbanized. Becker et al. (1994) argue against the idea of over-urbanization in Africa and assume that like the West and the newly industrialized countries in Asia, Africa will also go through a process of urbanization; as such there should be no alarm as to Africa's rapid urbanization. Absolute poverty in African nations and the conspicuous poverty in the cities which have not attracted as much investment (foreign or local) as those in Asia when it was urbanizing makes comparison of the two regions unbalanced. Dismissing "over-urbanization" and romanticizing urbanization in Africa misses the point, especially in this era of Structural Adjustment Programs, which translates as less public support in areas of health, transport, housing and employment, and thus more glaring urban poverty. Over-urbanization may be relative and indeed in some parts of Africa, Becker et al. (1994) may be right. However as an African rural-urban migrant to the city of Nairobi in the late 1970s, I have witnessed the city's high population growth due to both migration and natural increase. I have also witnessed the decline of services and the increase of the poor, underemployment and misemployment, informal settlements and the informal economy . The latter has become a partial solution to the over-urbanization problem. Urbanization should not be deliberately stopped by government policies because as I argue in this book, migrants make rational decisions and will move to the city despite the alleged problems. Indeed, this book discusses why despite awareness of the unemployment situation and the lack of housing, for example, the rural people continue to migrate to the cities. I have relied on information from the various African cities that I have visited, in which I observed business activities in the informal economy. These cities include, Johannesburg, Pretoria and Porchestrom in the Republic of South Africa, Arusha and Moshi in Tanzania and Lagos and Ibadan in Nigeria. Specific findings from studies in Nairobi, Kenya and Harare, Zimbabwe form the core discussions in this book.

The puzzling fact is that rural migration into African cities continues

in spite of over-urbanization. The African cities are the fastest growing
in the world and continue to do so despite inadequate amenities and
notable urban poverty. Labor-markets, hospitals, schools and housing
systems are saturated with people. Rural-urban migration, however,
continues. Factors that push rural people to leave their homes and
undertake long trips toward the city, without, apparently, the prospect of
a better life, must therefore be brought to light. The underlying
assumption in this book is that rural people are rational. They make
rational choices. This book rejects the hypothesis that myths, emotions
or other forms of potentially faulty economic reasoning cause migration.
It presumes rationality and seeks to find an answer to the puzzling
behavior of migrants who have now become city dwellers.

The main thesis of the book is that the informal economy is dynamic
and growing in Third World cities and particularly in the African cities.
Rural migrants pour into the cities because they hope that the informal
economy can offer them the possibility of a better life. They rely on their
social networks for initial accommodation and entry into the informal
economy.

The book is organized into ten chapters. Chapter 1 introduces the
problem of urbanization in Africa. I discuss the "Third World city" in
general and describe its major characteristics. The chapter also presents
a discussion of explanatory theories of urbanization and examines the
classical theories and their relevance to the Third World city. A
discussion of colonialism and urbanization in Kenya puts the colonial
origin of African cities in a particular perspective. Chapter 2 discusses
the general economy of Kenya and Zimbabwe with an emphasis on the
poor performance of the formal economy. A discussion of the cities of
Nairobi and Harare is also included. A discussion of the effects of the
Structural Adjustment Programs (SAPs) shows the continuing hardships
that the African urban and rural people have to deal with—among others,
engagement in the informal economy.

Chapter 3 defines the informal economy and discusses the
methodology used for the Nairobi study. To show the heterogeneity of
the informal economy, various sub-sectors in which Nairobi residents are
engaged are discussed. Chapter 4 continues from this and more
specifically discusses the *Jua Kali* sector in Kenya and its contribution to
development. Specific issues like the starting capital for those operating
various sectors, areas of concentration, definitions of *Jua Kali* (especially
the popular and the technical usage of the term) and the organization of
the *Jua Kali* and the Associations are addressed to show the various

dynamics that go on in this sector.

Chapter 5 discusses the role of the State, its contradictory role in promoting the informal economy, its passive and active support and its selective support for various informal economy activities. I explore an explanatory theory specifically for the Kenyan state's support for the informal economy after many years of its lack of support and periodic harassment that included jailing or imposing fines on those arrested for having been engaged in various informal economy activities. The importance of state support for the informal economy is emphasized in this chapter. Chapter 6 discusses the notion of informality pushing the discussion beyond the informal economy *per se* and looking at the informalization of the State in particular. The discussion in this chapter shows that the tolerance of the State toward the informal economy is as a result of the dynamics between the formal and the informal in all spheres of life and much more so in the African political system.

Chapter 7 discusses the significance of the social networks in the development and growth of the urban informal economy. The concept of trust leading to the formation of social capital that later translates into the real capital used to run the enterprises in the informal economy is documented here. The social functional use of ethnicity, rural place of origin, kinship and friendship are examined closely showing how each contributes to the proliferation of both urbanization and the informal economy. The social dynamics of the informal economy are highlighted in this chapter. Data from the original Nairobi study (1989), in which I interviewed 200 informal economy operators, with updates in the early to mid-1990s are presented and analyzed to show the importance of social networks.

Chapter 8 takes the idea of social networks further and specifically brings in a gender perspective in the full understanding of the dynamics involved in the urban informal economy. The functional uses of various social networks by women as they differ from those of men, the unequal representation of the men in the better paying informal economy enterprises and the limitations that face women on a daily basis are discussed here. Chapter 9 discusses the effects of small enterprise development (the informal economy) specifically in the alleviation of poverty. A discussion of what organizations like UNDP and the Kenya government could do to promote small scale enterprise as a possible way to alleviate poverty is given here. Lastly, Chapter 10 discusses conclusions and policy recommendations.

Those familiar with past literature on the informal economy may be surprised to find out that the State, in spite of its traditional opposition to any form of non-formal economy, has in fact selectively supported certain informal economic activities. To the image of government officials demolishing shopping stalls and kiosks in Nairobi, residential quarters and their confiscation of merchandise, one must superimpose the image of metal artisans and taxi-drivers receiving the favors of co-ethnic politicians, administrators and police officers. One must, in addition, recognize the changing nature of that relationship. Food sellers have in the past been allowed to operate near factories at a time when their cheaper prices would have lowered factory workers' cost of living and therefore enabled factory owners to pay lower wages. The "neurotic or unhappy marriage" (Smelser 1989) between the State and the informal economy is fully discussed in Chapter 5.

Whereas African urbanization and urban problems have been studied previously, this book builds on specific work started by the Manchester school of sociology (Gluckman 1960). Mitchell (1967) specifically tried to explain the importance of rural social networks for the new migrants in the urbanizing African environment. The Manchester school of sociologists and anthropologists studied the new towns in Zambia's copper belt, exploring among other things the readjustment of the rural African in the new urban environment. Other selected studies like Abner Cohen's (1969) focused on urban ethnicity and introduced the theme of "detribalization" and "retribalization" of the Hausas in what was a "foreign city" to them, Ibadan (which is predominantly Yoruba). It was another clarification of the ways Africans in the new towns had to deal with their "sameness" where "difference" among the many migrating ethnic groups was the norm. In East Africa, Hake (1977) studied a similar theme examining how "sameness" was useful in the self-help city that he described in his book, *The African Metropolis*. This book builds on some of the previous work to show the ever-increasing social functions that "sameness" exemplified via ethnicity, kinship, rural place of origin and friendship not only for settlement in the city but also in establishing entrepreneurial activities in the urban informal economy. The book also builds on the work that has been generally associated with the "informal sector" (Hart 1973; ILO 1972; King 1977; Horn 1994) by connecting the interplay between the State and the society's social networks in producing the dynamics that continue to produce the urban informal economy.

King (1996) revisited his earlier study following up on some of the artisans he had interviewed twenty years ago. Stren's work on housing

(1978) and on urban management crisis (1989) as well as his bibliographic essay on research studies done on African cities (1994) adds to our knowledge of the specific problems with African urbanization; Gugler and Flanagan (1978) among others have also contributed to the general understanding of Africa's changing urban phenomenon. The mentioned studies above did not discuss the social dynamics of the informal economy the way this book discusses it.

Most of the previous studies in African urbanization and the informal economy, particularly in Kenya do not discuss the social and political dynamics in the way these issues have been discussed in this book. Either such dynamics were taken for granted or the focus was on the economic significance of the informal sector. Whereas this book acknowledges the economic significance of the urban informal economy, especially in view of the poor performance of the formal economy, it also discusses the sociology of the informal economy, specifically the importance of social networks and how the operators use them in the founding and developing of their enterprises.

Students of development, both at universities and research institutes, should find this book to be a useful addition. Political scientists and sociologists should find the novel, network-based, perspective on the State challenging. The State's alleged role in the informal economy will probably cause some surprise and, to some, a sense of disbelief. My treatise of the African state as informal itself (hence its tolerance of the informal economy) should provide a challenging perspective in the conceptualization of the African state.

My special concern in writing this book, however, is to bring attention to the importance of the informal economy in a continuously rapidly urbanizing African continent. Indeed, the informal economy can be seen as a major attraction (pull factor) and an "indirect" causal factor for much of the rural-urban migration and the direction of economic growth for many Third World cities. The topic should prove valuable for further empirical research in other geographical areas and further theoretical elaborations. It remains one of the hopes for the majority of Africans who cannot get jobs in the formal economy both in the urban and the rural areas.

1

The Third World City

This book seeks to explain rapid urbanization in Third World cities. In light of that goal, a definition of Third World city is needed. The Third World city can be defined as an urban conglomeration characterized by a high degree of informality in the decision-making processes and the practice of the economy. Informality means reliance on nonofficial networks (ethnic, kinship, friendship-based). This is a sociological definition of the Third World city; it differs from geographical or other definitions in its emphasis on the activities of society and the roles of interpersonal relationships based on various kinds of social networks. It views all major social activities in the city as stemming from those networks.

MAJOR CHARACTERISTICS OF THIRD WORLD CITIES

Besides the informality of Third World cities, which I will discuss in greater length later, other major characteristics set them apart from other types of cities, especially those in the West. Drakakis-Smith (1987) identified these traits as over-urbanization, economic stagnation and low employment. I offer a similar, but expanded, list, as discussed below.

Primacy

In Third World countries, there tend to be one or two cities that have grown to enormous proportions when compared with other conglomerates. This is true for almost every country. Some striking examples are Bangkok, whose population is fifty times that of the second largest town in Thailand; Nairobi in Kenya, whose population is about five times that of the second largest town. The "primacy tendency" has an historical explanation. People migrating from the rural areas still go to the more established city where they hope to get a job faster than in the newer cities. Most of the primate cities are capitals of their countries and are expected to create jobs faster than the other places. Multinational companies tend to build their industries in these cities, afraid of venturing in new areas, and therefore create low-paying jobs because they realize they have an oversupply of labor. They can afford to underpay. Unfortunately, these multinational companies tend to have the backing from the leaders of the Third World governments who ensure weak trade unions that cannot possibly bargain for higher salaries. The leaders are also more keen on showing statistical numbers of those employed without really showing concern of the fact that the salaries are very low. It works out well as a political campaign to quote the numbers of jobs created without going into the details of what those jobs really entail.

Overcrowding

Much more than Western cities, the Third World city is conspicuously overcrowded both in the streets and in the housing estates. This is a result of continuous rapid rural-urban migration causing a condition of over-urbanization. The latter could be defined as a situation in which too many people migrate to the cities and the resources of the city cannot possibly suffice to accommodate the migrants. There are too many urbanites with too few resources. The overcrowding in the streets is very acute, especially among the low-income earners, the unemployed and those involved in the informal sector. Cases of shift sleeping in tiny rooms rented in various parts of town is common in some areas where mainly singles live and alternate work shifts.

In 1981-82, while conducting a study on women who work in industries in Kenya, I found room sharing organized around the work-shifts to be particularly the case of women workers in the Del Monte

Pineapple Canning factory in Thika, a town that is about thirty miles Northwest of Nairobi. Up to four women, some with children, shared a ten feet by ten feet room, sleeping on double decker beds and the children literally under the bed. The boarding roommates ensured that at least two of them worked at different times to decrease the actual number of persons present in the room at any one time. However, the overcrowding was still felt during public holidays or when the factory was closed for cleaning, and all four women and their children were in the tiny room. The overcrowding situation was made worse when unannounced visitors arrived. If they were overnight guests, this complicated matters even more, as it meant that the roommates may have to go out and seek an overnight stay with friends within the neighborhood or farther away in another part of the town.

One way that these women would ease the overcrowding in their room was by going to visit their rural home (especially those who were in a radius of about twenty miles). The other alternative was to visit a boyfriend for those lucky to have one and this could also ease the overcrowding. For the men in similar overcrowded rooms, I found that some chose to go out and spend the night in a club. This was always considered risky as there was a big chance of being booked by the police for "being drunk and disorderly," a common misdemeanor that the Kenya police have been known to use to harass urban dwellers at night and to some extent during the day time. It is also an expensive venture for somebody who is trying to save money because the night club operators expect those who stay overnight to be constantly drinking and not to use the club as "simply an alternative for a lodging place." Indeed the waiters will constantly go around to ensure that the reveler has a drink at all times and is not just dozing off to sleep. This can be expensive and eventually unaffordable for someone who was escaping an overcrowded room because he could not afford to rent a larger room in the first place.

Unemployment and Underemployment

Unemployment is everywhere in the world, but its degree is much higher and more conspicuous in Third World cities. Again, rapid urbanization has contributed to high unemployment and underemployment. An alternative explanation is that these cities were mostly established to serve the core countries (i.e., formerly Western colonizing nations like France and Britain). European and American industries during the colonial period were profit maximizing and capital oriented and therefore did little to solve the unemployment problem. After independence, efforts in most countries have been made to create labor and capital intensive industries, but the high population growth in most of these cases (both rural and urban) has continued to frustrate the job-creating efforts. The problem of unemployment becomes more conspicuous in the urban areas where most rural people move with the hope of getting a job.

Underemployment is a situation described as spending much time and energy for very little pay. A few examples will elaborate on this phenomenon which is common in Third World cities. A porter in Karachi International Airport will get up early in the morning "to go to work." There he hopes to carry a passenger's luggage from the baggage claim area to the airport bus and get "a dollar." With enough requests, he will make sufficient money to clothe and feed himself. A hawker in a Nairobi street will start to display his wares to the commuters as early as six o'clock in the morning because his products either cost so little that to accumulate enough money takes a long time or because so few buyers are interested in them. A Mexican man will wake up early, walk his donkey to the Revolution Street in Tijuana with the hope that some visitor will want to ride the donkey or just take a picture of it and give him some money.

In the three selected illustrations which I observed in three different continents (parts of the Third World), each person described woke up very early in the morning "to go to work." As I can tell, the returns may not be high, but the energy the individual puts in is enormous. Such are the many cases common in Third World cities which conspicuously represent underemployment.

A third reason for unemployment or underemployment is the low educational and technical skills of most rural-urban migrants. Self-employment in the least income-generating marginal activities becomes the only viable option, causing high levels of underemployment. I should point out here that self employment can be very well paying and very attractive especially due to the freedom it gives those running their own businesses. This has been reported to be the case with small scale entrepreneurs like the drum sellers in my sample, welders and metal artisans and those middlemen traders who would not exchange their current positions for any other form of employment. The more lucrative a business is, the more attractive it is for the self-employed. On the other hand, the less income the business generates, the less attractive it is and the more likely it is that underemployment, or "misemployment," exists.

The Shanty Town/Informal Settlement Phenomenon

While most Western cities have old dilapidated houses and slums, the shanty town phenomenon is especially common to Latin American, Asian and African cities. Whereas informal settlements may have existed at the time European and American cities were forming, it must be clearly explained that the Western cities had more capital coupled with industrial development which created jobs and ensured relatively comfortable incomes for the new city dwellers. Thus, the extent of shanty town development in cities of the developing countries was never realized in the developed countries.

While the comparison to the present situation between the Third World cities and the Western cities may be unfair because of the different current prevailing conditions, I argue historically that the cities in the West were never as badly hit by urban poverty, and the informal settlements never became homes of close to half of any given city's population as is the case in cities of developing countries. The shanty "urban homes" are replicas of simple makeshift houses typical of the rural areas from which urban migrants just recently came. In the shanty towns, one finds that the housing and lifestyle are profoundly different from those of the downtown areas, presenting a rural-urban feel, yet they are within the town boundaries. One may be working in a modern factory in the Industrial area of a given city but literally living in rural conditions in the same town. His or her social life in the domestic enclave follows most of the rural rituals.

Mathare Valley in Nairobi or Kiandutu in Thika, are good illustrations of these kinds of rural lifestyles within the urban areas. In such shanty towns, the lifestyle is similar to that in the rural areas: housing styles are the same although usually with poorer materials like polythene papers; they fetch water from nearby rivers (usually more polluted than the rural rivers); their diet is a replica of the rural diet, although probably less nutritious than the rural one. For many, in the shanty town, they are torn between wanting to go back to the rural areas and staying in their new "found homes." The choice is a difficult one because they may have left nothing behind to go back to in their rural homes.

Informal, unplanned settlement is very typical in African cities. In Latin American cities, invasion of land by squatters has been well documented (Castells 1986; Peattie 1987b). The description of informal settlement in Lima by Hernando De Soto (1987) is a case in point. The equivalent is not found in Europe or North America presently or even during the time the cities there were forming. The Western countries were richer—having been the colonial masters, exploiting most of the Third World countries; they did not have the debt crisis that has been cancerous in all the developing countries weakening the national economies and small budgets for urban development, especially housing for low incomes which in turn produces the shanty town phenomenon. I should add that the Planning Divisions of the City Halls of most Third World cities are as strict as those of the West, but the reality is that however strict, they cannot control for shanty town development without provision of adequate housing. Demolitions that were popular in the 1960s and early 1970s have been found counterproductive, and although they are still carried out occasionally, they have not possibly controlled the growth of informal settlements. In Nairobi, for example, the National Cooperative Housing Union (NACHU) has estimated that 45% of the population lives in informal settlements; in Lima, De Soto puts the estimate at 60%.

Poor Transport and Communication Systems

Poor public transportation and communication is another Third World city phenomenon. Transport systems are either inadequately maintained or nonexistent. The low income groups are usually the worst hit, as they rely heavily on public facilities. In most major cities, like Harare, Karachi and Nairobi, there are municipal buses. Their number is insufficient for the large quantity of passengers seeking their service. In addition, only a few reach the shanty towns, far from the downtown area, where most low income groups live. The geographical location of these shanty towns is, of course, the result of a conscious effort made by colonists to keep blacks and other minorities away from whites, who resided around the downtown.

Some townships, for example, are too far for anyone to walk to work. Chitungwiza, outside Harare in Zimbabwe was built for the expressed purpose of keeping Africans away from the former Salisbury (today's Harare). Residents of Chitungwiza were nevertheless expected to work, or at least to look for work, in Harare, which is 26 miles away. In Nairobi, residents of the shanty towns of Kibera and Mathare must walk along a four-mile trail that leads to the industrial area, despite poor weather conditions. Public transportation is available to a limited number of city residents. Its costs, however, can amount to half one's monthly income; for that reason, most low income residents still prefer to walk. Furthermore, the official routes of the buses obviously do not take into consideration the needs of the low income groups. Most buses are in fact planned to reach the downtown area first and then the industrial area, requiring most workers to pass through downtown and practically pay for a double journey to reach their place of work and also change buses. It is both expensive and time consuming. A trip would have cost less, for example, if there were direct means of transport from the low income informal settlement directly to the industrial area where some residents have low menial jobs.

Public communication is a second major problem in most Third World cities. Obtaining service either for home or office takes many months. Public telephones are rare and, when in place, often do not work. Faxes, computer electronic mail and other new forms of communication are present, but the majority of residents are still excluded from their use as many cannot afford such services. Rates for all services are very high, making it cheaper to use the telephone in a First World city than in a Third World city. For example, it costs a Nairobi resident three times as much to make a call to the United States in comparison to an American resident calling Nairobi. Apparently those more endowed economically and where there are many companies offering similar services tend to pay less than their counterparts in Third World cities. Oftentimes such services do not work in many Third World cities. In a recent (1994) trip to Nigeria, my attempts to make a telephone call from Lagos and Ibadan to the United States were impossible as the operator kept saying all the lines were jammed. The local people told me that I was lucky even to get through to the operator!

Uncontrollable Traffic and Corrupted Police

Undoubtedly, traffic congestion is as much a part of any city as trees are part of the forest. In most cities, traffic is usually heavy during morning and evening rush hours. In many Third World Cities, however, traffic congestion takes place throughout the day and the early part of the night. This is of course as a result of the large number of vehicles and an inadequate infrastructure. Caracas in Venezuela, Cairo in Egypt, Lagos in Nigeria, Karachi in Pakistan, Bangkok in Thailand and Nairobi in Kenya are notorious examples of cities with over-congested traffic. In some of these cities, too much automobile volume blocks narrow and poorly maintained roads. Taxis and minibuses compete desperately for passengers, abusing both traffic laws and pedestrians.

The names of *matatus* for Nairobi, *dala dalas* for Dar-es Salaam (Lugalla 1995), "Emergency Taxis" popularly called "ETs" in Harare and "Taxis" in Johannesburg should sound familiar to Third World travelers who have been on a trip in any of these cities. City residents have become reluctantly accustomed to the uncomfortable and congested means of transportation on a daily basis. Traffic police are powerless in these situations. They are too few in numbers and poorly paid. They are prone to accept little money as bribes in exchange for favors. In East Africa, the acceptance of *chai* or "tea," in the form of cash by the officers awards drivers "an automatic license" to break all traffic rules. Fatal road accidents due to either a poorly maintained public service vehicle, drivers driving under influence of alcohol and drugs or overloading a vehicle frequently occur. Ideally, the police should have reprimanded such drivers, ordered evacuation of the extra passengers or grounded the vehicle for the sake of ensuring road safety. However, the little *chai* the traffic police officers get compromises the ideal situation.

What is worrisome is that such are not isolated cases but commonplace in such cities as Nairobi and Lagos and many other Third World cities. In Lagos and Ibadan, the two largest cities of Nigeria, traffic congestion is such a big problem that residents talk as much about it as they talk about the weather in New England (the North Eastern part of the USA). Traffic lights do not work, and traffic police, commonly called "yellow fever" (a derogatory term) because of their yellow uniforms are literally ineffective. Motor vehicles literally bulldoze their way with constant hooting that can be very irritating and uncivil. I witnessed many traffic offenses being committed in both Lagos and Ibadan as well as in Nairobi, Kenya, despite the presence of the traffic police. In Harare on the other hand, the traffic management was relatively better handled than in Nairobi and Lagos. The fact that the city highways in Harare were better planned may explain this (they have more lanes); in addition, most of the workers work in the fringes of the city with their formerly segregated residential areas also outside the city center. The bus station used by most workers was also planned outside the city center with the idea of reducing traffic in the center.

While this was the plan before Zimbabwe's independence in 1980, it appears to have worked well so far. With the increase of population in the city and the zoning restrictions being less stringent as they were during the colonial period, there are presently signs indicating that Harare in another ten years may be just as congested with traffic like the present day Nairobi. Unlike in the United States, for example, where a traffic offense will instantly earn one a ticket, the readiness of the driver with some monetary exchange is all that it takes to ignore the offense. The driver almost instantly earns a warm smile and a salute from the officers. The irony is that many accidents have occurred by the "excused offenders," taking much toll in human loss in many of these cities.

Over-urbanization

Most Third World cities are experiencing over-urbanization, especially African cities. This is the situation of too many people migrating into or being born in the urban areas to the extent that the services are inadequate for the new urbanites—housing, water, electricity, transport facilities, sanitation, employment. In other words the urban areas are stressed out as a result of the many people who have come to settle there. O'Connor's work (1983), *The African City*, called attention to the fact that African cities are fundamentally different from their European, Asian, or Latin American counterparts because they are the fastest growing in the world. Since independence in the 1960s, African cities have been growing at world record rates. The United Nations (1988) estimated that 39 percent of all Africans will be living in urban areas by the year 2000. Although Africa's absolute level of urbanization is low compared with the world's (46.6 percent), Africa has the highest urban growth rate in the world. The World Bank (1989, 224-225) report showed that from 1980-1987, Africa's urban population grew at an annual rate of 6.9 percent. Latin American cities reached their highest growth rates in the 1950s, at which point more than 50% of those countries' population resided in urban areas. African cities are today experiencing the highest rates of urbanization in the world, making them a unique phenomenon. The poverty level among the new urban migrants is also the highest in the world. Specific country studies on the urban crisis and poverty, for example, in Tanzania (Lugalla 1995), exemplifies this situation.

African cities, in addition, are relatively young. A few started in the late 19th century (Ibadan in Nigeria, Kano in Northern Nigeria, Lamu and Mombasa on the Kenyan Coast to name but a few), but most, like Lusaka, Ndola in Zambia, Harare in Zimbabwe, Nairobi in Kenya formed early in the twentieth century. Newer cities have continued to emerge, such as Abuja in Nigeria, which was born in the 1980s as the new capital of Nigeria with a centralized regional advantage and away from the overcrowded old capital, Lagos; Dodoma in Tanzania, proposed by the CMM (Chama Cha Mapinduzi or the Revolutionary Party) as the capital. The reality of Dodoma becoming the capital city is still a far cry as the country has undergone deep financial crisis and has not been as lucky as Nigeria to discover oil. Profits allowed for the construction of Abuja. It looks like the idea of Dodoma as the future capital might be abandoned due to financial incapacities of the Tanzanian government. In the current multiparty democracy era, the wisdom of the former one-party government CCM (under Julius Nyerere's leadership) may be questioned by the newer parties. Dodoma was recommended as the future capital alongside the Socialist principles adopted by the party at the Arusha declaration of 1967; given that the Tanzanian government has in the last eight years abandoned the socialist (Ujamaa) development path, abandoning the idea of moving the capital to Dodoma will not be unimaginable. Socio-politically, it made sense to try to centralize the capital to make it accessible to all the citizens. Economically, it does not make sense because it means incurring lots of money to move the offices and residential areas for the workers and building a new infrastructure. Such funds could be better used to improve conditions of the many poor citizens. Indeed, with modern technology and with proper decentralization programs, the capital does not need to be in a central physical location. With advanced means of communications, telephones, cyberspace, roads, airways and rail lines, all of the citizens can easily access the capital city.

This example from Tanzania shows how difficult it has been for African governments to secure adequate budgets to finance their urban projects and as a result are impeded in dealing with the over-urbanization problem. Dar Es Salaam, because of the "no-move" to Dodoma, continues to be an overcrowded city, with many problems with which to contend: housing for the low income groups; unemployment and underemployment; a poor transportation system. Despite the informal transportation system, by which the residents use the *dala dalas*, complaints still abound.

REVIEW OF CLASSICAL THEORIES OF CITIES AND THEIR RELEVANCE FOR THIRD WORLD CITIES

Can classical theories of cities explain the presence of the problems in Third World cities, and in particular over-urbanization? Can one explain the formation of the Third World cities and the problems they face from different perspectives besides those used by Max Weber or the Chicago School to describe the formation of the Western cities?

Urban studies is a very recent field in both Western and developing countries. In Western countries, an interest in studying urban life as unique form the rest of the society started in the 18th and 19th centuries and grew in the 20th. In the developing countries, interest began in the mid 20th century. Most of the writing took place at the end of the 19th century and the beginning of the 20th, at the time when many European cities were reaching alarming sizes. Earlier scholars had viewed the city as an integral part of rural life and remained untroubled by the formation of small urban centers. Only when problems associated with cities in areas like public health, housing and education began to grow did scholars turn their attention to cities and began to develop explanatory theories. These were new problems, entirely different from those experienced by pre-industrial small towns and ancient cities (Sjoberg 1960; Weber 1905). None of the classical theories, however, can adequately address the Third World city's characteristics and problems.

The major contributors to the newly founded field came from the German School, more specifically from Max Weber, Georg Simmel and Oswald Spengler; from the Chicago School, with its leading theorists Robert E. Park, Louis Wirth and Robert Redfield; and from the Marxist School, Karl Marx, Friedrich Engels and, later, the neo-Marxists David Harvey (1989), Manuel Castells (1977) and Immanuel Wallerstein (1974) who pioneered the World System theory.

Max Weber offered the first contribution to the field of urban studies in (1905, 48) with the publication of his book, *The City*. In that work, he defined the city as "the set of social structures that encourage social individuality and innovation. The city is a social form that permits the greatest degree of individuality and uniqueness." To define the city for Weber "is not to describe one style of life, but one set of social structures that can produce a multitude of concretely different styles of life" (Sennett 1969, 23). As such, the city fosters individuals capable of leading their societies into new directions. The city becomes the instrument of historical change. Weber's efforts concentrated in the identification and typification of social structures, found in cities, that advanced the individuality and diversification of their members. Following this method, known as ideal-typical, Weber could compare bureaucracies, markets and laws from ancient China to city-states in Greece and to 19th century London.

Weber sought to understand the city through the social forms that lay beyond it. The same approach was adopted by the other members of the German School. Simmel, for instance, recognized that bureaucracies, markets and other social structures gave the city its nature. Simmel and others disagreed with Weber, however, on the origins and consequences of these structures. For Simmel, urban life was inescapably impersonal and overwhelming for its citizens. As a defense against the complexities of urban life, men tried to live "in a non-emotional, reasoned, functional relationship to other men; this defense was to break life into separate, neat compartments in order to be in control over each one of them separately" (Simmel [1905] 1969, 47). The reaction to those feelings was a turn inward by most urbanites into themselves. Simmel believed that men could, in a city, come to free their spirit from their acts; they would be able to understand that "who I am" is not simply "what I do ordinarily" (Simmel [1905] 1969, 52).

The Chicago School of urban sociology offered a diametrically opposed approach to understanding the city. They investigated the internal character of the city, believing that its different parts, and the way they interacted, were its defining characteristics. Unlike their German colleagues, the Chicago theorists did not define the city in light of the general social structures that existed within it. Park (1952), for example, saw the city as a human organism with parts that are competitive with each other but that, at the same time, act in the interest of the whole. A heightened sense of competition sets the city apart from other forms of human settlement. Competition, in turn, determines the spatial allocation of the different parts. Heavy industry, for instance, can successfully cut a niche for itself near a main river or water location and ensure a constant water supply, or near a railway, to have easy access to transportation. A car dealer will instead choose empty lots near parts of the towns where customers reside. The resulting distribution of space and resources is a by-product of competition, yet it also guarantees an efficient use of land and population. It was the outcome of a large-scale division of labor that ensured the maximum productivity of each part and of the whole. Like Simmel, Park argued that the city profoundly affected the life of its members. Ultimately, Park believed, when the division of labor is at its highest, an individual belongs to many spheres or groups, making it impossible to enforce a uniform set of standards on anyone. While Simmel believed that members of the city would turn inward to find freedom, Park argued that citizens would seek new moralities and social standards and become innovators and sources of social change.

Wirth's ([1938] 1969) major contribution to the Chicago School was his attempt to envision the effects that the division of labor would have on the relationship between urban economics, urban land use, urban labor patterns and urban political structures. Wirth, like Park, emphasized the internal dynamic of cities, giving the Chicago School its "ecological" trait.

Yet, their approach, built on the premise that natural competition occurs in the city, could not possibly apply to African cities. In Nairobi, for instance, space distribution has not resulted from complimentary or collaborative competition. There was instead a deliberate allocation of space by the colonial administrators as early as 1899 when Nairobi was at its infant stage. The arbitrary allocation of this space was enforced by harsh government rules that endorsed segregation. It was not, then, through complimentary competition that the residential areas of Milimani, Kileleswha, Kilimani, Lavington Green and Muthaiga became exclusive white residential areas while Kariokor, Bahati, Shauri Moyo, Pumwani and Kamukunji became homes of the few Africans allowed in the city.

Similarly, the German School could not apply to African cities. The fundamental assumption that particular social structures, like the market and bureaucracy, determine urban life assumed that all citizens can access those institutions. There is clear evidence that those institutions affected only a part of the urbanites living in African cities. In the case of Nairobi and other African cities, Africans were considered temporary sojourners whose life in the city was seen as a misnomer and a displacement from their comfortable familiar settings in the rural areas. No institution emerged from the African presence. Current problems among Africans in cities, such as housing and unemployment, must be seen as resulting from a lack of institutions, like a market, that would have emerged naturally without impediments. It remains even a question whether Nairobi itself would have become what it is today, a prominent city, if Africans had been able to freely choose to live and grow in that area. A different argument altogether must then be constructed to explain African urban life.

A class-based competition, where space is socially determined, proposed by neo-Marxist theorists of the 1970s, like Castells (1977) and Harvey (1973), may more successfully explain the organization of Nairobi and Harare and other African cities. Competition was unfair, favoring one side, the upper class colonialists. To the class factor in Nairobi and Harare, one must add the race factor, a crucial determinant of space allocation indeed, as colonial administrators openly enforced the "color bar" philosophy and actually implemented residential racial segregation. The crucial role played by race should be the basis of a new theoretical account of the history of the African city.

The World System theory, developed by Wallerstein (1974), has been a powerful tool for understanding the existence of the Third, Second and First Worlds. It introduced the idea of an international division of labor and sought to explain the emergence of poorer and wealthier countries, the presence of dictatorial regimes in the Third World and slow economic growth considering that division. Cities grew within the core and periphery to serve the interests of the core. In the periphery, cities were first centers of administration for colonial purposes and later retained that role as centers for multinational corporations and foreign investments. The theory came as a reaction against the functionalist modernization theory developed in the 1960s by Western thinkers like Rostow (1960), McClelland (1961) and Parsons (1958), among others. It re-elaborated and added an historical, racial and international dimension to the earlier theories of Andre Gunder Frank (1967), Fernando Cardoso and Faletto Enzo (1979) and David Harvey (1973) , proponents of the Dependency theory who first applied Marxist tools to the development of cities and argued that the spatial arrangement of cities is a result of internal competition between classes. Drawing from examples of their native Latin America, Cardoso and Frank described clearly how the Spanish colonial regime extracted resources from Latin America and when cities like Sao Paulo and Mexico City were developed, they depended on functions served out by the capitals of the colonial masters, Madrid and Lisbon respectfully. The cities in Latin America did not grow to serve the interests of the native Latinos but the Europeans in distant lands. This was to cause enormous problems especially after independence when the poor native Indians started migrating to the cities which had been historically exploited and did not have enough resources to hold upon the new migrants.

Yet, the World System Theory, despite its articulation of historical economic integration of different world economies, suffers from some shortcomings. By focusing on the relationship between core and periphery, the theory does not take into account the nature of class struggles and conflict that brings about social change in the Third World. Not all the ills of a country can be blamed on the world market. Many corrupt regimes have tended to blame the world market instead of taking responsibilities for their poor planning and misappropriation of profits earned from the same world market. Secondly, Third World leaders have an active role in shaping their country's conditions. Hence, in the case of cities, these leaders may have a bias toward particular cities concerning the location of foreign investments.

A good example is the development of the town of Eldoret (about two hundred miles from Nairobi) in Western Kenya which has had more infrastructure invested in it due to the favoritism of the head of state, President Moi and his close associates who come from near there. In 1995, for example, there were plans to put up a third international airport in Kenya (*Weekly Review* [Nairobi], 17 June 1995) at the expense of the taxpayers yet the two existing international airports in Mombasa and Nairobi were in need of improvements and are still under-utilized. Opposing views from opposition politicians and donor agencies like the World Bank have been leveled toward this proposed project, but the government in power has vested interests. It seems that the plan will actually be implemented at the expense of developing other towns that are genuinely more deserving. Instead of upgrading the nearby national airport of Kisumu to save on costs for a country that is still far from being self-sufficient, more foreign debts will be incurred with the Eldoret project. This is biased planning, politically motivated and perpetuating unbalanced development and wrong national priorities. The world system theory could be incapable of explaining these internal dynamics in the Kenyan political scene.

Such decisions later affect a country's trend of urbanization. Thus, some Western (world system) theorists have paid insufficient attention to the role of states as institutions that are somewhat autonomous from the world economic system (Skocpol 1985, 3). The theory essentially states that all Ministries of Planning and Treasury passively make decisions in direct response to the fluctuations on the world market. A socio-historical approach, specific to each city, that takes into account its colonial past and the active roles of states and acknowledges their urban problems must be developed. The German, Chicago and World System schools individually cannot meet all of these requirements. The Third World city is different from Western cities and cannot be reduced to a by-product of the international capitalist system. The next section sketches my approach to urban studies, one that highlights the importance of colonialism and the State, and one that can offer an account for the problems that are afflicting these cities. This approach also looks at the African in the 1990s and into the next century as an activist in his/her own city—not anymore as a sojourner awaiting to go back to the so-called African reserves.

COLONIALISM AND URBANIZATION IN KENYA

Towns in Kenya, as in most other African countries on the East African region, were established mainly to serve British colonial interests. Three distinct functions of the cities can be identified: (1) trade, (2) administration, (3) and settlement and agriculture. To best serve these functions, towns were founded along the railway lines. Indeed, in one sentence it could be said that "the history of urban development in Kenya follows the history of the railway, or put in another way the railway brought the towns." For obvious reasons, railways, being a commercial venture, were developed in those regions that were potentially productive and promotional of trade. By trade I refer to that which was beneficial to the British Crown and to individual British settlers and not beneficial to the indigenous Kenyan economy. The latter was given no priority and it developed not by active policies and programs to promote it but by mere chance. The African's trade became more needs-driven than official policy-driven.

Prior to the arrival of the British, most of Kenya was rural. Minor settlements along the coast existed due to the Arab trade. These included Mombasa, Malindi and Lamu in the far North Coast. These settlements were sufficiently dense to be considered towns. Inland, there were a few market centers used as stop overs for ivory traders trekking from the interior to the coast. These settlements included Voi and Machakos. They could hardly be considered towns, however, especially in comparison to the much bigger settlements of the indigenous West Africans, such as the Yoruba in Ibadan, who lived an actual urban life well before the arrival of the British (Mabogunje 1973). It is therefore accurate to state that most of the present towns in Kenya grew during the colonial period. Mombasa, though existing in earlier times, grew as a strategic harbor and railway stop on the Indian coast and served as a gateway to the rest of the world during the British colonial rule.

Nairobi was at first a warehouse for railway construction materials.

Before the British occupation, it was "a no man's land," lying at the border of the Kikuyu and the Maasai as an unsettled bush only useful then for grazing. The Maasai, perhaps had more control over the area because, as a pastoral society owning large herds of cattle, they occupied the area for longer periods, especially during droughts. The climate of the Nairobi area was cool, temperate and not as dry as other locations inhabited by the nomadic Maasai. The name itself, "Nairobi," means cool waters in the Maasai language.

The colonial government in Kenya, along with the settler community, established itself in the best farming lands of the country (the former white highlands) typically with farms and in the city with town homes. There was no policy for making Nairobi an African city. The city was initially a major railway workshop; it later became an administrative center and eventually the capital of the Kenya colony in 1920. The ideology and actual planning of the city were to create a comfortable town for colonial administrators. It was also meant as a center for gathering coffee, tea and other raw materials from neighboring hinterland en-route to Mombasa for shipment to the processing centers of London. The first Africans to live in the city were men recruited by the colonialists to undertake jobs which settlers considered below their dignity. Africans were imported primarily as cooks and gardeners (shamba-boys). Laws were passed in the colony requiring any African coming to Nairobi to display a pass indicating that he had a job and was working for specific employers. Their state of residence was absolutely temporary (Soja 1970). Nairobi existed independently of any African's influence. It was a rendezvous for the white settlers and colonial government officers where the likes of Lord Delamere (the white settler leader), Denys Finch Hatton and Baroness Karen Blixen met either in Muthaiga Club or the Norfolk Hotel. (See *Out of Africa* by Isak Dinesen 1937).

As such, Nairobi was the city of the *Mzungu*, Swahili for European, and later, of the *Mhindi*, Swahili for those South Asians who, although ranked as second citizens, had shops and small businesses they administered independently. Nairobi was never the city for the *Mwafrika*, Swahili for African, until 1963! The social structure of Nairobi remained essentially the same until then. The socio-political and economic structure of the city was dominated by whites and secondly by those few Asians, mainly from India, who were absorbed into agriculture and administration over a period. The African ranked always a distant third, with clearly no access to housing provisions, jobs, education, health care, transportation and other amenities typical of city life. Indeed, the law itself decreed the segregation.

Despite all the measures taken against the influx of Africans, especially those without jobs, and despite such laws as the Vagrant Act (1949), which ordered the expulsion of illegitimate Africans from cities into rural areas, a few thousands found their way to the city and even settled informally in Mathare Valley during and after World War II. Luise White (1990) has documented that women prostitutes had settled in the valley as early as the 1949. In 1954, during the Mau Mau emergency, a large scale operation was undertaken to expel Africans from the city, particularly the Kikuyu ethnic group and force them back to their rural homes (Barnett and Njama 1966). The operation indirectly revealed that despite many laws Africans wanted to come and work in Nairobi and possibly settle there. The formation of Mathare Valley as an informal settlement was one of the indicators that Nairobi was to transform itself into an African city and that its European character was to be lost by the 1990s (O'Connor 1983). Yet, before that time, Africans crowded illegally in designated areas with single housings, such as Kariokor, Pumwani, Bahati and Makandara.

Most of the jobs in Nairobi favored Europeans in the higher administration.   Later, the Asians who were educated in the discriminatory colonial education system obtained jobs as accountants, clerks, police officers and teachers. Africans were the last to be absorbed in those kinds of job markets, beginning in the 1950s and 1960s. For the majority of would-be workers, Nairobi was not really an industrial town. It therefore had a weak employment base which made matters worse for the African worker, given the discriminatory process of hiring. Asians were not immune to the "color bar" that treated them as only second to the European in all spheres of city life. Those who could not get a white collar job started artisanry work and became "fundis," making furniture, repairing cooking pots and metal pots, making lanterns and other kinds of artisan work (King 1977, 1996). These Asians later hired Africans as helpers. The latter learned the skills as apprentices, beginning a tradition of metal and wood artisanry which is today popularly known as *Jua Kali* and is at the heart of the informal economy that will be analyzed in details in this book.

The biased education system, in which the schools offered the best education to the Europeans followed by the Asians and much later by the Africans, did not do well in preparing African students for the job market that would be facing them upon graduation. The colonial administration was not interested in developing the mind of the African students toward high intellectual levels. The lucky few who attended school were expected to be loyal to the colonial system and to work for that system as clerks and junior level administrators. The education system therefore did not prepare students for the largely agricultural economy of the country. A few technical schools were established in the 1950s, and Asian shopkeepers continued to train African workers; yet in both cases, only a few Africans were involved. Women were under-represented in the education system. Many who reached the cities turned to prostitution, and only much later after independence when zoning was relaxed a bit did they engage in trade and food selling (White 1990).

Up to the time of independence the situation in the city of Nairobi had not changed since the early colonial days, and the social ranking of the races described above held true throughout the colonial period. In the rural areas, prior to independence, as large tracks of land were sagged and assigned to white colonialists, rural Africans had their movements confined to African Reserves. Many of these reserves, such as those of the Kikuyu of the Central Province, could not contain the swelling population. The situation was made worse by the Mau Mau emergency (1952-1956), which restricted not only travel to the city but also travel from one rural area to another. For better or for worse, and increasingly after independence, the city became the place to seek a new life with new opportunities. As independence approached, Nairobi became a busy "host" for rural migrants, many of whom came with almost no skills suited for the few jobs available in the now politically African city. By that time, most quarters in the city had, on informal levels, become African. It was at this time that the problems discussed above as features of Third World cities, began to afflict heavily occupied African towns like Nairobi.

After independence, the formal sector, which comprised mainly the civil service and private companies, employed most of the Africans who had at least a high school diploma. Absorption in this category went on smoothly, with almost everybody who had good qualifications getting employed. The same could be said for the few university graduates, probably numbering a couple of thousands. The existence of a good job market for them was the result of many Europeans abandoning Kenya and returning to Europe or moving South to then Southern Rhodesia (Zimbabwe) or South Africa, which at the time continued to be the bastion of European supremacy in the continent. The absorption of Africans into the formal sector served a dual function: to provide

Africans with jobs and to create a trustworthy civil service. During the 1970s, however, both the government and private companies had reached maximum capacity and could no longer employ the many thousands of new high school and college graduates. The formal sector had in fact never created new jobs but simply replaced Europeans with Africans.

The less educated and the uneducated formed the bulk of the new migrant waves into Nairobi. Almost no jobs existed for them. The only choice available was the informal sector, which employed them as street hawkers, shoe shiners and food sellers, the latter being open especially to women. The informal sector offered opportunities for learning new skills, as waste metal and tins were aptly utilized to make items like cooking stoves and lamps, and as metal rods annexed from building sites were used to make bicycles. The informal sector also required little capital. For these reasons, it flourished, employing thousands of new arrivals. Similar situations were taking place in other Third World countries. Studies sponsored by the World Bank, United States Aid for International Development (USAID), International Labour Organization (ILO) and United Nations Development Programme (UNDP) have shown, for instance, that most of the urban skilled labor force in Senegal was trained in the informal sector (Lubell 1991). The informal sector accounts for 70% of the entire work force of Kenya (Republic of Kenya 1986).

Yet, no official explanation has been given for the continued flow of immigrants into Nairobi, which took place despite the well-known fact that the formal positions in the city were closed and continued to diminish despite the continuing rural-urban migration. If the motive for the continuing migration could be identified, then a host of other variables and problems that afflict Nairobi, and other African cities, could be explained in an effort to understand not only the characteristic of Third World cities but also the remedies to those problems that characterize them. Indeed, inadequate educational, communication, employment and transportation systems are the by-products of too many users, as well as the original purpose for which they were designed. In the next chapters, I propose that the informal sector can be seen as responsible for attracting enormous quantities of migrants to the cities and for over-flooding a system of infrastructures that, from the start, was designed to accommodate the needs of the colonialists. I suggest that the growth of sectors of the informal economy is the direct result of the selective support of the State. I start by discussing Kenya's poor economic structure and the origins of the push from the rural to the pull

in the urban areas, as well as the economic realities in Harare
(Zimbabwe).

2

The General Economy of Kenya and Zimbabwe: The Cities of Nairobi and Harare

Although Kenya is mainly an agricultural country, less than 20% of the total land is arable. The poor soils found in most of northeastern Kenya, which is also semi-desert, have led to uneven distribution of agricultural production. This has caused high population densities in some provinces. In 1976, for example, the Central Province had 256 persons per sq. km. followed by Western Province and Nyanza with 232 and 226 persons respectively. (These provinces were also the homes of most of the respondents included in my original research, 1987-88). The low density provinces, which are also less arable, include Eastern Province with 87 persons per sq. km. and North Eastern with a low of two persons per sq. km. (Faruque 1983).

Agriculture provides two-thirds of the country's exports. The main exports are coffee and tea. Others include sisal, pyrethrum, hides and skins and horticultural products. Given that Kenya has no substantive minerals for export and the industrial sector is still forming, agriculture is the backbone of the country's economy. The performance of the economy depends on the pace and pattern of this sector. Agricultural growth slowed in the 1970s, averaging 2.7% per year over the period, 1972-1979. This was substantially below the rate of population growth which was around 3.8 in the same period (World Bank 1983). This disparity can have potentially serious implications for wages, employment and the country's balance of payments. Poor weather (e.g., drought) was responsible for much of this performance. Besides cash-crop growing, food crops like maize, beans and potatoes have to be encouraged to avoid famine disasters that can weaken a country's economic development. While most of the government's plans are to improve agricultural production with the hope of retaining most of the population in the rural areas, this has not been achieved, and the influx of the population to the urban areas has continued.

Kenya's industry is still at a very early stage of development. It includes processing industries such as milk production, food, tea and coffee. Other industries have been connected with the State's policy of import substitution which encourages industrial manufacturing in the country of goods that would otherwise be imported from outside. This policy has encountered many problems because of over-protectionism (Langdon 1981; Himbara 1994). During the 1970s and early 1980s, this policy led to tremendous losses. In several industries (e.g., vehicle assembly plants), domestic production involves higher net foreign exchange costs than would importation.

Manufacturing in 1983 employed only 2% of the labor force and cannot be expected, at any feasible rate growth of output, to provide employment for the almost nine million people looking for jobs in the year 2000. The nation, on the other hand, is in dire need of manufactured items like tools for agricultural production. Part of the informal economy that I studied in Nairobi is contributing to some of the country's manufacturing needs, although on a small scale. Using lower technology and locally available material (therefore saving foreign exchange), the metal artisans have been selling agricultural tools and other household items all over the country for at least the last 20 years. The artisans have established their individually-run manufacturing industries into a big industry, popularly referred to as the *Jua Kali* or "hot sun" industries. These artisans in the government's view are the best representation of the informal sector, mainly because they conserve scarce foreign exchange and require very little capital to create jobs. They also make and produce much needed farm equipment.

In an industrializing nation, employment of the economically active population is of great concern to planners, policy makers and political leaders. High levels of unemployment in Kenya, particularly in the city of Nairobi, were noted in the 1970s and early 1980s. The employment situation in the mid-1980s, especially 1986, improved moderately compared with the previous year. Wage employment in the modern sector increased by 46,100 new jobs or 3.9% (Republic of Kenya 1987). Employment in the small-scale enterprises (the urban informal sector) expanded significantly by 10.4% compared with 9.1% in 1985. Another positive economic indicator for the country was that inflation hit a low level of 5.7% from a high of 10.7% in 1985. The low inflation rate may have been due to increased agricultural and manufacturing production and low world oil prices.

The Sessional Paper No. 1 of 1986 (Republic of Kenya 1986) emphasized accelerated employment creation in the private sector and a gradually decreasing rate of employment creation in the public sector. The urban informal sector for the first time is officially seen to be a potential source of new jobs for the expanding labor force. Its growth is much more rapid than that of the formal sector. Although most people live in rural areas, urban wage employment accounted for 51.7% of the country's wage employment in 1986. The government realizes the need for more job creation to accommodate the nine million job seekers estimated by the year 2000. It also realizes that limited capital will require that most jobs be created in agriculture and the informal sector. It is estimated that, even with rapid growth and continuation of the high investment rate of 25% of Gross Domestic Product, Kenya will have only 23 billion Kenya pounds (approximately $20 billion) to invest from 1984 to 2000. It takes approximately $14,000 to create one new job in non-agriculture, modern wage-earning activities. If all the $20 billion of the savings went to finance investment in the modern sector and none of it was required to replace aging capital, only 1.4 million new workers would find employment over the next 15 years, leaving six million workers, or 40% of the labor force, without jobs in the year 2000. Obviously, the modern sector cannot be depended on to employ much of the growing work force. To employ people on small farms, in very small scale industry and services, or in self employment takes only a fraction of the $ 14,000 per worker required in the modern sector. Clearly the bulk of the work force will have to be productively employed in these activities (Republic of Kenya 1986).

A major problem facing Kenya's economic development is the rapid growth of population over the last twenty years. In 1962, for example, Kenya's population was eight million, and in 1969 it was 11.5 million.

In the last census (1979), the population had risen to more than 15 million. The current population is estimated at 25 million, a high figure for a nation that is still developing and without adequate resources. It is estimated (Republic of Kenya 1986) that by the year 2000, Kenya will have a population of about 35 million people—78% more than lived in Kenya in 1984. This population increase will include 14 million workers, 6.5 million more than in 1984. There is, therefore, a need to double jobs in Kenya in the next 15 years. The increase affects both urban and rural population. At current trends, urban population will reach nine to 10 million people by the year 2000, over one-forth of the total population. This is a big change compared with three million urbanites (15%) in 1984. The role the urban informal sector will play becomes more significant.

In the 1970s, Kenya's population expanded at an estimated 3.8% a year. Today's total fertility rate (TFR) is eight children, which is one of the highest in the world. If this TFR is constant until 2000, Kenya's population would grow by 4.3% a year to reach 38.5 million in 2000. Rapid population growth is probably the single most important obstacle to raising living standards in Kenya over the long term.

Despite the State's official recognition of family planning methods to check on the population increase in Kenya, their acceptance, especially in rural areas, has been weak. Children in most Kenyan societies are seen as social security during old age. They are also an important part of the agricultural labor up to their teenage years. Some families have more children in fear of the existing ones dying at a young age. High population growth is a constraint to both formal and informal sectors in Kenya.

A discussion of the nation's economic performance would be incomplete without including the international factors that have usually slowed economic development. Kenya relies on agricultural exports for its GNP and foreign reserves, but the prices of products like coffee and tea are decided in the world market. The fluctuation of such prices has affected the country's whole economy. In 1982, for example, low coffee and tea prices were reflected in poor economic performance that were high and meant a better overall, economic performance. Other factors, however, have lowered the economic performance even when market prices for exported agricultural goods may be high.

Kenya's reliance mostly on imported energy has been disastrous, especially in the 1970s and 1980s. The escalating price of oil has absorbed most of the foreign reserves. This has been a major drawback for Kenya. It has raised the rate of inflation to a high of 20% in 1983 and to about 40% in 1992. However, high cash crop prices and low oil prices in 1986 lowered the inflation rate to 5.7%, its lowest in the last twenty years. The international market thus constrains job creation, especially in the formal sector.

Another international factor is the debt problem. As of June 30, 1986, the government had an external debt of $18,029.00 million owed to Western developed countries, mainly West Germany, the U.S.A. and Japan. The World Bank and the International Development Association (IDA) are among the leading lending international organizations in Kenya. The debt problem means that the government spends most of its earnings from agricultural exports and tourism servicing debts instead of investing in development programs both in rural and urban areas. For those becoming economically active (15-55 years in Kenya), it means looking beyond the formal sector for employment opportunities. The cities may also have to look more into the informal economy to cater to the increased number of job seekers in a country that cannot afford a social welfare system for the unemployed.

There is a tendency for many students of development to blame the weather, the international market and foreign debt (e.g., dependency theory: Gunder Frank 1967; Cardoso 1979) as the causes of poor social-economic development in Third World countries. Such external factors have been highlighted in policy papers and development plans issued by the government of Kenya and other related agencies. Nevertheless, local conditions also constrain the economy.

Officials and politicians that manage the city of Nairobi have often been held responsible for the deterioration of service. Accusations of favoritism, nepotism and ethnic preference in employment or allocation of city plots have been leveled at many officials. The Ministry of Local Government in 1982 responded to a public outcry in Nairobi by dissolving the elected city government. From then until 1992, a government-appointed commission ran the city of Nairobi. Yet the Commission has also been accused of corruption and of providing deteriorating services. An elected city council was put in place during the multiparty elections in 1992.

THE ECONOMIC STRUCTURE OF NAIROBI

Nairobi is the city with the most wage employees in public and private sectors. Its urban informal sector is also the largest. In 1994, for example, expenditure on all services in Nairobi was $56,688 compared with $8,746 for Mombasa, the second highest. Most of Nairobi's expenditure is in economic services. In 1994, the distribution of expenditure toward various services was as follows: 52% for economic services; 26% for social services; 11% for community services; and 10% for administration. In the same year, about 52% of all wage employees had their jobs in Nairobi. The nation's wage employees were 607,371 and 315,701 of them were employed in Nairobi (Republic of Kenya 1995).

Nairobi is the hub of the nation, a place of the government and commerce. With its current population estimated at 2.5 million, Nairobi comprises about 8% of the nation's population. Nairobi attracts a constant flow of migrants who come seeking work or simply the excitement of the city's "bright lights." For job seekers, the chance of employment in the formal sector is less than one in ten and the realities of urban survival are harsh (Miller 1984, 75). The presence of multinational corporations in Nairobi has not solved the employment problem for those seeking jobs in the formal sector.

A low-cost room in one of the city's transient areas will have problems of water, sanitation and security. This is true of most slum and squatter settlements. Even for the new migrant who may find work in the informal sector, life is difficult. The place of work may be miles from where he or she can afford to live. If famine or a poor crop season has impoverished the migrant's home area, emigration. Such pressure has caused economic hardships in Nairobi for many new migrants.

STRUCTURAL ADJUSTMENT AND ITS EFFECTS ON THE ECONOMY OF AFRICAN CITIES

From Cairo to Johannesburg and from Nairobi to Dakar, structural adjustment   programs introduced by the World Bank and the International Monetary Fund with the support of major donors have become almost synonymous with economic planning in Sub-Saharan Africa. They have had effects in almost every aspect of social, political and economic development. It is not surprising, therefore, that the last ten years have seen debates on the pros and cons of structural adjustment programs (popularly called SAPS) in conferences, workshops and publications (Himbara 1994; Grosh and Mukandara 1994; Due and Gladwin 1991; Lugalla 1995). Economic liberalization has also been accompanied by calls for political liberalization which has been notable in most Sub-Saharan countries. The latter has been characterized by the call for the previously one-party states to become multi-party.

Despite vehement refusal to accept the idea of multi-parties, President Moi of Kenya in 1991 succumbed to both local and international pressure and allowed for the repeal of the parliamentary law that had ensured only a single party in the country. Zimbabwe, on the other hand, has had a multi-party system although the ruling party is too strong for the others. For most governments in Africa, structural adjustments aimed at liberalizing the economy have not been readily welcomed. While the government had used the civil service and public companies (parastatals) to reward their supporters and to punish their detractors, the call for transparency did not set well with the heads of state because they were now limited in the reward and rent seeking system they had applied in the 1970s and 1980s.

Key areas of adjustment for most African states include the following: downsizing an oversized civil service; devaluing the currency; emphasizing trade; and more specifically, allowing the market to operate freely without price controls, farm subsidies and monopoly of agricultural boards to purchase, process and market certain products like maize, coffee, dairy and tea. Another direct measure introduced during adjustment was cost-sharing in public institutions that may have been previously free or with a very low nominal surcharge. Introduction of cost-sharing in hospitals and clinics in Kenya as well as in higher education brought about a huge outcry in the late 1980s and indeed caused a political blur as citizens were hurt financially.

Structural Adjustment Programs were mainly instituted by the International Financial Institutions (the World Bank and the International Monetary Fund) with the sole purpose of ensuring that the debts incurred by most African governments in the 1970s and remained outstanding in the 1980s to the present (1990s) were paid. One way to ensure such payment was to make sure the governments cut their subsidies, be it health or education, immunization and vaccination programs, basic water and electricity supply, and so forth. In their economic logic, adjustments made from such previous expenses would be used to pay the foreign debt directly. Once the signs of ability to pay the existing debt became clear, more loans could be advanced to possibly allow the governments to invest in their countries.

Unfortunately, the poor, the low income urban dwellers and the low income peasants in rural areas have been hurt most by such adjustments since by and large they were the recipients, albeit in small quantities, of some of the government's public spending especially in schools, health services, food, social services and infrastructure (very basic developmental needs in any society). Under SAPS directives, government spending on such services has had to be cut to save money to pay the rising debt. The cry of "the government is hurting us," coupled with rising inflations and high levels of unemployment became the order of the day for most African urban dwellers. The opposition of the SAPS came not only from local citizens but also from United Nations Agencies, particularly UNICEF, charged to prosper the welfare of children all over the world. UNICEF asserted that "hundreds of thousands of the developing world's children have given their lives to pay their countries' debts, and many millions more are still paying the interest with their malnourished bodies" (UNICEF 1990, 26).

Many agencies including UNICEF have called for "adjustment with a human face" suggesting that the adjustment be done gradually and without eliminating programs for the most needy citizens, which is what has been happening in Kenya most of the late 1980s to the present. Remarkable in the Kenyan situation is the increase of basic food prices like milk, bread and sugar by about 40%. Also the cost-sharing directives introduced in the schools and health institutions have hurt the poor and made them lose hope for the future especially if they are unable to send their children to school. An example of the negative effects of SAPS occurred in the University system in Kenya where in the early 1990s, a fee of Ksh. 6000 was required of every student. Students rioted to oppose the new fees, which they argued might lead to many students staying at home because they could not afford it.

THE INFORMAL ECONOMY IN ZIMBABWE:
CASE OF HARARE

Zimbabwe's formal economy, as in the case of Kenya, has been declining and has been unable to cope with the much needed employment especially for the rural urban migrants coming to the cities like Harare. The informal economy in Zimbabwe has been generating employment and income for many persons who have no alternative employment or income sources. This explains why the interest of the informal economy in the late 1980s to the present was heightened among the citizens and within the government apparatus. Historically, the formal sector, especially the civil service and the large scale agricultural sector, had been the major source of employment for most Zimbabweans. Since independence in 1980 however, formal sector employment increased at a rate well below that of the labor force. By 1980, the employment problem in Zimbabwe had reached a crisis; as much as one quarter of the labor force was officially estimated to be unemployed (Davies 1992).

The informal economy was to play a significant role in absorbing the job seekers in the labor force, and a different approach from both the central and the local government was to prevail. As in Kenya, and other African countries, the informal economy in Zimbabwe comprises self-employed entrepreneurs and micro-enterprises employing small numbers of paid full- or part-time wage workers and contracting out for household production. Zimbabwe has an official designation of the informal economy that appears in the Central Statistical Office's (CSO), an equivalent of Kenya's Central Bureau of Statistics (CBS) Labor Survey, as one of the employment categories under "paid or self-employed." The legal status of the activity designates it to be distinguished as "informal." There is always a grey area just like in the case of Kenya because all business activities especially in the main towns have to be licensed by the government. Indeed most of the informal trading activities require and do have licenses, but they are still subjected to operating from areas of poor sanitary conditions as well as being subjected to different forms of government censor than the formal business activities.

It is fair to say therefore that "licensing" business activities in the African cities does not by itself make them formal. Nor does it free them from police harassment. Their location of operation, especially for those operating in what was traditional "African quarters" in both Harare and Nairobi, is usually to date considered informal. However, as I argue in this book, such business operations have become so prominent in these cities to render the reference "informal" as synonymous with their economic system.

The socialist government of Robert Mugambe with its strategy of "growth with equity" has been threatened with development problems. Some of these are as a result of a decline in economic growth that has been notable since Zimbabwe's independence in 1980 (Drakakis-Smith 1986). Like in many other African countries, part of the economic growth problem was a result of cumulative external factors of the last years of the 1970s, such as the rising scarcity and cost of fuel which in 1986 accounted for 30% of Zimbabwe's imports by value, but internal factors have also contributed to the overall difficulties facing the socialist government. The rapid population growth standing at 3.6% per annum (Drakakis-Smith 1986) was one of the major contributors to the internal problems. Rapid population growth in Zimbabwe, especially in the already impoverished rural areas and in the so-called Tribal Trust land (TTL)—land allocated for the Africans after the better yielding land was taken by the white settlers, produced a heavy out-migration to the urban areas especially Bulawayo in the South and Harare in the North in search of better opportunities than those available in the rural areas. This compares well with the African Reserve (AR) where Africans were overpopulated in Kenya. Relaxed urban policies in both Kenya and Zimbabwe were to produce higher population growth in the main cities, especially in Nairobi and Harare in 1963 and 1980, the respective years of these two nations' independence. Although the government of Zimbabwe proclaimed socialism, the white settlers had been guaranteed that they could continue to practice capitalism by the Lancaster House agreement as part of the deal for the African independence. As a result of that guarantee, the investment of international capital gave Zimbabwe's macro development programs a more capitalistic mode of production than a socialistic one. This meant that those who came to the city could not expect to rely on the State for their daily survival, no social or economic welfare was ensuing in the urban system that, like in Kenya, was clearly a colonial creation and had almost no preparation for the new African urban dwellers who were moving into the city, jobless, unskilled and unprepared just like the city into which they were moving.

The urban population in Zimbabwe and especially in Harare was mainly white. However, there were Africans (predominantly males) who had worked for many years as domestic servants for the whites and who lived in separate residential areas, "the African quarters," which today are referred to as the "high density residential areas." Like in Kenya, before independence, only males in Zimbabwe were the preferred domestic workers, and the quarters built were mainly to accommodate male servants who were expected to leave their families in the TTLs. The sex ratio because of the male-preference policy was higher for the men, but in the mid 1980s and 1990s, the ratio had evened out with just about equal numbers of both men and women. As a result of landlessness and poverty in the TTLs, the African migration to the main cities like

Harare had begun to expand as early as the 1960s. Despite the wishes of the then white administrators, squatting and sub-letting was appearing in the more densely populated African townships. This continued with higher numbers after independence. Manufacturing or industrial development did not accompany the high population in the cities. This led to high levels of unemployment, a fact the new independent government had to deal with without much success.

THE GROWTH OF THE INFORMAL ECONOMY IN ZIMBABWE—HARARE

In all the Zimbabwean cities, the results of the impoverished unproductive TTLs led to heavy urban migration. The Zimbabwean economy, especially in the 1980s and the 1990s, was facing increasing difficulties and consequently, unemployment was large and growing. With the formal economy unable to absorb all the new entrants to the labor force, attention has increasingly focused on the informal sector as an important source of employment and income. Yet, as in the case of Kenya, establishing and operating a business in the informal economy of Zimbabwe is seriously hampered by an inhospitable environment and by limited access to key inputs. The informal economy in Zimbabwe, and especially in Harare, tends to be overwhelmingly run by women (comprising two-thirds of those involved) (Saito 1990). Most of these women are engaged in food and fruit selling, vegetable selling, knitting and sewing, (Horn 1994; Saito 1990). Most were previously in the predominantly black townships like Chitungwiza and Highfield, but in 1993-94, I observed dozens of women and men vendors who were now in the central business district of Harare, formerly the white section of the city and where the informal economy was legally and efficiently prohibited. Women entrepreneurs in the informal economy are to date additionally impeded by cultural and legal constraints and by the demands of their time and energy imposed by their dual responsibilities of family rearing and income earning (Saito 1991).

Like in the case of Kenya, the government of Zimbabwe has given rhetorical promises of recognizing and supporting the informal economy. Indeed after independence, the government recognized the informal sector in pursuing its national goals of "growth and equity." The government declared in the First Five Year Plan (1986-1990) that it would give strong support to the informal economy. Fifteen years later, the overall picture is that the informal sector is still treated as a secondary economy and as contributing less to the national economy. Hence, the informal economy is subjected to discrimination and occasional harassment as was narrated by the informal economy entrepreneurs, particularly by the women selling secondhand clothes who informed me of how they were never sure of whether the location they sold from today would be safe to sell from the following day given the inconsistency of the city officials. Saito (1991) and Horn (1994) on different research missions observed that many of the racially motivated restrictive laws and regulations governing economic activity in the pre-independence period have been retained unchanged, and the few institutional changes have been largely ineffective. One of the locations in Harare that I visited and interviewed the informal sector entrepreneurs was Dura Wall not very far from Mbari-Musika. In Dura Wall, the set up is very much like the *Jua Kali* sites in Nairobi which now have sheds. Instead of roof sheds, the Harare location had this wall made of a hard "durable" material, hence the local reference of "dura," short for "durable" wall.   While the entrepreneurs in the location were appreciative of having a location that they could safely conduct their small business (mostly carpentry, auto-repair, metal work), they were critical of the fact that this place had no basic infrastructure like electricity. The road to their work place was muddy and therefore a problem for them and their customers to reach to during the heavy tropical rains. Thus, one observed on the surface support of the informal economy in Harare but very little concrete government support.

Despite such constraints like in the case of Kenya, the informal economy in Zimbabwe and particularly in Harare has grown rapidly in recent years and displays considerable social and economic dynamism. This can only be attributed to the efforts of the individual entrepreneurs pursuing their social networks effectively for both information and starting capital for their various trades. Women in particular in Harare have shown a high motivation and entrepreneurial spirit given that they encounter more impediments than the men to achieve success in their small businesses.

3
Defining the Informal Sector

THE INFORMAL SECTOR DEFINED

In this chapter, I seek to understand what the informal sector is as well as give an explanation of its role in over-urbanization. What is the informal sector? In an attempt to answer this question, many researchers have offered different answers (explanations), most of which do not conform with my perception. The informal sector is not the opposite of the formal sector. I disagree with Geertz's (1973) classical distinction and separation between the bazaar and the firm economy. I also refute Sethruman (1981) and Mazumdar's (1976) view that the informal sector is constituted by the activities of the poor. The informal economy not only successfully advances many of its practitioners but also may be one of the most promising sectors of the economy. It does not, then, offer only occupations for survival, as De Soto (1987), Mingione (1991) and Portes, Castells and Benton (1989) have argued. The informal sector boasts some reasonable existing capital intensive projects, such as welding among metal artisans, and some of the most innovative practices, especially in the application of technological skills used to fabricate items that well-equipped modern factories have normally produced. The services offered by some informal sector operators in transport and in vegetable and food selling are competitive. Indeed, the

World Bank, United States Aid for International Development (USAID) and other international agencies and governments have increasingly recognized the informal sector as a major contributor to the overall economy of developing countries.

Much controversy has developed in the last twenty years over a definition of the term informal sector, which has become a universally recognized concept to most scholars, researchers and practitioners in developing countries. Those involved in the sector would in fact be amused to discover the number of scholars and policy makers who spend breathless debates and pages defining their work. In their own eyes, they are street hawkers and garbage collectors, as in Cali, Bogota; metal artisans in Nairobi's Kamukunji area; food sellers in Nairobi's industrial area; drum sellers in Nairobi's Shauri Moyo; and garment makers in either Shauri Moyo or Jogoo market.

It has become almost routine among scholars in this field to start the discussion of definitions by acknowledging the early work of Keith Hart (1973), a British anthropologist who worked in Accra, Ghana. I respect that tradition but point out that the different definitions are a matter of semantics and are irrelevant for a true understanding of the informal sector. Hart, working in a low income neighborhood in Accra, distinguished between what he called formal and informal on the bases of the legitimacy of the activities that were generating an income. Hart then called attention to the otherwise previously ignored illegitimate sector of the economy. In it, he saw survival mechanisms for the urban poor. He focused especially on traditional market activities that in truth were not unique to Accra but were interesting for the volume of income and transactions that they generated. He studied radio and car repair shops, shoeshine boys and street hawking. He did initiate an inquiry that would interest many scholars in the Third World cities who were preoccupied with understanding the economic survival strategies employed by most new and old urban migrants.

The work of the International Labour Organization (ILO) in Kenya on Employment, Incomes and Inequalities (1972) brought international attention to the subject of the informal sector. Going beyond Hart's description of various varieties of economic activities among the poor, the ILO report came up with seven different characteristics that distinguished the informal sector from the formal, some of which have been subject to heavy criticisms by researchers in the field. According to the ILO (1972), the following characterize informal activities:

1.   ease of entry;
2.   reliance on indigenous resources;
3.   family ownership of enterprises;
4.   small scale of operation;
5.   labor-intensive and adapted technology;
6.   skills acquired outside the formal school system; and
7.   unregulated competitive markets.

The characteristics of the formal sector are the obverse of those of the informal:
1.   difficult entry;
2.   frequent reliance on the market for resources, hence imports;
3.   corporate ownership;
4.   large-scale operation;
5.   capital-intensive and formal technology;
6.   skill acquired from specialized schools; and
7.   regulated competitive markets.

The ILO team was not preoccupied with a precise definition. The team's concern was mainly to explain income inequalities that presented barriers to growth.

The ILO's list is inadequate for various reasons. First, the availability of capital does not govern *entry* into the informal economy only but requires complicated social network connections not available to everyone with some financial resources. For some sub-sectors, for instance, entry is more difficult than for the formal economy. The scale of operation may cover entire cities. It was Moser (1984, 136) about ten years later who challenged the imprecision of the ILO's list by offering a new definition:

> The informal sector is still too broad to be meaningful; at one end is a pool of surplus labor, at the other skilled high income earning entrepreneurs; at one end the proliferation of residual enterprises evolutionary in nature, at the other end of the spectrum dynamic evolutionary enterprises.

Moser was correct: the heterogeneity of the informal sector cannot be overemphasized. Some sub-sectors are better paying than others; some require large capital to start while others require a small amount. Males dominate some, like metal artisanry in Nairobi, while women overwhelmingly run others, like food selling. Some involve political activities (indirectly or directly) and future promises of growth, while others are truly marginal and stagnant. Indeed the informal sector is a smorgasbord of economic activities varying in size, products produced, levels of capital investment and gender of those predominantly producing.

Besides Moser, other scholars have criticized the term informal sector for being analytically weak. Peattie (1987a) suggested that the term has popular appeal but, due to the many economic activities it encompasses, it is not useful for analysis. She argued that it should be abandoned altogether. Khundker (1988) criticized what he considered Peattie's extreme position but recognized the impossibility of arriving at a precise definition of what the informal sector is.

The Central Bureau of Statistics of the government of Kenya offers yet another definition of the informal sector. The informal sector is "those self-employed persons in open markets, in market stalls in undeveloped plots or on street pavements within urban centers" (Republic of Kenya 1992a). Naturally, this definition, too, has its limitations, in particular the fact that the informal sector is known to exist in rural areas and not exclusively in urban centers. Also, those who tailor or finish their products in their own homes do not operate in any of the locations mentioned by the definition. By using the above definition, the government under-reported the existing number of informal sector activities.

In light of so many criticisms, the ILO (1991, 6) revised its earlier definition and suggested that the informal sector:

> is understood to refer to every small-scale unit producing and distributing goods and services and consisting of independent, seller, employed producers in urban areas of developing countries, some of whom employ family labor and/or a few hired workers or apprentices, which operate with very little capital, or none at all, which utilize a low level of technology and skills, and therefore operate at a low level of productivity . . . they are for the most part unregistered and unrecorded in official statistics; they tend to have little or no access to organized markets, to credit institutions, or to many public services and amenities; they are not recognized, supported or acquired by the government.

Like its predecessor in 1973, this definition has some serious flaws and does not keep up with the times and reality in the ever-changing cities both in developing and developed countries. The informal sector, for instance, is not only found in developing countries. It is prominent in New York City (Saskia-Sassen 1989), Madrid (Benton 1989), Miami (Greiner and Stepick 1989), Los Angeles (Fernandes-Kelly 1989) and London (Standing 1989), as well as in many Italian cities (Capecchi 1978). In addition, at least in Kenya, one cannot say that government support is nonexistent for the informal sector. The Sessional Paper No.1 of 1986 and later official research papers have urged the government to involve itself in the informal sector to try to strengthen it. Certainly, the government has also acted against the sector, through the demolition of working premises and residential places, for instance, but there is continuing overwhelming evidence that without detailing the motives, the governments in Kenya and Zimbabwe have been giving some kind of support toward the informal economy.

In this book, I take the position that definition problems may exist, but that such problems in themselves do not suggest that the informal economy does not exist. It exists in many forms albeit most of them, informal. Informal networks, for instance, play a critical and important role in recruitment, one that classical economists could never take into account. Recruitment done, for instance, on the bases of friendship or co-ethnic affiliation is not what a mainstream economist would be expecting. It is with this understanding that I offer my definition of informal sector.

> The informal sector is all those small scale business activities that operate without direct state regulation. They are considered illegal because they do not pay taxes and they operate in spaces not zoned for what they do. They are illegal but not illegitimate in the eyes of society. Thus I distinguish between the illegitimate ones, which include criminal activities such as drug selling, soliciting or engaging in prostitution, and so on. The small scale businesses of my definition face harassment from city and local council police, yet they are a viable and a dynamic part of the national economy.

My definition does not discriminate as to whether the small business is manufacturing using technical skills or in trade. The major variable of the definition is the State, and whether or not it regulates the economic activity. Castells and Portes (1986) and De Soto (1987) have offered similar state-based ideas of informal sectors. The same can be said of Preston-Whyte and Rogerson (1991, 2), who define the informal sector as "institutionally unregulated income generating activities."

During the last two years, the literature from Kenya has distinguished between the informal sector and what has been popularly called the *Jua Kali*, a term that international agencies, like the World Bank, have adopted. It means "hot sun" and refers to those operators that have their premises in open places. They include carpenters, tinsmiths, welders, auto mechanics who have been working in the hot sun most of the year. Some of these operators have distinguished themselves from other informal sector operators by gaining the semi-official recognition of the Ministry of Technical Training and Applied Technology through the founding of trade associations, commonly known as *Jua Kali* Associations. Kenya non-governmental organizations (NGOs), like the Kenya Rural Enterprise Programme (K-REP), Kenya Industrial Estates (Informal Sector Programme), Kenya's women Finance Trust (KWFT), refuse to recognize these associations and categorize *Jua Kali* with the rest of the informal sector. The existence of *Jua Kali* reveals the importance of state recognition, the inability of most definitions to categorize the phenomenon, and the value of my definition. Chapter 4 more fully discusses *Jua Kali*.

The informal sector has developed in most countries as a response to the inefficiencies and the saturation of state-regulated (formal) labor markets. The failure of the Kenyan government to create jobs in Nairobi during the late 1970s (no more than 300 were created), for instance, inferred that the growing migrant population had to find employment in activities other than those recognized by government officials. The newly created informal labor market enjoyed no governmental regulation, required no official qualifications and no special levels of education. Informal activities rely on traditional skills, although that is not their main characteristic. These skills are applied to modern technological products.

Informal activities vary from country to country. In Kenya, they include the following: metal and wood artisans, open air auto garages, shoe shining, maize roasting, vegetable, fruit and food selling, newspaper vending, hawking, garments making, rubber stamps making, taxi and *matatu* operating, car parking and car washing and drum selling.

METHODOLOGY

To gain a better idea of the activities of informal sector operators and their links to the State in Kenya, I conducted simple and participant observation among four subsectors. This involved daily presence in the work places of metal artisans and garment makers (production), food sellers (services) and drum sellers (actually middlemen). The four subsectors are distributed mainly in the eastern side of Nairobi City. I initially posed as an interested customer and, once a rapport was established, identified myself as a researcher and asked related questions (see questionnaire in Appendix). In the third month, I hired two research assistants. Besides the qualitative data collected during the observations, an interview schedule (questionnaire) was administered by the author and the assistants from the fourth month to the operators in the various subsectors. A random survey of the operators, mainly the owners of the small-scale business activities they were doing, was done and 200 respondents in Nairobi answered the questionnaire that formed the basis of the quantitative data of the study. The distribution was as follows in each subsector: metal artisans (62); drum sellers (29); food sellers (46); and garment makers (63). For details of sampling procedure see Macharia (1989). I conducted this part of the study in Kenya between 1987-1989. The goal was to explain the growth of the informal sector in times when the Kenyan state was openly against it (ILO 1972).

Recruitment in all subsectors cannot follow official methods, such as the market, credit facilities and so on. It is instead carried out through social networks, mainly kinship, ethnicity and friendship. Information flow concerning resources, markets and suppliers also rely heavily on networks.

Income varies with occupation. Most of the entrepreneurs, full-time employees or those working on a piece rate reported higher incomes than the minimum official salaries. They however complained that the work they do is physically harder than that done by those employed in the formal sector. It was more tiring, for example, to make a washbasin from hard scrap-metal than to work as a messenger in a government office. I would briefly characterize the subsectors I studied in terms of income in the following ways:

1.   Drum sellers make huge profits. The same holds true for entrepreneurs, middlemen, investors in rural farming and urban plots. Garment makers reported high profits, although

lower than those in the occupations just mentioned. All
these informal sector operators invested their profits in
property and their children's education.

2. Food sellers, particularly those operating in the kiosks, make
    incomes that are reasonably high, but are lower than all
    those in the first group. Those operating in the streets do not
    make good profits. In fact, most of them have to rely on
    their spouse's salary to make ends meet, especially those who
    have children in school. Others admitted that they have
    other kinds of income generating activities, mainly illicit
    beer brewing.

3. Metal artisans make sufficient amounts to maintain a
    moderate life style. Their assistants make reasonably good
    incomes compared with the minimum legal salaries in the
    formal sector which was about Ksh. 750 per month (about
    U.S. $50 per month).

According to the Economic Survey of 1994, 45% of Nairobi's two
million people are engaged in the informal sector, although that figure
could be as high as 50%. Participants come from a variety of
backgrounds. A large percentage comes, however, from poor economic
backgrounds and rural areas. Many of these have learned over time new
skills and expanded their practices, to the point that one can compare
their achievements to those of Koreans in Los Angeles (Light and
Bonacich 1987). Thus, a percentage of informal economy operators are
fairly wealthy individuals who managed their activities successfully. My
records showed that more than half of the interviewees had improved
their conditions over the years. Their pride was understandably high;
one stated that "no matter how much money I could be offered, I would
not leave this dusty place for an office job." Those employed by others
received, on average, wages higher than the minimum set by government
regulation.

Most informal sector operators were between 25 and 65 years of age.
Women were more active in food and vegetable selling. Men favored
technical employment. Education levels were low, often not beyond
primary school. Formal education appeared to have no correlation with
ownership of a business activity. In some cases, very successful
entrepreneurs had no formal education at all. One illiterate drum seller

reported making an equivalent of $900 a month. They felt they were more successful than the average University of Nairobi lecturer, who makes $450 per month on average.

Of the 45 Kenyan ethnic groups, only ten were represented in Nairobi's informal jobs that I studied. Two of the largest groups, the Luo and the Kikuyu, are almost equally distributed in the garment making industry, food selling and metal artisanry. Historically, these are the two ethnic groups who have lived longest in Nairobi. Their distribution in subsector specificity was particularly interesting as evidenced by the few examples here showing which group dominated most: maize roasting is mainly Kikuyu; shoe repair, Luo; shoe shining, Kikuyu; watch repair, Kikuyu; car washing, Kikuyu; roast peanuts sale, Luo and Luhya; tire shoes and woodcraft, Akamba.

The analysis of ethnicity in the informal sector is significant both theoretically and practically. Theoretically, a class analysis of the informal sector cannot be sufficient for understanding labor markets. Ethnic ties play a large role in determining the assignment of jobs. Practically, awareness of ethnic distribution is useful for sound policy-planning, especially if the informal economy becomes the major employer in Kenya (a trend confirmed by the government in its Sessional Papers No.1 of 1986a and 1992b).

The ILO (1973) suggested that informal sector operators were pushed from the rural areas into the city because they were unemployed in their villages and were attracted by the ease of entry that the sector offered. I strongly challenge this theory. My evidence suggests that friendship and ethnic ties mainly made entry possible. The evidence also suggests that new migrants were only a small percentage of those working in the city's informal economy. Most had lived in Nairobi for many years and had opted to work in the informal economy because of the possibility for higher incomes, making this particular economy not a mere choice for survival, as the ILO report seemed to suggest. Indeed, more than one fourth of the interviewees had formal employment before. They rationalized in favor of the informal economy activity based on the sizable income they got, as well as the personal freedom *vis-a-vis* a formal employment that may have been less paying and with stringent working hours like 8:00 a.m. to 5:00 p.m., as was the case with most jobs in both Nairobi and Harare.

It must be made clear that, in spite of their informality, these sectors are intimately linked to the formal sectors of the economy. This is of course true for Nairobi and Harare as well as many other Third World cities (see Mattera 1985; Bromley and Gerry 1979). One drum seller in Nairobi had connections with East African industries as a former employee that ensured a steady supply of drums. Metal artisans are connected to the *Jua Kali* Associations formed through the Ministry of Technical Training and Applied Technology. Goods and clients of the informal sectors are often from the formal sector. Middle class women buy from Singapore, Hong Kong and European cities clothing which they then sell informally to Kenyan middle and upper class customers. Money made in the informal sector is invested in the formal sector through established banks. Money is also used to purchase services from the formal sector, such as education for young children. The interdependence of the two sectors can be complex, leading Laugurre (1993) to suggest that sometimes one or the other is dominant, interstitial, or peripheral depending on the angle of the study. Similar observation has been made from the studies of the informal sector in the Republic of South Africa as to the close linkages and interdependence between the formal and the informal (Preston-Whyte and Rogerson 1991). Men active in the informal sector learn, through regular interaction with sections of the formal economy, about finance, investment and government activities. Put simply, none of the two operates in a vacuum!

It is this interdependence that has recently pushed governments in both Kenya and Zimbabwe to accept the existence of informal activities. The Kenyan government, for example, has looked upon metal artisanry as a nucleus of indigenous industrialization and entrepreneurship that can almost be classified as "capitalist." The nation's President has repeatedly visited work sites and promised government loans to foster growth.

Informal sector operators work in different trades, some of which I have already listed. These are hierarchically organized (owners, permanent employees, casual employees) and can be organized into two general categories: production, a more recent phenomenon, and services, a more traditional activity. On the bases of this categorization, I gathered some important facts about each subsector worth individual mention.

Metal Artisans

Metal artisans are mainly involved in the production of tin boxes (suitcases), frying pans and farm equipment (like hoes and machetes).

Figure 3.1 Tin boxes, or "the informal suitcase," popularly used by high school and college students nationwide. They cost less and are more durable than the vinyl (formal) suitcase. Note the artistic decorations to make them more attractive.

Welding various tools is also common practice among the metal artisans, especially making cooking stoves, tin lamps (the only source of light in squatter settlements). Two characteristics of the metal artisans deserve attention. First, the artisans are conspicuous in the city because the goods they produce have a competitive edge over the imported ones. Their products compete with those formerly imported by Kenya's Asian businessmen who run large stores in downtown Nairobi. These Asians have started to buy metal artisans' products to sell them in their own shops, creating a direct link between informal and formal economies.

Second, metal artisans are mostly fully integrated in the larger Kenyan economy, receive the support of the State (discussed in detail in the next chapter) and serve as testing grounds for new technologies and international organizations. Although some skills used among the metal artisans are traditional (e.g., welding) modern industrialization heavily influences this sector. The United Nations Environmental Program (UNEP) has relied on the metal artisans for producing "energy *jikos*," or energy saving cooking stoves. They are considered both environmentally safe and affordable to most urban dwellers. They use less charcoal or firewood which in turn saves trees from destruction. Because of their (metal artisans) importance, the Kenyan government has, since 1986, legalized the working sites of most metal workers.

Garment Makers

Garment makers produce women and girl dresses, children's clothes and occasionally men's clothes. The most interesting aspect of this subsector has been its marketing strategy. Having lost competition in urban markets to Asian businessmen and to second-hand clothes sellers

Figure 3.2 Energy-saving charcoal- or wood-operated cooking stove. These have become common both in urban and in rural areas. The drums are the main raw materials.

(commonly known as *mitumba* in Swahili, garment makers have successfully turned to the interior rural areas of Kenya to find thousands of customers. Their suppliers are legal textile industries, also run mostly by Asians. Like the metal artisans, they rely on established contacts with the formal economy. The entrepreneurs in this economic activity are mainly women who will usually have two to three sewing machines with the same number of employees. They all do the sewing while the owner of the business keeps busy with ensuring that there is enough material for sewing and that the orders keep coming to keep the business running. The owners also have to keep up with market day schedules in the city and outside to arrange to transport the garments there on the exact day and on time for sale. In Harare, the garment industry though dominated also by women like the Kenyan one had the distinction that most of the women garment sellers in Harare were foreigners from neighboring Zambia to the North. The garment sellers in Harare were given a low social status and esteem and this explained mainly why most of those involved in this trade were foreigners. Most of the Zimbabwean women were involved in green vegetable and fruit selling (Horn 1994).

Women Food Sellers

In the service sector, I chose to study cooked food sellers, in particular those serving factory workers in the formal industry. I discovered two important facts. First, food sellers have established long-standing relationships with formal workers, therefore creating another solid bridge between the formal and the informal economy. Secondly, by producing inexpensive food, food sellers lower the cost of living for factory workers, enabling factory managers to lower wages. Thus, the contribution of food sellers to the overall Kenyan economy is much subtler than it may appear at first. Its role may explain why the government has protected the operation of some of these food sellers, a topic discussed in detail in the next chapter.

Drum Sellers

Drum sellers cannot be categorized as either production- or service-oriented. They are in fact middlemen. They are closely linked to metal artisans, who are their main customers. The drum sellers buy empty oil

Figure 3.3 Drum selling professionally arranged. The drums are raw materials for metal boxes, cooking stoves and woks, among others.

barrels (or drums) from the industries that use chemicals, and they transport them to locations that they have occupied for the past twenty years free of charge. Their activities are startling for one reason: profit. They usually buy a drum in the Industrial Area for about Ksh. 100, transport it at a cost of at most Ksh. 10 and sell it for Ksh. 150, thus making a net profit of Ksh. 40. Most of them have had more capital to start their small business than any other group that I studied. They are more confident of themselves. Their monthly income level is Ksh. 8000, which is more than the amount the average middle income employee makes in the formal sector. They, of course, pay no taxes, no licenses of any kind, and have few harassment complaints. Their main concern is the possibility of being asked to vacate immediately from their business location because of real estate development. I found more educated men and women in this activity than in any other that I analyzed. A majority had transferred jobs with the hope of being self-employed and wealthier.

They export their products to Uganda and Tanzania. Different usages of the drum include water reservoirs, roofing material (especially in rural areas), cattle feeding containers, raw material for cooking stoves, pots, woks and frying pans among others.

Other researchers have noted the important contribution that informal economic activities, like drum selling, make to the overall economy (Portes and Saskia 1987). Drum sellers buy their drums from chemical industries, oil refineries, food processing industries, and they sell the drums to metal artisans, who then sell their products to customers in the formal sector. Thus, the formal supplies the informal, which in turn supplies the formal. They are middlemen and -women who form a perfect axis between the formal and the informal.

The informal sector is dynamic. It has evolved with time from the peripheral, small-scale businesses to large-scale enterprises active in major parts of cities. It has extended its reach to middle and upper class customers, and it has gained the selective support of the State. Indeed, its growth cannot be understood without a close analysis of its relationship to the State.

4

The *Jua Kali* Sector in Kenya: Its Contribution to Development

WHAT IS *JUA KALI?*

The term *Jua Kali* in Kenya has become synonymous with any kind of work that people do to make money outside their regular formal employment (for those employed) and small scale business activities for those who are not employed either in the public or in the established private sector. The term connotes, on one the hand, hardships, perseverance, survival, unpredictability and long-working hours. On the other hand, it also connotes independence derived from the self-employment, self-supervision and flexible hours, albeit longer than an eight-to-five job. The images are implied by the Swahili language's literal meaning of the term—"hot sun." As can be seen below, it has gained currency in development circles in Kenya and the outside world that has contact with the country. This is mainly because at least 40% of the economically active population in major cities like Nairobi and Mombasa are earning their living from a variety of *Jua Kali* activities much more in the 1980s and 1990s. The white-collar jobs of the 1960s and 1970s in Kenya are rare to come by these days even for the educated. This is also true of the blue collar jobs in the few processing industries in the major cities. Self-employed street hawking, selling second hand-clothes, repairing an automobile on a street corner, repairing furniture or cooking pans, family business or working as an apprentice are the more likely places for the youth coming out of school looking for jobs. These kinds of job opportunities are popularly referred to as *Jua Kali*. I will make further distinctions below as appertains to the usage of the term *Jua Kali*. I will discuss research findings based on sample surveys in four towns in Kenya to give the reader the reality and extent of *Jua Kali* development and growth.

Figure 4.1 Frying pans in the foreground followed by woks and wash basins—also made from drums by the metal artisans. Note the makeshift corrugated iron store. Note also the unsurfaced road which becomes impassable during the rainy season and almost unbearably dusty in the dry season—the *Jua Kali* (hot sun) season.

In this chapter I make the argument that given the poor performance of the formal sector of the economy (both public and private) in the

1980s, particularly in the creation of new jobs and in raising per capita income, the *Jua Kali* sector, an individualized entrepreneur-driven economic activity, will offer an alternative for many Kenyans in the years to come. The necessary support and an enabling environment must be given for this sector to progress to the limits that are yet unknown. However, evidence from East Asian countries, which have become economically strong through their fashion of *Jua Kali* (mainly information technology based on small family firms), may offer an idea about what the limits in Kenya might be. My emphasis is, therefore, on the positive contribution of the sector to the general economy in Kenya.

The last section of the chapter will discuss the organization of the *Jua Kali* sector focusing on the *Jua Kali* Associations—their merits and demerits and whether they have changed their goals with the closer collaboration some have adapted with the government through the Ministry of Technical Training and Technology. I argue that the *Jua Kali* sector should be given a center stage in any realistic programs of Kenya's economic reform toward the 21st Century. This argument is based on field research I carried out in Kenya (1992-1993) which will form the bulk of the discussion below.

Other studies—Kinyanjui (1996), Macharia (1989), McCormick (1994) and Ngethe and Wahome (1989)—have shown the largest concentration of informal sector activities is in the urban centers. Indeed, Ngethe and Wahome (1989) noted that those operating the informal sector in small rural centers have been wanting to migrate to the larger towns. The explanation for this is that the informal sector/*Jua Kali* operators are businessmen and women looking for availability of materials they use for their production and above all looking for a market. In larger towns, the demand for *Jua Kali* goods is higher due to the larger consumer population. Their salaries may not be enough to buy imported products. This makes for a larger market in these towns when compared with the small rural towns.

Nairobi has the highest numbers of *Jua Kali*/informal sector activities in the country. Heavy concentrations, especially in low income residential areas, are noted. A good example for this is Kibera where a recent K-REP survey (Parker and Aleke-Dodo 1991) counted 7,350 small scale enterprises. The Central Bureau of Statistics (CBS) figures below still show a lead for Nairobi in informal sector activities. The Kamukunji *Jua Kali* Association officials were helpful in facilitating my entry here, minimizing the inquisitiveness and political association that prevailed in other parts of the city. I was therefore able to cover the metal artisans, the drum sellers and other small traders like charcoal sellers in Gikomba, Kamukunji and Shauri Moyo.

CONCEPTIONAL DEFINITIONS

Informal Sector

Various definitions of the informal sector have been given by different organizations (e.g., International Labour Organization (ILO), CBS and different researchers). The definitions vary slightly, and among those who are working in this area, the definition has ceased to be a priority as there is a general consensus that "we know what we are referring to." Other issues like problems faced, policy strategies and organization of the sector have become more pertinent issues than definitions *per se*.

Republic of Kenya (1986b, 5-6), the official government body in charge of statistics defines the informal sector as "self-employed persons in open markets, in market stalls in undeveloped plots or on street pavements within urban centers." This definition has its own limitations, among them, the fact that an informal sector also exists in rural areas; also, those who tailor or finish products in their own houses may not be operating in any of the locations mentioned in the above definition. This complicates matters more for anyone wanting to come up with precise numbers of existing informal sector activities. The CBS definition excludes businesses that have more permanent premises and employ one or two extra workers. The ILO in a recent definition (1991) advanced from their 1972 definition which I have criticized elsewhere (Macharia 1989), defines the informal sector as follows:

> The term "informal sector" will be understood to refer to every small-scale units producing and distributing goods and services and consisting of independent, self employed producers in urban areas of developing countries, some of whom also employ family labor and/or a few hired workers or apprentices, which labor with very little capital; or none at all; which utilize a low level of technology and skills; which therefore operate at a low level of productivity . . . . they are in the sense that they are for the most part unregistered and unrecorded in official statistics; they tend to have little or no access to organized markets, to credit institutions, or to many public services and amenities; they are not recognized, supported or acquired by the government.

This definition has many flaws—for example, the informal sector is not only in developing countries.   One finds it in New York (Saskia-Sassen 1989) and in Madrid; indeed, Portes, Castells and Benton (1989) disapprove such a definition. At a later stage in my own work, I plan to compare the informal sector in Africa and American cities. Parts of the ILO definition may not also qualify for Kenya today (e.g., the lack of support or recognition by the Government as there is recognition and even support albeit minimal).

I define the informal sector as:

> all those small scale business activities that operate without direct state regulation. They are considered illegal, because they do not pay taxes, they operate in spaces not zoned for what they do —hence illegal yet they are legitimate in the eyes of the society. I distinguish between the illegitimate ones which would include criminal activities (e.g., selling or trafficking drugs, soliciting or engaging in prostitution). The small scale business activities have faced harassment from city and local council police yet they are a viable and dynamic part of the national economy.
> (Macharia 1989, 5a; 1992a, 222)

My definition here encompasses what I will distinguish below as *Jua Kali*. In other words it does not discriminate about whether the small business is in manufacturing using technical skills or in trade. The bottom line is that it is a small scale enterprise. Despite the limitations of the term itself—narrowing down precisely what is informal—my definition is in line with what other international scholars have called informal (e.g., the works of Portes (1989) and De Soto (1987)). Thus in the case of Kenya and what my study included as *Jua Kali* sector, such trades as carpentry, charcoal selling, drum selling and others were included in the larger term, informal economy. I call it the larger term because, as I will argue below, what I refer to as *Jua Kali* is a subset of the informal economy.

Jua Kali Sector

This term is quite appealing and very distinct as a Kenyan creation. Its Swahili translation refers to "hot sun." The adoption of the term to refer to artisans—be they carpenters, tinsmiths, welders, etc.—is quite fitting given that when these people were without sheds, they did their business outside in the hot sun or in rain during the rainy season. It happens that there are more days in the year when the sun is hot in Nairobi and in most parts of Kenya. Thus, the "hot sun" description is quite fitting.

Its usage in the discourse of small scale enterprises has become more prevalent in the late 1980s and in the 1990s. Initially it came into use as a way of substituting the term informal sector, which was deemed inappropriate. It gained more momentum in usage when the Ministry of Technical Training and Applied Technology was created in 1988. It was then and is now popularly referred to as the *Jua Kali* Ministry. The term has two kinds of usage, *popular* and *technical*:

The Popular Usage

In many people's minds *Jua Kali* simply refers to any small business operating in areas not zoned for it or one that is not recorded with the government authorities. The popular usage of the term is almost equivalent to the term informal sector. Indeed, talking with officials from CBS who supervise their survey for the small scale enterprises in the country, their definition of informal sector given above is understood to be the same as the popular usage of the term *Jua Kali*.

The Technical Usage

The technical usage of the term *Jua Kali* has been advanced mainly by the Ministry of Technical Training and Applied Technology. It is not surprising that the *Jua Kali* Associations, the Kenya National Federation of *Jua Kali* Association or its rival group the Kenya National *Jua Kali* Organization, all of whom have some formal relationship with the Ministry, understand the term *Jua Kali* in the same way. The technical usage defines *Jua Kali* as "all those business activities that use technical skills and know-how to manufacture goods, or use technical skills in provision of various services (e.g., an auto repair, electrical repair, shoe maker)." This definition then encompasses those dealing with metal (e.g., welders, tinsmiths, carpenters). The technical usage of the term is almost becoming standardized particularly in the Ministry of Technical Training and Applied Technology. However, based on my interviews with officials of some non-governmental organizations (NGOs), the popular usage of the term is still preferred by those involved in this area (e.g., Kenya Rural Enterprise Programme, K-REP, Promotion of Rural Initiatives and Development Enterprises, PRIDE and Kenya Industrial Estates Informal Sector Program, KIE (ISP)).

For this chapter, I have adopted the technical usage to understand the term *Jua Kali*. Thus tailoring, carpentry, welding and tinsmith are *Jua Kali* activities (see Table 4.1). Other activities in this table would be what is defined as "informal sector."

SAMPLE SURVEYS ON *JUA KALI* DEVELOPMENT IN SELECTED TOWNS

The data discussed in this chapter were collected in December 1992. In the four towns selected—Nairobi, Mombasa, Kisumu and Karatina—I counted a total of 4083 business activities in various sub-sectors mainly those in what has been referred to as *Jua Kali* (Macharia 1993).

I managed to cover in my sample 8,741 persons engaged in the 4083 business activities. Among the 8,741 persons, I managed to administer a questionnaire to a sub-sample of 261 persons, mainly owners of businesses. These were distributed as follows in the various towns: Kisumu—95, Karatina—46, Mombasa—86 and Nairobi—34. The information from the sample was relevant especially as a resource for employment and investment data. The interviews represented 5% of the total activities. Each interview represented an actual business activity. The sampling method I adopted was systematic whereby I interviewed the first activity and every fifth thereafter that I counted. I feel therefore that this is a reliable, valid and representative sample.

Size of the Informal Sector in Kenya

A reliable complete census of the informal sector in the country is still lacking. I also note that pocket studies done by various NGOs—for example, Promotion of Rural Initiatives and Development Enterprises (PRIDE), Kenya Industrial Estate (Informal Sector Programme) (KIE (ISP)) or Kenya Rural Enterprise Programme (K-REP) (e.g., its study by Parker and Aleke-Dodo (1991) on Kibera)—are at best specific to some interests, mainly credit oriented. They are therefore not reliable in giving the overall sum of those engaged in the informal sector. I relied on the only census that is apparently complete given that there has been a survey team especially charged with doing annual censuses of informal sector activities. This is the Central Bureau of Statistics. Their definition does include the *Jua Kali* activities which could fall in the categories described as manufacturing, construction, transport and communications.

Although CBS's definition may be narrow as I have criticized above, for example, not including those in the rural areas and those in the urban areas working from their houses (Tomecko and Aleke-Dodo 1992), I felt that for lack of any other complete census at this time, I should rely on the CBS data. I could as Tomecko and Aleke-Dodo (1992) boost the CBS figures by 20% or 30% which would probably give a more realistic estimate of the size of the *Jua Kali*. I hesitated to follow this procedure because the raised figure is still an estimate.

Table 4.1
Informal Sector, 1988-1991. Number of Persons Engaged, by Activity

Activity	1988	1989	1990	1991
Manufacturing	66,096	73,167	84,876	101,109
Construction	128	144	170	200
Wholesale and Retail Trade, Hotels and Restaurants	219,131	242,574	274,585	308,455
Transport and Communications*	5,540	6,187	7,047	8,015
Community, Social and Personal Services	55,467	61,439	69,916	79,378
Total	346,362	383,511	436,594	497,157

*Includes mainly support services to transport activity.
Source: Republic of Kenya. 1992. *Economic Survey.* Nairobi: Government Printer.

The sample survey I did in the four towns compliments the national figures published in 1992 (see Table 4.1). I have also taken the average percentage increase between the years and estimated for the 1992 persons engaged in the informal sector.

As Table 4.2 shows, 497,157 persons were engaged in this sector in 1991. Tomecko and Aleke-Dodo's (1992) boosted estimates by 20% gives the figure as 598,513. Either of the figures suggests that at least half a million Kenyans in towns are actively engaged in the informal sector. In the estimated figures nationwide for 1992 (see Table 4.2), I estimate the persons engaged in the informal sector to be 561,004.

Table 4.2
Number of Persons Engaged 1990-1992, by Industry

Industry	1990	1991	1992*
Manufacturing	34,876	101,109	116,554
Construction	170	200	221
Wholesale and Retail Trade, Hotels and Restaurants	274,585	308,455	345,706
Transport and Communications*	7,047	8,015	9,065
Community, Social, Personal Services	69,916	79,378	89,458
Total	436,594	497,157	561,004

*Estimated figures

The categorization like manufacturing would be what qualifies to be *Jua Kali*. Some examples would include construction, transport and communications. These activities are, however, not common among the *Jua Kali* activities identified in Kenya. From the available data nationwide, it is evident that wholesale and retail trade, hotels and restaurants (which includes kiosks) are more dominant in the informal sector (see Table 4.2). To get the proportional distribution and to get the composition of *Jua Kali* and informal sector, I did a percentage distribution of the different major categories. My analysis shows that the wholesale and retail (including women food sellers especially in large markets like Karatina) hotels and restaurants represent about 62% of the total informal sector. From the figures in Table 4.3, there appears to have been a slight fall in this percentage. This may be explained by the generally poor economy experienced in Kenya in 1992—a year that will be remembered as the year of "big time politics in Kenya" leading to the multiparty elections on December 29. What would be referred to as *Jua Kali* (i.e., manufacturing, construction, transport and communication) is 22% of the total informal sector, the remaining 78% being in wholesale and retail, community, social and personal services.

Table 4.3 below shows the distribution of activities in the four sampled towns. As mentioned above, I chose areas of high *Jua Kali* concentration but nonetheless with other trade activities like wholesale and retail, shoe shining, grain selling, charcoal and drum selling. (Drums are empty oil barrels used as raw materials by the metal artisans. See Figure 3.3.) I argue that the sample is quite representative of what one may expect to find in other Kenya towns. Some major business activities that I enumerated as *Jua Kali* included tailoring, carpentry, welding and tinsmithing. I also have a category of other manufacturing not compared in the four main ones. Open air garage is a service using technical skills although it is not manufacturing *per se*. Other activities include those that identified as the informal sector (i.e., wholesale and retail trade, market selling, etc.). Different towns tend to have a predominance in certain sub-sectors (or business activities). Nairobi appears to have more people involved in metal work, especially welding. One should be aware, however, that this may also be because of the area I sampled. In Nairobi as explained above, the Kamukunji, Shauri Moyo and Gikomba area were sampled and this may explain the distribution of different sub-sectors. Carpentry, tailoring and welding predominate in Kisumu while in Mombasa tailoring and carpentry were the major business activities. Karatina, where I carried a total census given the small size of the town, appears to have an almost even distribution of the *Jua Kali* activities.

It is interesting that my sample corresponds with the national figures especially in the category of other activities which here refer to wholesale and retail trade, hotel and kiosk operation. This predominates in all the towns, with Mombasa having more than half of the business activities I counted (i.e., 1363 in this category compared with the total of 1795 activities). I managed to include in the sample 4083 business activities, a size I consider reasonable and representative (see Table 4.3).

Table 4.3 Distribution of Activities, by Town					
Activity					
	Nairobi	Mombasa	Kisumu	Karatina	Total
Tailoring	—	129	183	57	369
Carpentry	79	116	209	69	473
Welding	114	37	124	16	291
Tin-smithing	12	21	91	29	153
Other Manufac.	9	83	27	65	184
Open Air Garage	1	46	241	45	333
Other Activities	207	1363	594	116	2280
Total	422	1795	1469	397	4083

Composition of Women in the Informal Economy

My data, like the national data and other studies (e.g., Macharia 1989; McCormick 1994; Ndua and Ngethe 1984; Ngethe and Wahome 1989), indicate that women are still much lower in number, especially in the manufacturing sub-sector. This had not changed in 1992. I enumerated very few women in welding, tinsmithing and in other forms of metal fabrication. The majority of the women were in trade, the sub-sector represented here by wholesale and retail, hotel or kiosk operation.

In Karatina, for example, there are many women traders much more than men who predominate the Karatina open air market. In an interview I did with the Karatina Branch officials of Kenya Women Trust

Fund, I learned that there were more than 1000 women in this small town engaged in active trade. Most are involved in market selling of food and other agricultural products. This included mainly dry food, green vegetables and fruits. Although I did not focus fully on this group, suffice it to say that they are a group that cannot be ignored when discussing promotion of small scale enterprise development in Kenya. Otherwise, one may assume women are not actively involved in small scale business if one only looks at the *Jua Kali* activities where they are under-represented. Ngethe and Wahome (1989) in their study of the informal sector in rural areas found that women there were more represented than in urban centers. This may be due to the same reason I have explained above, mainly that most of those women are involved in simple trade, which predominate the rural informal sector compared with the urban informal sector that may be characterized by manufacturing as I have noted in some towns.

Figure 4.2 Water pails (containers). This one is owned by the woman seated waiting for prospective customers. Note the wire mesh windows and the door for night security.

Tailoring, especially in Kisumu, Mombasa and Karatina, appears to be the main domain of women (369 in my sample) as opposed to tinsmithing where I only found one woman in Nairobi or in carpentry where the total sample produced only five women. Engagement in other activities, including wholesale and retail trade, is predominated by women, as can be seen in Table 4.3 where 1412 (61%) women were involved in trade out of the 2280.

From my sample, which did not discriminate against women but, rather, counted every business activity in sampled areas, I still find that women were under-represented. Out of 8741 persons engaged, 1860 (i.e., 21%) were women while 6881 were men.

LARGEST CONCENTRATION OF *JUA KALI* IN KENYA

The largest concentration of *Jua Kali* in Kenya is found in the largest towns. Most people involved in informal sector and *Jua Kali* activities rely on heavy populations to purchase their goods and will therefore try to locate where a consumer culture is more developed and above all where purchasing power is high.

Jua Kali activities also need to be located where they are accessible to the raw materials that they need for their manufacturing, near large industries as some *Jua Kali* specialize in using leftover materials from the large industries; they also need to be near electrical power especially those involved in welding. Thus, I find a bias for *Jua Kali*s to want to be in the large towns. This was my finding which concurs with that of Ngethe and Wahome (1989) who found that those informal sector operators in small rural centers would prefer to move to major urban areas.

My findings suggest that the heaviest concentration of *Jua Kali* in Kenya is in the leading towns in population size: Nairobi, Mombasa, Kisumu, Nakuru, Thika, Eldoret. Thika is an interesting case in that it is not the largest in population size but historically it has been a major industrial town with such industries like Metal Box based there. There has been an outflow of formal employees of these industries going on their own and starting their *Jua Kali* workshop.

Most of the business activities in small towns and rural areas are mainly trade oriented. Thus, it is safe to say that most *Jua Kali* activities are concentrated in the major towns.

CAPITAL, INVESTMENT AND EMPLOYMENT CAPACITY IN THE *JUA KALI* SECTOR

The main activities that I will discuss include tailoring, carpentry, welding, tinsmithing and open air garages. These fall in the general categorization of manufacturing or what may be called *Jua Kali* proper. Table 4.4 presents the average recent and expected investments. By recent, I referred to the last six months from the time of the interviews. Thus, for many of them they were giving their last investment in June/July 1992. I was also eager to learn from the owners of the business activities what they considered to be the needed capital to create only one additional job in their business based on their practical experience. I have summarized all this information in Table 4.4 below.

Table 4.4
Average Recent and Expected Investments and Average Funds Required to Create One Job, for the Selected Activities

Activity	Avg. Recent Investment (Ksh)	Avg. Expected Investment (Ksh)	Avg. Funds Required to Create One Job (Ksh)
Tailoring	6,498	42,163	7,902
Carpentry	1,463	43,774	9,881
Welding	25,882	120,294	31,824
Tinsmithing	3,807	40,769	9,321
Open Air Garage	19,805	194,844	29,750

Taking all those (369) involved in tailoring, for example, the data show that the average recent investment in Kenya shillings in June/July 1992 was Ksh. 6,498; the carpenters in general had not invested as much. The data show that they had only invested Ksh. 1,463. Those involved in welding and open air garage had invested more than the others, i.e., 25,882 and 19,805 respectively (see Table 4.4).

By "average expected investment," I mean the amount of money (funds) one would consider realistic to invest in their business to boost it to a higher level. I made it clear that I was not interested in what they considered to be their "dream" business but instead one that they could feel comfortable with, and if it was a loan they were to get to invest, one they could also afford to repay. The welders again from evidence in Table 4.4 happen to have been the ones involved in a business activity that required a lot of investment. They expected an investment capital of about Ksh. 120,294. However, the open air garage activity appears from the data to have been the one requiring the most, as they reported Ksh. 194,844. On pushing them to tell me why they needed this much money, they explained that motor vehicle tools and parts prices have gone up so high that to run a viable business one needs quite a lot of money. The tinsmiths on average reported the lowest average expected investment of Ksh. 40,769.

I was interested in finding out how much money the Jua Kali businessmen in the various sub-sectors or activities thought they would need to realistically enable them to create one job. These results are in column three of Table 4.4. Not surprisingly, the welders reported the highest amount needed to create one job (Ksh. 31,824) compared with the lowest reported, the tailors (Ksh. 7,902).

Noting the differences among the sub-sectors is important. This would make one avoid the simple generalization of *Jua Kali* or the informal sector without being specific about what sub-sector is being referred. There are varying needs in different sub-sectors. This is a point that this sample survey has helped to emphasize,

Most of the business activities had an average of one employee except the tailors who reported to have started on their own with no employee. It is interesting that the tailors also on average started with the least capital of Ksh. 7,018 compared with others like welding where the average initial capital was Ksh. 37,386.

The findings showed that with an increase in capital, there is also an increase in the number of employees in any given business activity. Those in tailoring, for example, who reported having had no employees at all when they started with Ksh. 7,018, increased their number of employees from zero to two when their average capital rose to Ksh. 15,804. I noted the same increase with all the other business activities with welding topping the list. While the welders had an initial capital of Ksh. 37,386 with only one employee, with the average capital of Ksh. 190,944, the number of employees had increased to six. From the data, open air garages appear to be the other major employer in this *Jua Kali* sector with five employees at an average capital of Ksh. 148,750.

From the sampled businesses, the calculated average reported income is Ksh. 11,976,451. This is derived from the current average capital for each activity multiplied by the number of activities that I interviewed during the survey. It is therefore correct to assert that there is much capital that is in this sector given that the almost Ksh. 12 million presented here is just part of the sample of 201 respondents who also represented business activities. Table 4.5 is self-explanatory, but I include it here for readers who may be interested in the average age of the business activities in the sample survey. This is quite representative of what one may get nationwide. The point to note is that *Jua Kali* activities have been around for some time as represented in the category of those aged 10 years and above. Indeed I did interview a few that had been around for more than twenty years. It appears from the data that not many *Jua Kali* activities started in the years between 1982-1987. This may be due to the harassment of this sector noted during these years (Macharia 1992b). As can be observed from the findings, between 1988 and 1992, at least 98 *Jua Kali* business activities started, which is a higher figure compared with 78 and 85 for the previous years.

Table 4.5
Age of Business

Activity	<5 yrs	5—10 yrs	>10 yrs	Total no. of Businesses
Welding	4	6	9	19
Carpentry	21	24	16	61
Tailoring	26	9	14	49
Tinsmith	8	10	20	38
Other Manufacturing	7	4	6	17
Open Air Garage	10	14	10	34
Other Activities	22	11	10	43
Total	98	78	85	261

DEVELOPMENT AND ORGANIZATION OF
THE *JUA KALI* SECTOR

The *Jua Kali* development in Kenya has been ongoing since the 1960s. Those involved in it have been artisans and other small scale entrepreneurs who have been more concerned with the products they develop and where to get the market for them in order to make a little money for their families. Those involved have in almost all ways relied on informal systems to establish their business including informal training of skills through apprenticeship, informal banks (mainly from money lenders who are relatives or friends) and informal marketing, that is not necessarily through the Chamber of Commerce branches of the various towns. These people have utilized their informal social networks to enter their trade and to develop them.

The government started showing some interest in this sector in the mid 1980s as evidenced by such policy papers as the 1986 Sessional Paper No. 1, which emphasized the development of the informal sector/*Jua Kali* as the answer to the unemployment that was increasing in the country and also as a way of increasing income opportunities for the country. Some intervening measures introduced toward achieving that goal included provision of infrastructure symbolized by the *Jua Kali* sheds like the one in Kamukunji (which was among the first of many to come up in various Kenyan towns), provision of land for the *Jua Kali* artisans in various towns and recognizing the sector by, for example, having a Directorate in charge of *Jua Kali*, relatively lessening the harassment that was more the order of the day for the *Jua Kali* businessmen before 1986. Suffice it to say that such harassment has not disappeared and can still be recorded in almost every town in Kenya. While the government promised to create an enabling environment for the development of *Jua Kali* and small enterprise in general, the promise is yet to be achieved. This may explain why there has been a development of *Jua Kali* Associations. Similar to civic associations, they have been founded to rally together the *Jua Kali* artisans in particular, and more so to act as lobby groups for their grievances.

The *Jua Kali* Associations that are now to be found in most towns in Kenya grew up informally as a result of artisans and other traders coming together with the aim of speaking with one voice whenever the city police, as was common in Nairobi, demolished their kiosks or the sheds from which they operated. They were ideally loose associations. Some performed the function of bailing each other out financially in case one of the members had a problem like lack of school fees for a child, sickness, confiscation of goods by authorities and, at times, laying marketing strategies for their goods.

In recent years (1990-1992), these informal associations have been taking a new formal role, not only in the organizing of small-scale businessmen and women, some of whom are artisans, welders, mechanics, and so forth, but also in acting as a link between the government, donors and the artisans. This attempt to formalize the formerly informal associations is the subject of the remaining pages of this chapter.

The Ministry of Research, Technical Training and Technology through the Directorate of Applied Technology has been behind the mushrooming of *Jua Kali* Associations in Nairobi as well as other towns in Kenya. These Associations have acquired a new formal role of liaison with the government. This would be a very good role, but if played wrongly, it could be a problem. It is in this context that I ask the question, "Whither way for these associations?" which are acting formally in a traditionally informal environment that is introducing too many formal requirements, thus losing touch with the original ideals of the informal associations. Officials of the Associations are too quick to look up to the donor community which poses the question as to whether it is for the common man *Jua Kali* operator, or if it is for the officials who lead the now formalized *Jua Kali* Associations in the disguised role of civic associations.

EVIDENCE FROM THE FIELD DATA ON *JUA KALI* ASSOCIATIONS

From October 1992 to 1996, I had an interest in the rise and development of *Jua Kali* Associations in Kenyan towns which in a broad sense fits the above discussion of the African city. While doing research on *Jua Kali* and small-scale enterprises in six towns—three small ones, Siaya, Muranga and Karatina, and three big ones, Nairobi, Kisumu and Mombasa—the role of *Jua Kali* Associations, especially in promoting the development of the *Jua Kali* sector itself, or the small enterprises in general, has been a major concern. A working hypothesis to answer this question has been, *Jua Kali* Associations may promote small enterprise development; the alternative hypothesis is that *Jua Kali* Associations may kill the entrepreneurial spirit among the *Jua Kali* entrepreneurs.

More precisely, are the *Jua Kali* Associations, both local and national ones, doing more harm than good to the small enterprise development in this country, particularly in the towns where the majority of them are? The experience from the local associations is that there are mixed feelings among the *Jua Kali* operators themselves. A minority of those who are members of the associations said they benefitted from being members, most of them now for about two to three years. An interview with those who said they benefitted revealed that they had got a space to work in sheds that have been put up in their towns and believed their marketing had been improved by the fact that through the association they could be concentrated in one area which made it easier for the customers to reach them.

Those who reported that they did not find the association beneficial said they felt exploited to be paying on average Ksh. 50.00 per month and an extra Ksh. 10.00 payable to the national body, of which the local Association is usually a member. They felt this was a rip-off, especially those who had not benefitted from any space in the *Jua Kali* sheds, had not got any loan or grant through the initiatives of the Association, had not got any plot, though some members got some (as in the case of Mombasa *Jua Kali* Association), and had to attend endless meetings called by the officials. The group with such dissatisfactions preferred the "good old days" when the association was so informal and attended to quite localized needs than the latter ones which some *Jua Kali* artisans accused of being too politicized instead of showing concern of the members needy problems.

Some members also complained that besides paying some money to the local and national associations, they also had to register with the Directorate of Applied Technology and that also cost money. For these small scale entrepreneurs, any little amount taken away from their businesses hurts. They felt that the Associations were becoming the extended arm of the government, with the officials acting like extension officers to propagate government policy. They also feared that these associations may be the entry point of the income tax official with whom the *Jua Kali* have so far avoided contact.

The Mombasa *Jua Kali* Association, for example, at the time of research in December 1992, claimed to have a membership of 1600 members, the largest in the country. This may be explained by the fact that unlike in Nairobi or Kisumu where at least three *Jua Kali* Associations are registered, the whole of Mombasa, that is, on the island, Likoni, Kisauni and Changamwe all belonged to one *Jua Kali*

Association. The officials painted a rosy picture of their association and were ready to enumerate their achievements, mainly acquisition of land for the *Jua Kali* in Likoni, Kaa Chonjo and Miritini where they took me to witness. They also have *Jua Kali* sheds near the refinery from which a few of the artisans operate; the sheds were also the home of their office.

The Kaa Chonjo site is the most developed, partly because it is on the island and adjacent to the main Nairobi-Mombasa highway. The government official charged to overlook the activities of such organizations was not as pleased with the association as the officials were. The government official has the title of Provincial Technical Training Officer and is an employee of the Ministry of Research, Technical Training and Technology. He was unhappy with the way the officials had allocated for themselves large plots in the best sites, at the expense of majority of the members. He also accounted cases of nepotism, and open favoritism of those allocated, some of whom were not members of the association, but were well known or related to the officials. During the visit to the Kaa Chonjo site, I noted the disproportional large plots allocated to the senior officials compared with the small plots of the rest of the members. An interview with a majority of the members revealed a lot of dissatisfaction. Many had still not been allocated any plot, and they had decided to withdraw their membership by refusing to pay their membership fees.

The few women who were members of this association felt exploited by the men officials and were planning to form their own association that could address the women's concerns better than the Mombasa *Jua Kali* Association. They were unhappy with the allocation of plots. Ironically, land promises is one major factor that has rallied most of the *Jua Kali* operators to want to become members of these associations. When there are outcries of corruption during the allocation process, this indeed ruins the association and demoralizes the previously excited artisans. This is true of the Mombasa *Jua Kali* Association.

In Kisumu, there were three *Jua Kali* Associations, one at the famous Kibuye market and two formerly bitter rivals near Kisumu's industrial area where there is a proposed site for the *Jua Kali* artisans. A reconciliation of the two rival associations was facilitated by the Ministry of Technical Training with the senior most civil servant in that Ministry, the permanent Secretary, going to Kisumu to settle the differences. The Kenya National Federation of *Jua Kali* Association official also went to Kisumu to help settle the differences. This is a case of the formal system intervening with the informal. The approach for the reconciliation bordered intimidation from these officials from Nairobi who told the two Kisumu *Jua Kali* Associations that "if they did not unite, the government would not assist them because they would not know which Association was legitimate." In Kisumu, since there was a promise of plot allocation in the site at the industrial area, the members there were very enthusiastic about the now merged Association and expressed support. On the other hand, the association based in Kibuye market was not supported much by its members and most of the members claimed that they did not see the use of it because only a few individuals who were close to the officials benefitted from it.

The carpenters and the women tailors in this market who used to be members had already ceased to be members. They decried the membership contribution which they felt benefitted the welders and metal artisans who were mainly the officials. There was no promise of land allocation in Kibuye, and this may explain the lack of enthusiasm. One can deduce from the Kisumu case that there has to be certain incentives to join these formalized *Jua Kali* Associations and once those incentives are not delivered, the collapse of the association becomes imminent. Due to disappointments and frustrations that may befall such members who do not realize the promises given, the entrepreneurial spirit could be destroyed among these small scale entrepreneurs.

In the other towns, the members expressed similar sentiments. In Nairobi there are many Associations, as almost each area of operation has its own: for example, in Kamukunji, there is the Kamukunji *Jua Kali* Association; in Mathare, there is a Mathare *Jua Kali* Association; along Rabai Road near Buruburu there is a Rabai Road *Jua Kali* Association; and so forth. In the small towns like Karatina and Siaya, one Association purports to represent all the *Jua Kali* operators in these towns. In Muranga, there are two: one in the main town called Muranga *Jua Kali* Association and another one, Mukuyu, which was not active during the time of the research since there were disagreements among officials. The Muranga case is also interesting in that the *Jua Kali* Association that is active happens to be the recipient of the *Jua Kali* sheds that have been put up by the government—another kind of incentive to formalize into an Association. This raises the question of the sustainability of these Associations in the small enterprise development in this country, particularly in Kenyan towns.

One thing that was common with all these associations is that they looked down upon artisans, tailors or carpenters, for example, who were not current (all dues paid) members. To the officials of these associations, those who are not formally registered and paid up on the membership dues, were not *Jua Kali* operators. In one exercise where I was enumerating all *Jua Kali* operators in some of the towns mentioned here, the officials would openly skip an operator who is his immediate neighbor simply because they are not paid-up members. This attitude has developed as a result of those leading the associations believing that outside aid from the government will only come through the associations, a point that has been emphasized by the Ministry of Technical Training. It is, therefore, a system of reward and punishment where one is rewarded for being a member of the association and punished if one is not, or if one chooses to continue operating in the informal way one had always known, before the introduction of the formalized associations. This is wrong. Most of the associations in the towns visited tend to be exclusive and, therefore, not fully accommodating all the *Jua Kali* operators in these towns.

NATIONAL *JUA KALI* ASSOCIATIONS

Besides the local *Jua Kali* Associations that are based in various towns, there has also emerged in the last three to five years what may be referred to as National *Jua Kali* Associations. They may be referred to as such since it is not evidently clear that they are representative of all the *Jua Kali* operators in the country.

The first of these national associations is the Kenya National Federation of *Jua Kali* Associations with its headquarters in Nairobi. This "Federation," as it is popularly referred, came into existence at the beginning of 1992. It has the support of the government through the Ministry of Technical Training whose officials were instrumental in legitimizing it and organizing the first national elections at the Kenya Polytechnic in February 1992. It is also the organization that is closely associated with the Ministry of Technical Training in organizing the Annual *Jua Kali* Exhibition sponsored largely by the British American Tobacco (BAT). My association on an advisory/consultant capacity for about three months at the Federation's headquarters exposed me to the strengths and weakness of this "national organization." Unlike the others that do not enjoy direct government support, the Federation, while enjoying this, also suffers legitimatization from the ordinary *Jua Kali* who, as I have continually argued, had always organized themselves along informal lines.

Most artisans I talked to refer to this Federation as "a government unit," and many argued that the elections were rigged in favor of those who were seen as willing partners with the Ministry officials. This has been hard to verify as the government officials usually allege that a fair election was conducted and the best men and women won. This is not what most *Jua Kali* operators believe. The Federation, again with the support of the government managed to get a foreign donor in the name of Friedrich Ebert Stiffung (FES), a German-based donor that has been quite conspicuous in Kenya funding those with activities that could be generally referred to as social democratic. The foreign donor gave funds for the elections and also for establishing the offices in a posh section of downtown Nairobi on Harambee Avenue, sharing the same building with the Indian High Commission in Kenya.

In an interview with the director of FES, I learned that they see their role as the donor for the Federation as one way of educating the *Jua Kali* operators about their political rights. Their logic is that once you know your political rights, you may also demand better working conditions, and you may eventually raise your economic well-being. For them, therefore, the Federation is like a civic institution which should be politically astute to lobby for the common man who in this case is the *Jua Kali* operator.

The problem with this particular conceptualization is that when the Federation is so closely linked with the government, one wonders when it will stand out against some of the government's oppressive regulations toward the *Jua Kali* sector. I am not suggesting some kind of adversary role between the two. It could be complementary, but from the experience in the three months there, the Federation was more in tune with what the Ministry of Technical Training was suggesting. It was either elaborating on or advancing the Ministry's ideas and rarely did the Federation's officials show some originality to keep up with the donor's idea that they should lobby for the *Jua Kali* operators.

The leadership was itself unprofessional, although this may be seen as part of the teething problem of any new organization. The local *Jua Kali* Associations had not been quite convinced that they should become members because they were concerned about what benefits their membership would be awarded. In brief, the Federation did not represent all the *Jua Kali* operators, and their close association with the government was turning out to be more of a liability than an asset in terms of recruiting membership. Again, it must be understood that the local *Jua Kali* artisan is more concerned with making a new product, coming up with a more competitive design, marketing the product, and not the national politics, which seems to be the preoccupation of the Federation.

Another national association is the Kenya National Organization of *Jua Kali* Associations with its headquarters in Eldoret. This Association, popularly called the "Kenya National," has tried to gain legitimacy with the government through the Ministry of Technical Training without much success. The Ministry, even in this era of multi-party democracy, is still insisting on one representation. Interviewing some officials in the Ministry, I found that they feel other national associations should be allowed to operate and compete among themselves in their delivery of services to the *Jua Kali* operators. This view is held by middle level civil servants in this ministry, but not by the senior-most ones who make the final decisions.

The Eldoret based national association is seen as a rival of the Federation and has continued to play that role of the rival. They claim to have national representation, but I would say they are disadvantaged by being so far away from the national capital. They, however, do have representation in Nairobi and indeed a number of Nairobi's associations like the Rabai Road, the populous Kamukunji *Jua Kali* association, belong to the Eldoret-based association. Their ideology is different from that of the Federation—they believe more in getting their mandate from the local *Jua Kali* operators, and not necessarily being closely aligned with the government through the Ministry. To some extent, they are still keeping up with the informalized way of dealing with their members. They have been talking of possible donors, but none had been identified as yet early in the year (1993) when I spoke with the officials. One area of rivalry between these associations is that the "national organization" existed much earlier than the "federation" which was a recent creation.

The third registered national organization is the *Jua Kali* Co-operative and Kazi organization, with its headquarters in Nairobi. This one has been a bit on the low profile due to illness of its chairman who was very articulate on *Jua Kali* needs prior to falling ill. It started like a co-operative, as its name suggests, with members contributing money that would be shared or that would be invested jointly. It has members countrywide, and it is quite practical in its approach. Like the "national organization" above, it, too, has no direct association with the Ministry of Technical Training who also views it as a rival of the Federation, though it performs a different role (i.e., bringing the *Jua Kali* together as a co-operative).

Advantages of Associations (National and Local)

Some advantages may be deduced from the operations of these associations that have come up in the last few years, including the following:

1. They could be helpful in organizing the small-scale entrepreneurs to keep up with the rapidly changing economic system in the African cities, especially with the influence from outside the structural adjustment programs.

2. If run properly, and without corruption, they could be trusted to put scarce resources from either foreign donors, the government or private companies together.

3. They could be particularly useful in disseminating information either for marketing or improving products of their members.

4. They could also, if unbiased, act as lobbyists for the *Jua Kali* operators and, hopefully, promote production and sales.

Disadvantages of Associations (National and Local)

Disadvantages of these associations, some of which I have already mentioned, include the following:

1. The danger of exclusion or ostracizing those *Jua Kali* operators who are not paid-up members of the associations, thus benefitting only the few who can afford membership.

2. Nepotism practices, especially during allocation of sheds or plots at the expense of other members. This is more practiced by officials of these associations.

3. There is a clear gender bias favoring men and giving a raw deal to the few women who are members. The women see these associations as a men's world and are not willing to become members, meaning that they will also get excluded when sharing of rewards comes.

4.   Tribalism, especially by officials in those associations, like in Mombasa and Nairobi where multi-ethnicity is commonplace among the *Jua Kali* operators.

5.   Withdrawal of members because of various disappointments, thus killing their morale, especially when the promised incentives are not delivered.

6.   Exploitation by officials and their close associates when the membership dues are misappropriated. This also kills the entrepreneurial spirit among the *Jua Kali* operators.

The role of associations needs to be redefined and should take into account the local socio-cultural environment in every town that they operate. If the close association with the government does not go well with the members, then the association should refrain from it. If there are no rewards forthcoming, the officials should be direct and forthright so as not to kill the hopes of would-be co-operators in the future. Empowering the associations by letting them advocate their real needs and concerns should be the goal. All aspects of informality that worked prior to the introduction of the formal *Jua Kali* Associations should be incorporated to attract more members.

CONCLUSIONS AND IMPLICATIONS

I have clearly shown the significance of the *Jua Kali* sector in Kenya's economy giving it a center stage in a program of economic reform and development in Kenya through the 21st Century. I have also called for the need for a more comprehensive census of the informal sector and *Jua Kali* business activities in this country. As shown in the sample survey, coming up with actual figures for this sector is possible. Hopefully, soon an interested organization (e.g., Swedish international Development Agency (SIDA), Overseas Development Agency (ODA), the World Bank) will commission a complete exercise independent of that planned by the Central Bureau of Statistics. This will be important as actual programs are implemented. Specificity of size, location and type of activity are important and need to be known for a successful reform.

I have raised a crucial concern and recommended an approach in this sector mainly studying its heterogeneous characteristic. Thus, I have avoided generalization of talking about informal sector or *Jua Kali*. I have instead looked at actual business activities or sub-sectors like tailoring, welding, tinsmithing, open air garages and the wholesale and retail trade. This approach, whether one is thinking of credit for the sector, infrastructure, training or whatever other component, should be adopted. This is because the different business activities are of different sizes and have different needs; this may be overlooked if one simply talks about *Jua Kali* or even the other term informal sector.

My approach of including different towns is also not accidental, but one of methodological significance. What this suggests, also, is that Nairobi *Jua Kali* should be understood as such while, for example, Kisumu or Mombasa should be understood from their own localities. Such an understanding of the needs in different towns will help policy makers come up with a national policy guided by local needs as identified in different towns and in the different sub-sectors.

In my analysis of initial capital required, estimated investment and the number of employees, I have noted varying results depending on the sub-sector examined. Welding appears to require the most capital, but it also has the most employees. These are the kinds of issues to be examined clearly to develop national strategies to train or to increase employment in the general *Jua Kali* sector. There is more analysis that could be done, and this chapter should be seen as having opened what could be followed. The sector with over half a million people engaged in it, and with over Ksh. 10 million invested among only 201 business activities in the four towns I sampled is definitely large and worth national attention.

The findings should be taken as representative of what is out there nationwide, and being one of the recent field surveys, it will, hopefully, give further guidance about whom the *Jua Kali* are (see previous definitions), where they are, the gender composition and their absorptive capacity of both capital and employment. Of course, this should fit in well with my argument of looking at the *Jua Kali* sector as an alternative and complementary economy. Information contained in this chapter should help us in understanding the ordinary man and woman out there in Karatina or Kisumu involved in different kinds of *Jua Kali* business. This is what I refer to as an individualized policy approach whereby the aggregates should still aim at improving the business and the welfare of that individual *Jua Kali* operator. This will go in the direction of strengthening the policy statements in the government Sessional Papers, No. 1 of 1991, No. 2 of 1992 and the earlier one of 1986, all of which address employment creation in Kenya through the small-scale enterprise—informal or the *Jua Kali* sector.

The last part of the chapter has examined *Jua Kali* development and organization. I have, in particular, analyzed the significance of the newly formed *Jua Kali* Associations which are acting in a formalized version (especially their close association with the formal government organs like the Ministry of Research, Technical Training and Technology). I have discussed the problems with this arrangement, especially when imposed on a section of the economy that has thrived on informal lines during its past. The leadership problems in the Associations may actually be more harmful to the sector's growth. I suggest that there should be cautionary embracement of the leadership of these associations establishing their loyalty to the ordinary *Jua Kali* practitioners and not the almost hyper-embracement portrayed by the Ministry of Technical Training and Technology in 1992 whose concern appeared to be more the number of registered associations rather than what was their legitimacy to the local communities. Establishing a national association also appeared to be at the Ministry's top priority as evidenced by what has been referred to as "hurried elections" sponsored partly by the Ministry at the Kenya Polytechnic, Nairobi in early 1992. For the Ministry, penetrating the sector through the national organization was a priority. It is not surprising that many of the ordinary *Jua Kali* operators are still skeptical of the government's proclaimed good will and are generally dissatisfied with the Associations. Reforms that target individual artisans in local towns will be, in the long run, more helpful than the "powerful" associations seeking national limelight at the expense of ordinary members at the local levels. This will contribute further to the development of the *Jua Kali* sector and contribute to the overall socioeconomic welfare of low income earning groups in Kenya.

5

The Growth of the Informal Economy: The State's Selective Support

The State and the informal economy cannot be separated. There have been contradicting ways in which the State policy has sometimes supported and at other times harassed the informal sector. The African state is a neo-patrimonial entity whose roots are found in its colonial past (Young 1994). Patrimonialism, which in Kenya has been along ethnic lines, has determined whether the State would support or prevent the growth of subsectors and, at times, the whole of, the informal economy.

Whatever the subject of study in the Third World and especially in Africa, the State both at the macro (monolithic) and at the micro (local government) levels ought to be understood in discussing various processes of development. Although not writing directly about the State and the informal sector but on development overall, Rothchild observed correctly:

To fail to understand the role of the State in the Third World is to fail to
gain an insight into the dynamic place of domestic decision makers in the
development process or their possible role in mediating conflicts and
confrontation among different interests in society (Rothchild and Chazan
1988, 56).

Unlike most of the literature on the State which emphasizes the formal
bureaucratic nature of the State in Max Weber's tradition, I argue that it
is by understanding the informal activities of the Kenyan state that one
can explain the continuous growth of the informal sector despite legal
statutes that the State has formally had against the informal economy.
This closely parallels Weiss' (1987) argument on the development of the
Italian informal sector and the informal activities of the Christian
Democratic Party. Weiss showed how the State in Italy promoted the
informal sector by encouraging a dense network of patron-client ties
throughout the Italian society. The State finds itself supporting the
informal sector because many of its clients are informal employees or
employers. In the Kenyan case, too, the State, in its attempt to build
alliances, has become a neo-patrimonial entity and has undergone an
informalization process that has developed parts the informal economy.

How, then, did the informal sector thrive and become a major source
of employment for urban migrants in the 1970s and early 1980s, a time
when it had no official recognition or support by the State? Why has the
informal sector grown so rapidly in the early 1990s? Why were some
bylaws against the informal sector strictly enforced during the colonial
state and unofficially "relaxed" during the post-colonial period? Or, in
the city of Nairobi, why did food sellers in the streets of the industrial
area not thrive until the removal of a predominantly Kikuyu city council?
Why were *matatus* (shared taxis that are usually uninsured and
unlicenced for public service and owned by an upcoming middle class)
in the 1970s suddenly allowed to operate on the Kenyan roads? If
wavering State support is the answer to these questions, more questions
must be posed concerning the causes of that uncertainty. Why, for
instance, did President Moi in the 1980s direct official recognition of the
low level informal sector like the metal artisans to the extent of having
the government put up roof sheds for them?

The answer to these questions is found in the thesis that the State has,
especially through social networks, acted informally (i.e., in a style not
consistent with official policy) and has indirectly *supported* the growth
of the informal economy, even at times when it produced official policy

impediments, such as harassment, meant to eradicate sectors of that economy. In this chapter, this thesis is supported empirically by data from two subsectors: the metal artisans and the food sellers. These, with their subdivisions, most clearly demonstrate the interaction between the State and the informal sector in Nairobi. Before the presentation of the research findings, a brief history of the Kenyan state is appropriate. Only by understanding the State's heritage, is it possible to comprehend its patrimonial character and therefore its informal, selective, involvement with subsectors of the informal economy.

THE ORIGINS OF THE KENYAN STATE

The African independent state in Kenya from 1963 inherited the power structure, laws and bylaws established by the colonial state. This change of power from the British to African elites was essentially what took place in 1963 but the structural system and biases especially among the urban unemployed were still within the system. Clapham (1985) observes that what distinguishes the Third World state (like Kenya) from its equivalent in other parts of the world is the combination of its power and its fragility. Of these two elements, the power is the most evident. Like the colonial state from which it is descended, the Third World state has to maintain itself by extracting resources from the domestic economy, and especially from the trade generated by the economy's incorporation into a global structure of exchange. A poor economy in such a state would mean a weakening of its power base and more fragility especially in acquiring legitimacy from the unemployed and the under-employed, a noticeable group in cities like Nairobi after independence.

The nature and role of the new African state were also linked to the expansion of the urban sector. This occurred through the critical part played by the State in employment creation (ILO 1972; Young 1982). It also resulted from the then unrestricted rural-urban migration that was previously characteristic of the colonial state. Rapid and uncontrolled urbanization had dawned in the new state and socioeconomic problems in such cities like Nairobi were to become a concern of the State and other international organizations sooner rather than later. The city's essential amenities like housing, transportation and sanitation were strained. Werlin (1966, 192) observed that "after the lifting of emergency restrictions in Kenya in 1960, some 50,000 Africans, mostly Kikuyus, entered Nairobi, severely straining the city's facilities." Werlin in 1966 predicted correctly that "even before 1960 the City Council had been attempting to halt migration to the city and the new Kenyan leaders may be forced to restrict it--exactly what they condemned colonial governments for trying or wanting to do." This prediction at that time was to be proven right for in the years of late 1960s and early 1970s, the first President of Kenya, Jomo Kenyatta, advocated "going back to the land" as the State policy in an attempt to reverse migration from urban to rural areas. This example shows the inherent problems that the independent state took over from the colonial state and the irony of using the same measures, though in a less punitive way while compared with the colonial state.

Implicit in the writings of many economists on development is the liberal assumption that the State is a neutral and even a benevolent arbiter whose role is to promote the national interest in economic growth, efficiency and social welfare (Sandbrook 1982). They do not take into account conflicting interests of social classes or regional-ethnic groups who dispose of differential political power. An opposing view conceives the State as a set of public institutions that reflects in its activities the interests of the dominant forces rooted in the structure of production.

The independent state, however, was faced with major contradictions that were insignificant in the colonial state as far as the informal economic activities in the towns like Nairobi were concerned. Unlike the colonial state, whose interests were far from those of the Africans, the independent African state had both direct and indirect responsibility for its people who were previously oppressed, banned from certain places and positions in both the central and the local government, represented in one case here by the City Council of Nairobi. The independent state had to seek legitimacy from the majority of its people since power alone would not help pacify an indigenous administration which was sought after independence. The contradiction then is that whereas the African leaders would prefer a clean city without street vendors, artisans and others who comprise sections of the informal economy, they also felt a responsibility toward the many new urban migrants and had to be realistic about the fact that the State could not create enough jobs for them. Needless to say, the leaders who took over from the colonial masters enjoyed many privileges and wielded much power and respect from the society. For politicians both at the central and at the local government, this was the moment to use those powers to solicit more support from the electorate and indirectly struggle to legitimize their positions in the civic society. Like the nation-state in Europe, the independent state ideally owed responsibility to the civic society. The client-patron relationship was starting to take off in respect to informal sector activities.

The contradictions mentioned above in respect to the new independent state where the leaders wanted to maintain efficiency and cleanliness in the city, for example, and on the other hand felt indebted to help their friends, kinsmen or co-ethnics in acquiring jobs or surviving in some way in the city brought about what I refer to as the neo-paternalism state, borrowing from Clapham (1985) and Medard (1982). Neo-paternalism can be defined as a form of organization in which relationships of a broadly patrimonial type provide a political and administrative system which is formally constructed on national-legal lines. Officials took positions in bureaucratic organization with powers which are formally defined, but exercise those powers, as far as they can, as a form not of public service but of private property. This happens, both in central and local government levels, as empirical findings in Nairobi will show later in this chapter.

The State in Kenya after independence, like all the others in Africa, was characterized by clientelism in the form of patron-client relationships and political patronage. Medard (1982, 162) briefly defines "clientelism" as "an exchange relationship between unequal partners." Medard argues that the patron-client relationship, from the point of view of the anthropologist, is a relationship of personal dependency, excluding kinship ties, maintained by reciprocal exchanges of favors, between two persons, the patrons and the clients, who control unequal resources. Patronage, from the point of view of the political scientist, refers, according to Alex Weingrod (1968, 377), "to the ways in which party politicians distribute public jobs or special favors in exchange for electoral support." My sociological interpretation of patronage, as it applies to this study, is a situation where those in public office have allocated jobs, plots for business operation and other favors to kinsmen, friends or co-ethnics in exchange for political support or legitimation of these favors. In all cases, the exchange is between unequal partners, but political patronage remains less formal and diffuse, more specific than patron-client relationships. Political patronage adapts easily to the formal political structures, whether parties or administration, as in the city of Nairobi.

In the absence of legitimacy, political patronage is the core of underdeveloped states. Coercion alone or harassment in the informal sector is not enough. At the state level, a skillful leader has to learn how to reconcile his own search for booty and spoils with the redistribution of those resources necessary to get political support and strengthen his position. Through patronage, the leader can co-opt his potential opponents and regulate the recruitment of the ruling class. This kind of description fits the State as it operated in independent Kenya. While the leaders in the central government practiced patronage-clientelism as the way to reward supporters, friends, relatives, co-ethnics or clansmen, this was carried out at the local government level by the Mayor of Nairobi. Political leaders who use public office or public property to reward their supporters get legitimacy which they so much need. They also, in a general election, get assured of being voted in by those they have rewarded. Those rewarded, the clients, benefit also by getting a position that they probably would not have gotten had a universalistic process been followed. At the city level, the city leaders may allow residential construction on what would have been a lot for public use, like putting up a health clinic; they may turn a blind eye to violations of city bylaws if this is to their political benefit. Members of a dominant ethnic group, for example, may reward their co-ethnics to ensure reelection in office.

This may also be interpreted as corruption, that is, the use of public powers to achieve private goals. Smelser (1971) defined corruption as a particular kind of "crossing over" of economic and political rewards. He sees it as a contrivance that flourishes particularly under conditions of unevenness and inequality in structuring social rewards—unevenness and inequality that arise typically but not, of course, as a consequence of developmental leads and lags. In summary, I find that the patron-client system has operated around and outside the monolithic, Western state ("normal state") much like the informal economy itself has operated around and outside the formal sector.

THE INTERACTION BETWEEN THE STATE AND THE INFORMAL SECTOR

Five possible theoretical explanations could help explain the relationship between the neo-patrimonial African state and the informal sector. One such theoretical argument is that which emphasizes economic crisis. The thesis is that the State may liberalize its policies to avert an economic crisis. In a situation where big industry or the formal economy are doing poorly, the State may support directly or indirectly the growth of the informal sector.

The second possible argument emphasizes the political populist appeal. This assumes that the leader or leaders of the State may want to attract popular support by allowing or liberalizing rules and laws that would otherwise have hindered the free economic participation in the economy by the common man or woman (the low income groups) who especially in cities may violate land zoning bylaws.

The third argument emphasizes the patron-client relationship. The thesis here is that the informal sector in general, or certain sections of it, may be operated by those who are clients of certain leaders or patrons in the State. This could be either at the central or local government. To maintain the patron-client relationship vital to state leaders, the informal sector draws support and continues to grow informally. Various social networks, like ethnicity and clanism, exist before the establishment of the patron-client relationships.

The fourth argument emphasizes the importance of a subsector to the national economy. This suggests that the State may consider some subsectors to be more important than others. That means some sections of the informal sector may flourish with the State's blessing while others, considered less important to the national economy, receive the State's wrath.

The fifth argument emphasizes gender differences. This suggests that the State may support or discriminate on subsectors. The common trend in African countries has been the tendency of attaching much lower value in informal economic activities dominated by women and much higher value to those dominated by men. The State may therefore be negative or positive in its interaction with certain sections of the informal sector depending on which gender dominates.

Singly, none of the above theoretical arguments can explain the situation in Nairobi. None of them is an adequate model by itself. Based on the data to be discussed below, I develop an alternative model of the interaction between the informal sector and the State which combines some of these arguments. In its simplest version, the model proposes that the State informally may support specific subsectors of the informal economy because of ethnic or kinship ties, need for political legitimacy, gender biases and/or economic crisis and recognition of the potential economic contribution of the informal economy to the overall economy of the country. Which of these factors is more influential on the State depends on the variables external to the model, such as the colonial past, international economic recession, legitimacy of the political elite, international diplomatic pressures and restrictions imposed by international donor agencies.

Thus, drum sellers, food sellers, metal artisans and garment makers in Nairobi did not start in the 1960s and prosper in the 1980s without some state regulation directly, or indirectly, and some blessings from an arm of the State. The existence of informal rules aimed at legitimizing leadership in Nairobi after independence could well have been an informal kickoff for the growth of the informal sector. The norms of reciprocity allowed during Kenyatta's regime (Rothchild 1973) developed between most state and ethno-regional actors in the cabinet and high party organs. This exercise was prevalent in the city of Nairobi in the wake of new African leadership, as Werlin (1966) observes. Bending rules, nepotism and co-ethnic favors were characteristic of the central government, especially in the distribution of white collar jobs in the wake of Africanizing the bureaucracy. Local governments emulated this pattern through their discrimination in the allocation of jobs (in the city hall, plots and kiosks) and in their turning a blind eye to the occupation of a city lot by some artisans. In this way, the city leaders could reward their supporters, friends or co-ethnics.

While these practices may explain the initial prosperity of the informal sector in Nairobi and its blossoming in the 1980s, the stability of the political leadership in the 1970s may explain the State's constant harassment in the 1970s of specific informal activities, since the support of the citizenry became less important to the life of the State. The informal sector was subjected to demolition, confiscation of goods and heavy court fines.

In the 1980s, the relation between the State and the informal economy in Nairobi took a different pattern. In 1982, the City Council of Nairobi councilors and senior administrative staff were accused of corruption, misappropriation of city funds and embezzlement of public monies. The central government, through the Minister for Local Government, abolished the Council and instead appointed a commission to run the affairs of the city. The predominantly Kikuyu council was replaced with a more balanced ethnic commission (*Weekly Review* [Nairobi], 19 June 1983). This change, according to my respondents in the food selling subsector, may have been responsible for an increase of Luo and Luhya women food sellers. There were some senior Luo and Luhya officers appointed in the new commission. Unemployment figures rose in Nairobi and in the rest of the country as the formal sector, private and public corporations combined to perform poorly. This may have led to the government's positive recognition of the informal sector contained in

Government's Sessional Paper No. 1 of 1986.

Before generalizing again on the role of the State in Nairobi's informal sector, I will illustrate the theoretical points already outlined by giving the evidence I gathered from studying specific subsectors: the food sellers and the metal artisans. The State's intervention is either supportive or harassment.

State Support

Some subsectors, particularly the metal artisans, received overt state support in 1986 and 1987. The one that was both dramatic and a living, long time proof of such support was the surprise visit by the Kenyan president at the work place of these artisans. The visit was in 1986 and was covered widely by both local and international media giving the metal artisans a place in the evolvement of a government policy toward the informal sector in general. What came out of the visit were the positive statements by the president of the importance of the artisans in national economic development. He directed that the artisans be set free from previous harassment especially evictions of the land they were accused by the city *askaris* (police) to have illegally occupied. A presidential directive revoked the formal law, which stated that the artisans occupied the land illegally, thereby legitimizing the artisan's occupation. More important, the president also directed that a roof-shed be constructed using government funds creating a semi-permanent work-space for the metal artisans.

State Harassment

Of the two subsectors discussed here, the food sellers, in kiosks and especially those women selling outside factory gates in Nairobi's industrial area, had more stories of state harassment to tell than those of state support. There are three possible explanations why they were harassed. The first may be because of their gender—there were more women food sellers than men. Literature on gender has shown that women have been unfairly treated by law-keeping officers who are usually men (Tinker 1982). Indeed the 23 women food sellers complained that the male police were against them and did not respect their trade. They also thought that the male *askaris* were envious of their being single and having a trade in the city, however small it was. The police saw this as a challenge to their masculinity.

The second possible explanation was the fact that unlike the metal artisans, the women food sellers did not have any political clout or a constituency that could have interested specific patrons who could have come to their support. They were fewer and had little or no political influence. Thirdly, the State might have considered the women's contribution toward the national economy as petty and without the potential of saving some foreign exchange as in the case of the artisans. Examples of other harassment not covered by this study but related are the Muoroto and Kibagare slum clearance which took place in 1990 (Macharia 1991). The two slum areas were largely homes of those engaged in the informal economy.

The State and the Food Sellers

I categorized the food sellers into two: mainly those who sell food in kiosks and have a permit to do so from the city authorities, and those women food sellers outside major factory gates. The food sellers in the kiosks have been established for about twenty years, whereas those outside have only been actively operating in the last four to six years. The State, both at central and local levels, has had both an explicit and implicit role in the establishment of these two sub-categories of food sellers. The policy toward these subsectors has been full of contradictions depending on the political and economic situation in the country, and specifically in the city of Nairobi. I conducted scheduled interviews with 26 food sellers in the kiosks and 20 of the women selling outside factories. In total they comprised 23% of the 200 informants on whom I conducted scheduled interviews in the Nairobi study. I also conducted unscheduled interviews with others in those subcategories. Of the two, those who sold food in kiosks reported to have had close interaction with representatives of the State, particularly officials from the city of Nairobi. Those who operated the food kiosks had a permit for occupation of the 10 feet by 20 feet space. They had to get this permit from the City Council. Otherwise, the kiosk would be declared illegal and would be subjected to demolition.

The fact that there is a permit for the kiosks may suggest treating the kiosks as part of the formal economy, particularly if the definition of informal economy is any "economic activity operating without state regulation." One may even suggest that the kiosks should be referred to as semi-formal. I continue to call the food kiosks informal economy like other researchers have done, Mukui (1979) and House (1984) mainly, because the issuance of the permit is as close as it gets between the City Council and the food kiosk owners, and therefore the State's regulation is very limited. It is certainly not there at the work place. Those independent entrepreneurs reported that the permit has, in fact, not protected them from demolition when the State officials (the city of Nairobi here) have wanted to remove them. The lack of security of tenure in their allotted spaces and the insecurity of closure by city health officials was persuasive enough for me to conceive of the food kiosk operators as being in the informal economy. They also think of and refer to themselves as *Jua Kali* operators, which is the popular reference of the informal sector in the country.

The need for employment opportunities in the mid-1960s, especially with rapid rural-urban migration in Nairobi, contributed to the development of food kiosks. Those in Nairobi's industrial area developed as a response to both the unemployment and underemployment phenomenon that was typical with the factory jobs undertaken mainly by the blue collar workers. The unemployed in search of economic survival in the non-welfare state sought refuge in selling food in these kiosks. The underemployed also sought refuge in the hot food from the kiosks which had been generally reasonably priced compared with food from the few restaurants around them. Few factories have cafeterias with subsidized food for their workers and salaries are extremely low.

The food kiosks have always been a subsidy for the owners of the factories in Nairobi's industrial area. Permitting the operation of the kiosks served two purposes: directly to create employment, and, indirectly, to subsidize expenses for factory workers by establishing cheap food services around the factories. This relationship between the formal and informal sector did not escape the awareness of the State authorities. The latter, usually interested in a harmonious relationship between itself and the owning class (in this case the factory owners) did not press for wage increases.

All the respondents operating food kiosks acknowledged the fact that they did not start their kiosks unnoticed. The contradictory nature of the State toward the food kiosk owners was apparent from the beginning, especially when the City Council was slow in fulfilling its responsibility to install running water. Periodic demolitions were reported on grounds of lack of running water. Ninety percent of the food kiosk owners reported to have made the necessary payments for water installation, but that did not stop the demolition squad from the city council.

It was also evident, as discussed elsewhere (Macharia 1989), that the city officials played a "direct" role in influencing who got the allotment. This was not acknowledged as such by a former city councilor that I interviewed, because official influence is not legal or "rational." Clientelism has characterized both central and local governments in Kenya in various sections (Leys 1975; Rothchild 1984; Kithching 1980). The informal economy has not been immune as the case of food kiosks above has shown. The role of the State in establishing the food kiosks in Nairobi's industrial area was through specific social networks, mainly ethnicity, kinship and friendship. The pioneer food kiosk operators reported having known or being introduced by a co-ethnic, a friend or sometimes a relative, to a member of the then City Council. The councilors were mainly the ones who gave out the spaces for kiosk establishment. Although the process was formal, the allotment was informal in practice!

At the time of the establishment of food kiosks in Nairobi's industrial area in the late 1960s, the central government was led by Kenyatta, who was from the Kikuyu ethnic group. The patrimonial-clientelist practice was evident in Kenyatta's government, particularly in cabinet-level appointments and other senior government positions. Sections of his ethnic group benefitted, and obviously, in return he expected support from them as the exchange factor (Kitching 1980). The Nairobi City Council had a similar situation in that there was a Kikuyu mayor and most of the councilors were Kikuyus, particularly those who represented wards in the industrial area and its neighborhood. This explains why more than 75% of the food kiosk operators in Nairobi's industrial areas are Kikuyu.

The role of social networks, ethnicity in this case, cannot be understated. The respondents freely disclosed that "to get the kiosk, you had to know or be introduced to the city councilor." Once this happened, allotment was assumed and occasionally *chai* ("tea") had to be given. *Chai* refers to a small degree of bribery which is considered as a way of the client saying "thank you" to the patron. Social closeness, especially in being a friend, kin or a co-ethnic from the same rural home, was a significant basis of *trust*. This was required for smooth allocation of kiosks. It also ensured political support for the councilor from a loyal clientele who benefitted from such allocation. This kind of support was invaluable to those in the city government, particularly at the time when there was a transition from the colonial to the independent state. New political alignments at both central and local government level were forming. Some ways that the city officials and the central government could legitimize the new acquired power included: city council distribution of city services to the financially pressed Africans; allowing these Africans who had recently migrated to the cities to do business in areas in which they previously could not; allocating residential plots and housing as well as food kiosks, as was the case in the industrial area.

The suspension of the City Council of Nairobi brought some changes among the food kiosk operators in the industrial area. The City Commission tolerated a new group that had previously been kept out of business by the city councilors. The City Commission was more ethnically diverse, Kikuyus being in the minority. The new group was the women food sellers outside factory gates. Although this group was operating on a small scale during the 1970s, their full presence, according to food kiosk owners, was felt after 1982.

Competition for customers was being felt and the food kiosk operators were usually at loggerheads with those women selling food outside. The former felt that it was their right to be the sole food sellers in the industrial area since they had permits from the city. The latter felt that they too needed to earn a living and their competition should be viewed positively by those in the kiosks. A competition within subsectors was encouraged indirectly by the State, mainly because of its interest in satisfying as many citizens as possible and building a larger clientele. It was clear from the women food sellers that their presence was because of the multi-ethnic nature of the city commission. Also, most of the women food sellers are from the Luo ethnic group (Macharia 1989). They have been tolerated and have not been subjected to as much police harassment as they faced in the heyday of the city council.

After 1982, the City Commissioners targeted groups that were not accommodated by the City Councilors. This explains the emergence of groups of women food sellers outside factories and a one-on-one competition with food kiosk operators. Patron-client relationships extend from the high office to the dusty street corner in Nairobi's industrial area as the patrons continue in the search for legitimacy in the civil society. This may take different forms, some of which is the State indirectly creating a situation of competition between subsectors and accommodating others that would be categorically illegal in a universal bureaucracy.

The State has been *inconsistent* and *contradictory* in its role toward the informal sector. The food sellers in the industrial area, and in other parts of Nairobi, have not experienced total support by issuance of permits. They have instead been subjected to threats of closure, demolition and unnecessary police harassment. The Public Health Act (Cap. 506 of the Laws of Kenya) has been invoked very often in Nairobi against various subsectors, even against those with permits like the food kiosks. Arbitrary demolitions that suit the State interests have been done in various parts of the city against hawkers and fruit and vegetable sellers in downtown Nairobi. A recent demolition was the case of Muoroto in May 1990 where the Public Health Act was used to justify demolition. Another earlier case was in the summer of 1987 when my original research was in progress. The city of Nairobi was host to the All-African Games. This meant thousands of visitors from all over Africa and media coverage from all over the world focused on Nairobi for at least three weeks. The government, both central and local, needed to keep Nairobi clean and attractive to the eyes of the visitors (*Daily Nation*, 2 June 1987). This was intended to present to the visitors a clean and beautiful hassle-free city with the purpose of attracting future tourists.

Food kiosks that had all along been operating without being accused of violating the Public Health Act were now under fire. The State was clearly using this act as an excuse to demolish the kiosks, thereby keeping the city "clean and attractive" for the visitors. Some party leaders in Nairobi were against this idea and were quoted as saying "it makes no sense to demolish the kiosks of the poor citizens because some of the visitors are coming from cities with a lower cleanliness record than Nairobi." Some compared the extensive slums and hawking in Lagos, Nigeria as worse than in Nairobi (*Daily Nation*, 22 July 1988). Indeed, my observation from a visit in Lagos Ibadan in 1994 confirms that slums and hawking disorder are much more a problem there than in Nairobi.

The food kiosk operators were unhappy with the State's collaboration with Asian capitalists who owned the factories next to them. Unlike those in the downtown area who faced demolition threats because of tourism, those in the industrial area attributed such threats and actual demolition to their rich neighbors—factory owners either multinational corporations or Asian businessmen. They reported that some factory owners colluded with the city politicians and relevant officials to have kiosks near their factory demolished. In such cases, the Public Health Act could be invoked even where it was inappropriate. Some food kiosk owners reported racial overtones in such demolitions. They said that the Asians were against Africans and were uncomfortable with their gathering in big numbers around kiosks they patronized which were adjacent to their factories. They believed the Asians could convince someone or some people in the City Hall about the 'nuisance' of the food kiosks which were then subjected to demolition.

The food kiosk operators told me, "We cannot understand why these Asians report to the City Hall that our kiosks are dirty and are eyesores, yet they themselves patronize them and their own workers whom they interact with every day are our regular customers." The City Hall officials usually side with the factory owners. This contradicts their giving permits to such food kiosks and "commitment" to protect the small businessmen. Here, I see another level of patron-clientelism, this one being mainly the State in support of the capitalist class who are usually supportive of the status quo. Such kind of support of the owning class was parallel with the State officials' rhetoric especially in the last two years proclaiming the need to support the growth and development of Kenya's and in particular Nairobi's, informal economy. The contradictory role of the State is revealed again in this case.

Women food sellers outside factories reported the problems the State gave them before 1982. They recall how they had to carry food on their backs for long distances to the Law Courts under the supervision of city police officers. They were usually charged for operating businesses without a permit and required to pay fines usually larger than their monthly income of Ksh. 500 (about $10). They were, however, more satisfied with the current situation by which they have not been taken to court. They strongly believe that this change came about with the multi-ethnic commission appointed by the Minister of Local Government in 1982. They still had a few complaints regarding some city police officers who threatened to take them to court in exchange for some *chai*. It could be as low as Ksh. 5 or 10, but given their daily earnings of only Ksh. 20 to 30 for most of them, this is a large proportion of their earnings.

The food sellers attributed this kind of corruption between the city police officers and junior city officials to personalities rather than the city's official policy. However, they wished the city officials could apprehend the police officers and the junior officials who required kickbacks from them. They also expressed an interest in being allocated food kiosks by the government. Half of them hoped that the government would get them jobs which could be more secure in terms of having a consistent income than the sporadic one they were getting from their food sales. They also compared themselves with the metal artisans of whom they were envious because the government was attentive to their requests. They felt arrangements like the roof-shed that the metal artisans got from the government should be given to them too since they were also part of the informal economy and in their opinion, contributing as much. Overall, they felt discriminated against in the overall governmental approach to the informal sector, especially in the last year when some positive measures have been accorded to some subsectors. Government loans to promote the informal sector were only being discussed among the metal artisans, drum sellers and the garment makers. The food sellers regarded this unfair of the State which, in their perception, should promote not one or two but all the subsectors of the informal economy.

The State and the Metal Artisans

The metal artisans have operated in the background of the city center since the times of the colonial state and during the independent state. During the colonial state, they could only be found in the neighborhoods of residential areas designated for the Africans. This may explain why up to this day, the Kamukunji area of Nairobi which has always been an African residential area, is the major hub of metal artisanry. Indeed it is where the new roof-shade, the first constructed by the government for these previously "hot sun" artisans, is located.

The metal artisans occupied empty lots of the city of Nairobi mainly in low productive areas, usually unsuitable for residential or office construction. These areas were mainly near river valleys, as in the case of Kamukunji which is beside Nairobi River, or those in Mathare beside Mathare River. The Nairobi location, as in the case of Kamukunji, was and still is right next to a major street and there is no way that the city officials or the central government could have been unaware of the "illegal site" occupied by the metal artisans. The fact that the occupied land was usually in high density areas may have helped to downplay the government reaction. There were, however, sporadic evictions and various kinds of harassment (e.g., tools being confiscated) which the respondents reported. This took place in the 1960s and 1970s and also the early 1980s.

Political aspirants in the area realized that the artisans in Kamukunji were an electoral group on which they could rely. They formed a strong and generally unified constituency. Political aspirants in the late 1960s and 1970s campaigned on issues that appealed to the artisans, mainly promising to lobby for their continuous existence in the illegally occupied land. They also promised to stop police harassment and arrests that led to heavy court fines similar to those of the food sellers. The patron-client system working at the central government found an extension between

Figure 5.1 A section of the roof-shed in Kamukunji from which the metal artisans work.

the local politicians and the metal artisans. The artisans were largely from the Kikuyu ethnic group. One local politician reported to me:

> the silent power of the artisans can be felt by looking at past local elected leaders from the area. They have all had an unofficial endorsement from the artisans and it is not surprising that local leaders and particularly the member of Parliament have been Kikuyu in the last five general elections. (field notes)

The metal artisans had therefore established a survival strategy by soliciting unofficial support by the local politicians who in return were assured of votes. The ethnic factor cannot be underestimated especially in the 1960s and the 1970s. In the 1980s, the metal artisans continued to survive in their illegally occupied land. In the 1990s, a process of legitimation has been in the offing. The City Commission in 1982, like its predecessor, the City Council, found an almost established group which was not easy to move. This did not save the artisans sporadic harassment and evictions, and being always on the lookout and ready to run when a city official was in sight. The political astuteness at a local level of these artisans and the wheeling-dealing with local leaders gave them a place in the growth of Nairobi. One pioneer artisan, a Mr. Mwangi, who is also a respected local politician who has voiced the artisan's problems, told me that "if we did not stand up and present our case to the leaders, this *Jua Kali* would not be here today and the President could not even have come here. It is through our persistence and logistical survival strategies that we have endured this long avoiding what was planned earlier as our extinction."

In 1986, the long-surviving artisans in Kamukunji were visited by the head of state and, like all his visits, this was covered by both national and international media. For the first time the term *Jua Kali* or informal sector started to have a positive image. Many Kenyans (Nairobians) who had only heard sounds of hammers now saw on their national television what products these artisans made. The chair of the Metal Artisans group had this to say about the presidential visit: ". . . it was the best advertisement we could ever dream of. It was free and reached the whole nation through television, radio and newspapers." He also reported that they started getting respect from the police after this visit. He continued, "I can now identify myself as a *Jua Kali* worker (metal artisan) without as much harassment as before. When I tell the police officers that I do not have a work identification number because I work in Kamukunji as a metal artisan, the immediate response these days is, 'Oh, the President's place,' and I am left free." The positive image has meant so much to the artisans and it has also improved their trade.

According to the respondents, the President's visit to the metal artisans created a positive image that they really need, not only to continue their artisanry in the illegally occupied land, but also to boost their sales. One artisan who represented the majority opinion had this to say:

From the time the president visited, we have witnessed an increase in
customers. The customers have also started trusting us more than before.
Previously, the customers were afraid of giving us a large bill in fear that
we will have no change. The customers also feared that we may never
have handled such a large bill and may therefore disappear with it if we
went asking our colleagues to give us change. (field notes)

This shows the new level of trust that the public had for the artisans and
the general negative images that were common at official circles and
among middle-class Nairobians who are mainly the customers of these
artisans.

The artisans reported that previously they had to sell most of their
products through a middleman, mainly Asians who had shops in the
downtown where the middle class felt free to shop. Selling through a
middleman obviously meant low returns and they are now happy that
they can sell from their Kamukunji site directly to the customers who are
now more at ease with the artisans. The roof-shed that was built as a
result of the President's visit has now ensured the "permanence" of the
artisans on this site. The illegality of the occupation of this land may
now be considered as temporarily being over. This is the closest the State
has come to accommodate the informal sector, but other than the land
occupation issue and the roof-shed, there is nothing more official that has
taken place. The metal artisans are therefore still informalized in their
day-to-day operation, although more confident of continuity and survival.

Ironically, there are still a large number of the artisans who are
outside the new roof-shed, for at least three reasons. First, the space in
the roof-shed is not enough for all the metal artisans. Secondly, there are
those who had established markets in certain parts of the city,
particularly certain corners of some streets. They did not want to
inconvenience their customers and therefore chose to continue in their
old premises. Finally, and most important, there were those who refused
to move to the shed because they were skeptical of the State's sudden
interest in their welfare. Some respondents asked me the rhetorical but
significant question, "Where were they (the State) all these years that we
have been in the hot sun and heavy rain? Why now and who needs
them?" Well, some needed them as evidenced by those who are currently
in the roof-shed. The skeptical ones were also afraid that the new
government interest would lead to formalization of their subsector,
leading to taxation, licenses to operate, health certificates and others with
which they do not presently have to deal. Such skepticism is not isolated

to only those metal artisans operating outside the roof-sheds. It was mentioned by other respondents among the drum sellers and garment makers.

The government roof-shed and the Presidential visit are political symbols coming about at a time of political economic crisis in Kenya of the mid-1980s. With high rural-urban migration and high birth rates both in city and rural areas, scarcity of jobs in the formal sector was too obvious for any economic analyst to ignore the contribution of the informal economy in job creation and employment. A government gesture in support of the conspicuous informal sector group (the metal artisans) could well be taken as a new government approach. The President's many political speeches reiterating that the government is on the side of the common man (or the low income group) could not be better demonstrated than to visit these metal artisans to show state support by directing that a roof-shed be built for them. The crisis of the State's need to identify and to establish legitimacy with the common man as opposed to the middle class bureaucracy, common during Kenyatta's era and the early years of Moi's regime, may not have been felt as much before and this may explain why such a visit never took place earlier in the 23 years of the independent state.

The political astuteness of the metal artisans may have captured national attention which brought the head of state right to their site. The President's rhetoric that he is on the side of the common man was ultimately boosted by this visit to *Jua Kali*, who are popularly seen as the representatives of the common man. Measuring the effect this had politically is hard, but suffice it to say that 70% of those in the roof-shed were very supportive of the President, as long as no taxes were going to be introduced. It appears that the President is appealing for support from the common man, and hence his support to the metal artisans. His predecessor, Kenyatta, appealed more to middle class and indirectly to the common man. Kenyatta's support of shared taxis (*matatus*) which were initially owned by the middle class was very well received initially by them and later by the average Kenyan. The common man also benefitted from the shared taxis which became a big relief to the poor public transport system in Nairobi and elsewhere in the country.

The Government's Move from a Passive to an Active Role

On the average, the informal economy has been creating jobs at the rate of 7% a year since 1982. In 1985, this rose to 9% gain in excess of other sectors in the economy (Republic of Kenya 1988). In 1995, the average job creation by the informal economy was reported to be 11% (Republic of Kenya Review 1996). *Jua Kali* workshops such as the metal artisan, or others not included in this study like carpenters and auto mechanics, are regarded as essential to Kenya's strategy for economic growth with unmatched potential for creating jobs to expand the work force. The informal sector is also viewed as a prime training ground for tomorrow's African entrepreneurs. From an economic standpoint, this perception circulating in government circles explains the State's move to indirect support in the pattern of patronage-clientele system to direct support at least in political statements and on paper. The *Kenya Times* (5 June 1987) reported that "the government hopes that the informal sector will provide more than half the non-farm jobs needed between 1987 and the end of the century and it sees the accelerating expansion of the informal sector as one of the challenges."

Richardson (1984, 4) sums it best when he argues that

> as long as governments are unable to create enough jobs to employ the urban population or to pay households subsistence welfare payments, it is very important that impediments on the informal activities should be as be as few as possible.

The Public Health Act is frequently invoked to the disadvantage of the informal economy in Nairobi. Traffic congestion arguments that are frequently used to justify harassment are rarely compelling; and even when they are, the problem could be dealt with through other methods (e.g., providing alternatives, well-located sites for an informal sector that blocks traffic). The advantages of supporting the informal economy outweigh the disadvantages of a crowded street in most African cities.

Market considerations should be considered when alternatives to move various subsectors are being considered. It would be unwise, for example, to move the women food sellers far away from the industries regardless of whether they may be seen as a nuisance by factory owners. This is mainly because their customers are the factory workers who have only thirty minutes to one hour for lunch. A longer distance would mean failure to reach the food seller which will eventually kill this subsector, a source of bread for many families. The drum sellers, for example, would not like to be moved into an area that is out of reach or inconvenient for the metal artisans who patronize their products. They would also prefer to be nearer the industrial area where they get the raw materials.

These considerations are necessary for the continued growth of the informal economy. Policy formulation for this economy should take into consideration such concerns as proximity to raw materials and customers as well as efficiency of communications and transportation. The role of the State in Nairobi's informal economy has been a passive one during the decades of the 1960s and 1970s. At times aggressiveness as police harassment, demolition and evictions have characterized the relationship between the two. The passive and sometimes supportive role of the State has come through junior or middle-ranked representatives of the State. This has been mainly through the patronage-clientelism system that has been operating in the independent state, first at the central government, and then, as an extension, in the local government. The informal economy operators in different subsectors as shown by the subsectors I studied have through various social networks secured support of their local leaders who have lobbied for them to continue operating even when they have been known to be illegal. The case of the metal artisans in Nairobi is a good example.

The State in Kenya, led by the president, has taken a new approach to the informal economy. This is as a result of the political economic crisis in the 1980s which has seen high unemployment figures (30% to 70%) and poor performance by the formal economy in maintaining the situation. The State has then turned attention to the development and growth of the informal economy. Government statements in support of this sector have been recorded in the media in recent years. A government blueprint, Sessional Paper No. 1 of 1986, describes the informal economy as one hope the country has about economic development as it enters the 21st century. The dynamics of the informal sector have been recognized by the State and it appears the passive role it has taken in the past might become active after all.

The skepticism of the new role of the State toward the informal economy still abounds among the operators and researchers of this subject. It is still unclear whether there will be systematic planning for this sector or whether it will be haphazard and responding to a crisis as was the Kenyan president's visit to the metal artisans. The extent the new role will have in "formalizing" what is now informal is still unclear.

Whether the new role of the State will undo the effective social dynamics that have made this section of the economy grow strongly in most developing countries is still unclear.

Finally, based on the discussion above on the possible theoretical arguments and the presentation of the two case studies, the informal sector can clearly be supported by the State on a patron-client basis without itself becoming "formalized." This is mainly the case because the State itself is "informalized" through the patron-client relationship and other forms of networks in the societies they operate in as was true of Nairobi.

Government Efforts to Integrate the Informal Economy into Mainstream Development Planning

A brief historical policy survey since Independence may help in the understanding of the evolution of the current positive policy toward the informal economy. The government's strategy for industrialization and commerce soon after Independence in 1963 was geared toward expansion of overall output. Industrial development policy was not designed to cater to either formal or informal sectors. The Kenya Industrial Estate (KIE) was created to look into matters relating to finance and technical aid to small industrial enterprises. It did not include the informal section of the economy as part of its portfolio. Although it was not a government policy paper, the International Labor Organization study in Kenya in 1972 influenced the government policy.

The International Labour Organization (ILO) staff studied employment, income and inequality in Kenya. The report used the term "informal sector" to describe the proportion of the urban economy that escapes enumeration in official statistics. It was a major step toward increasing government awareness and concern in the development of the informal sector. The initial response of the Kenyan government to the ILO Report as contained in the 1973 Sessional Paper on Employment was accommodating, at least in print. Since then, commitment to the expansion of the informal sector continues to be mentioned in all subsequent National Development Plans, although the methods for carrying out this commitment are far short of what is required.

In the 1974-1978 Development Plan, the informal economy received considerable attention as a result of the ILO report and the Sessional Paper on Employment. It stressed the need for promoting small scale-enterprises. This policy was strengthened through the establishment of programs in Industrial Estates, a Rural Development Center and the promotion of indigenous African entrepreneurs. The Plan further proposed ways of implementing the small-scale industries' policy. The strategies were to take three forms:

1.   To review central and local government regulations that were an obstacle to small-scale enterprises;

2.   To direct assistance to small business enterprises all over the country; and

3.   To establish an organization that was well-equipped to administer and provide extension services to the small enterprises.

To improve the quality and the coordination of services to small businesses, a new corporation to be known as the "Small Business Development Corporation" was to be established. This body was to incorporate the KIE and the Rural Industrial Development Program. The aim of such an organization was to coordinate all extension services and Research and Development as would have been required by small enterprises. Such services also would include local market research, accounting and product design, manufacturing techniques and other managerial methods. As of 1996, however, no such organization exists. This is a good example of a policy statement unfulfilled despite its positive promise (Republic of Kenya 1989).

The 1979-1983 Plan stipulated several measures to be taken for the implementation and promotion of the informal sector. Among the main ones were the following:

1.   Fund of Ksh. 50 million to help the informal sector enterprises to take advantage of the facilities available with Kenya Industrial Estate network and other Industrial Development Agencies;

2.   Massive expansion of KIE services to include at least one facility in each of the 43 districts, by the end of the Plan period; and

3.   Programming and Evaluation Section within the Ministry of
       Commerce and Industry to assist the District Development
       Committees in the preparation of coordinated programs for
       informal sector manufacturing units. This has not been
       established yet.

The 1984-88 plan envisaged the establishment of a full-fledged Small
Industries division in the Ministry of Commerce and Industry. This
division was expected to monitor the implementation of a small
industries development program and to provide assistance to the
industrial extension service in collaboration with the Project Studies
Division.   This division has been established in the Ministry of
Commerce and Industry. The plan also stated that there would be a shift
of emphasis from capital intensive modern industries to labor intensive
small and cottage industries.   Such emphasis is intended to increase
employment in the country.

Of all the previous government written statements, the Sessional
Paper No. 1 of 1986 on Economic Management for Renewed Growth
makes it clear that the informal sector has been given the "official
recognition" that its proponents have been advocating since the early
1970s. The Sessional Paper claims that the sector will feature more
prominently in the country's future development strategies and that it
will shoulder a much heavier responsibility than hitherto. The Sessional
Paper stresses that the sector has "a vital role to play in the growth of the
country."   In the Sessional Paper, the government recognizes, for
example, that farm productivity and incomes must be raised to stimulate
the demand for goods and services provided by the informal economy.
Since this section of the economy tends mainly to cater to the needs of the
low-income groups, who happen to be predominantly in the rural areas,
increased incomes would ensure effective demand for informal sector
goods. The government also wished to lower tariffs on raw materials,
semi-processed goods and other intermediate inputs, with a bias toward
those used widely by the informal sector. The investment incentives
outlined in the Sessional Paper encouraged the substitution of labor for
machinery which favors more informal sector activities that are
characteristically labor intensive.

The chronological survey of the government's policy shows that in
every development plan since 1974 there has been mention of how to
improve the informal economy. The programs to carry out such policies
have, however, been discouraging. It was not until 1986 that a stronger

official statement toward this sector had been outlined. Given the poor implementation record in the past years, it is hard to say that the informal sector will now benefit from the government's planning agencies. In 1987 when I carried out part of the original research for this book, the 1986 policy statement had not helped in stopping the police harassment of some sectors of the informal economy. Neither has it stopped in 1996, ten years later. There may be more support for the manufacturing sector of this economy but, if the policy is to be successful, it should be applicable to all the subsectors indiscriminately.

What is lacking in all the policy statements is the commitment toward the people who are actually operating in the informal sector. In other words, the social dynamics of this sector have received less attention. Instead the economic contribution has been emphasized. In this study, emphasis on social composition, ethnicity and kinship, is emphasized. Theoretical assumptions based on this understanding could be of relevance to the next government policy statement.   Such an understanding may also help to bridge the gap that I have identified between the policy and the implementation program of the informal economy. These are the issues that I turn to in the chapters that follow.

6

The Informalization of the State: The Unwritten Bureaucracy

In this chapter, I revisit the concept of informality. This time, I apply it specifically to the State and to local governments. I argue that the Kenyan state is based on a social structure permeated by networks that operate along familial, ethnic, friendship and overwhelmingly patrimonial lines. The rationality that Weber (1968) suggested should be part of the functioning bureaucracy of modern states; to a large extent, it is found in most Western states, but is yet to be achieved in most African states. In trying to account for this, scholars have viewed African states as corrupt (see Young 1982) and international agencies, like the World Bank, regard African states as showcases of bad governance (Landel-Mills 1992). Whereas I am not condoning corruption or "bad governance" as African virtues, I on the other hand argue that the blanket condemnation of bad governance in African states is exaggerated and at times misinterpreted by Western theorists who start from the assumption that the African state should emulate the Western state as the ideal one.

The Western conception of rationality and formality involved in dealing with state matters may be yet to take roots given the informal African cultural practices that are yet to find harmony in the Westernized formal style of conducting business or governing. In fact, the African state is characterized by an unwritten bureaucracy where many major decisions take place outside parliament, the cabinet and even the official state house (the equivalent of the White House in the United States).

In Kenya during the Kenyatta regime (1963-1978), for example, the official state house was under-utilized for state functions as most of them took place in Kenyatta's private home, which thus assumed public significance. Official delegations, local and international, became used to visiting the "unofficial home" of the President and conducting official business there. Kenyatta's successor, President Moi, followed the same pattern but with less success, possibly because his home in Kabarak, Nakuru is more than one hundred miles away from the capital, while Kenyatta's was only about thirty miles.   Being hosts to official delegations in their private homes for these two presidents gave the occasions such an informal character (symbolized by the casual attire they wore), off the cuff commentaries that were less typical of the kind of business conducted in the official state house where formal Western suits and ties were the norms. In the informal environs of their private homes, reading prepared speeches was less likely.

I argue, in addition, that it is the informality of the State, and the networks on which it functions, that can explain the "neurotic" relationship between the State and the informal sector. It is the same informality that explains why those sectors that receive support from the State do not become "formalized," as the World Bank, United Nations Development Programme (UNDP) or multilateral donors like United States Aid for International Development (USAID) and the Overseas Development Agency expect. Understanding the State's informality and its relationship (support or harassment) with the informal sector is therefore a vital part of any analysis of African states. Indeed, one might also argue that it is a vital part of analyzing states outside Africa. Linda Weiss (1987), for example, argues that the Italian state has promoted the informal sector by promoting a dense network of patron-client ties throughout Italian societies. Weiss argues further that the State partly tolerates informal activity because many of its "clients" are informal employers or employees. The State has contributed to a social structure permeated by networks operating along familial/friendship and patrimonial lines (Weiss 1987).

DEFINING THE CONCEPT OF INFORMALITY

I will define this concept using a mathematical principle of the "subset" as illustrated in Figure 6.1. I juxtapose the traditional and the modern as two major social, political and economic processes that have been competing with each other in the African state. It is not empirically clear which of the two is winning. In the realm of this competition is the subset where *informality* reigns as an additional player in this competition.

Figure 6.1. Informality

A   B

Informality is not strictly confined within the subset. It goes outside the borders of the subset (see shaded area in Figure 6.1). In most of the history of nation-states, modernism (read Westernization) is winning the competition with the "traditional." In the African case, the traditions are still strong and are reinforced by the very need to cope with modern competition. One, therefore, finds various forms of "resistance," explicit or implicit, staged by the "traditionalists." These forms of resistance are what produces the subset "informality" either in the economy (the informal economy), the government (the informal state) or socially (informal networks). The subset, "informality," is not static. It is a dynamic interface encroaching both the traditional and the modern. It is not quite clear which of the two has the upper hand in general, but in Kenya the traditional informality seems to have the upper hand over the "modern," especially in the so-called modern institutions. In other words the modern institutions are marred by traditional forces where nepotism, ethnic affiliation and locality (among others) rule over a meritocracy. In Kenya, for example, a case in point was in 1986 when President Moi appointed a fellow Kalenjin (his ethnic group), a historian with no prior banking training background to head (as Executive Chair) the biggest public bank in the country, the Kenya Commercial Bank. This led eventually to poor performance of the Bank in the eyes of many Kenyans but for the Kalenjin inner circle who could easily have loans approved, it was a success. After years of the bank's poor performance and public outcry, the chair was relinquished of his position and replaced with a professional banker (keeping up with the "formal," though late) and indeed the performance of the bank since then has been positive.

In African states like Kenya and Zimbabwe, for example, the "traditional" is more powerful than the modern mainly because the modern was only recently imposed on the society through Christianity and Colonialism. It is, therefore, exogenous to the African society. This suggests that informality is part and parcel of the evolving African social, political and economic processes. It is present in almost all aspects of the modern African state, the African city and the entire African society. The reality is that any analysis of the African state that does not zero in on informality will only ignore it at its own risk. It will also be an incomplete analysis.

Informality resists attempts by Western-educated planners to create formal nation-states or cities. The persistence of informality may explain some planning disasters, such as the Site and Service Scheme sponsored by the World Bank as the solution to the housing problems of low-income groups in African cities (Macharia 1985; Nientied and Linden 1985) or more modern efforts by the World Bank, the United States International Aid (USAID) and Britain's Overseas Development Agency (ODA) to train informal sector operators with the hope of promoting small enterprise developments that will raise the quality of informal sector activities and eventually eliminate urban poverty in African cities.

Informality, however, can also refer to a defiance of the formalized way to do things. The African state is still struggling to catch up with the West, yet it is very "African" in its social-structural composition. New waves of system processes usually hit the African state, but technical dilemmas and a continuous search for identity continue to pull the African state away from prescribed paths. For example, the current so-called Africa's second liberation that is taking place in many African states calling for multiparty democracy is an induced dose from the West with stiff conditions (as in Kenya where foreign aid was suspended for two years, 1991-1993) that are often resisted or ignored. The heritage of group negotiation is preferred and carried out occasionally. In such cases, the African state and society are acting informally: adhering to the official protocol but undertaking other activities on the side. Scholars of peace and conflict have also come to recognize the need to solve modern conflicts in Africa using some traditional and informal ways of approaching such conflict. A recent (29-30 March 1996) conference organized by I . William Zartman of the School for Advanced International Studies in Washington, D.C., underscored the significance of looking at informal ways Africans used to solve their previous conflicts. Positive contributions should be enhanced. Indeed, had the conflicts in Somalia and Rwanda been left to be solved through informal negotiations without Western, especially American, formal intervention, the problems would have been settled in their own African way like they had done hundreds of years before. The kind of genocide witnessed by the world in 1994 in Rwanda and the continuous warfare in the now stateless Somalia was unrecorded in the past and attests to the pivotal role informality could play even in modern African states. The past crises were solved informally between the different ethnic groups and clans. In other words, the informal ways used by many African generations to solve their conflicts and problems will still be preferred to a modern Western method, which has not worked in most parts of the continent. The 1994-95 U.S. interference in Somalia with the hope of settling the clan rivalry that had destabilized the Mogadishu government is a case in point. The solution, though taking long to arrive, will come largely from informal negotiations among the clan leaders less so from formal Western orchestrated negotiations.

THE INFORMALIZATION OF THE KENYAN STATE

In this section I will elaborate on the informal ways that the Kenyan state has operated, especially the power flow and general leadership in the management of the State. One can identify informality in the State at nearly all levels of its apparatus. Appointments and decision-making procedures are mostly conducted informally through ethnic, kinship or friendship ties. In this section I identify three major informal aspects of the Kenyan state.

Ruling Through an Inner Core

The inner core here refers to advisors to the government, especially the presidency. Some of these advisors do not have any legitimate government position. They acquire the inner core position through longtime friendships with the president, either as schoolmates coming from the same home village or having become relatives through marriage. Such trusted and at times influential persons may have more power and leverage than the Vice-President (technically expected to be the second most powerful person in the state after the President). In almost all cases in both Kenya and Zimbabwe, such trusted friends are co-ethnics. Their informality extends beyond their position in government: their duties go beyond written "Terms of Reference."

The Kenyatta regime (1963-1978), the first African government after the Colonialists left, had, for instance, as its inner core a few leaders from Kiambu district from where Kenyatta himself hailed. These confidants practically ran the government informally. There was an unofficial State House at his Gatundu home where critical decisions affecting the State would be made in disregard of the legislature or the judiciary, as the written constitution demanded. The Kenyatta regime, from one of those unofficial sittings in Gatundu, decided to support the *Matatu* transport system, that is, gypsy taxis that started competing with the public transport (mainly established buses) and that over the years has become part of public transportation in Kenya. That decision reflects the co-ethnic and patron-client ties between workers and leaders. The *matatu* system of transport became the first clear informal transportation system competing with the Kenya Bus Services (the formal official transport, especially in the city of Nairobi). This was happening with informal support from the Kenyatta regime.

The *matatu* today has become a more mainstream form of transportation with acceptance by the government although with many modifications to make it more acceptable. This is a good example of the informal economic activity graduating from informal to formal. It is also an example of an activity started on informal basis or directives like the Gatundu meetings, later becoming part of a formal parliamentary debate that called for the amendment of the Public Transportation bill which formalized the *Matatu* transportation. This bill, though formalized in parliament, had its informal beginnings in Gatundu. Informality can therefore come in the form of ideas that may be formalized later as in this example.

Another example of informality, during the Kenyatta regime, of this "unwritten bureaucracy" at work was his Minister of State, Mr. Mbiyu Koinange. He became very close to the president and was, unofficially, the number two person in charge of the country, although by law he was only a cabinet member among 26 others. He had been a longtime *trusted friend*, who knew Kenyatta from their early days in England in the 1940s. He was also a co-ethnic Kikuyu. He later became Kenyatta's kinsman through marriage (Kenyatta married his sister as the third wife). He came from the same rural place of origin, Kiambu district. By the 1970s, Mr. Koinange gathered so much power that he was literally running the government, despite his officially limited role of a Minister of State in the President's office.

In President Moi's regime (1978 to the present), again, the inner core is from his own ethnic group, the Kalenjin. In fact, its members are from a sub-group of the Tugen, the Elgeyo and the Marakwet. During Moi's regime, the strength of the inner core has been felt in all spheres of the state government—policies, programs and especially in all the key appointments, most of which have been given to co-ethnics. The example of the Kalenjin historian who was appointed to head the Kenya Commercial Bank although he had no banking experience has already been mentioned above. Decision-making has reflected the ethnic make-up of the informal bureaucracy. An illustration of this was the ethnic violence between 1991-1994, where Kalenjins were armed by the government to fight any non-Kalenjins (especially Kikuyus, Luos and Luhyas) to move out of the Rift Valley, which they regarded as traditionally Kalenjin land. Informally, ethnic cleansing was perpetrated by the formal mechanisms of the government to ensure that the Rift Valley remained ethnically Kalenjin, who were also seen as a block supporting the presidency.

A single influential personality has also emerged in Moi's regime. Mr. Nicholas Biwott, initially without a cabinet position, was in 1988 appointed Minister of Energy. After the death of the Minister of Foreign Affairs, Robert Ouko, in February 1990 and later investigations by the Scotland Yard Police that alleged that Mr. Biwott was a key suspect in the death of his colleague, Biwott was relieved of his duties as a cabinet member. Although officially he is only a member of Parliament, he has much more power than the Vice President or any other high ranking official within Kenya's formal bureaucracy. He has more influence in all levels of state policy decisions: it is alleged that cabinet ministers have to receive his approval to be appointed by the President. He has almost literally been running the government from behind the scenes and occasionally issuing open statements against anyone appearing to challenge the Moi government (see, for example, the *Daily Nation*, 29 March 1996, against Kipruto arap Kirwa, ironically a fellow Kalejin but from the majority Nandi, who challenged President Moi's "so-called democratic leadership.") Biwott publicly requested that Mr. Kirwa be reprimanded for his anti Moi campaign. On January 15, 1997, Mr. Biwott in a surprise cabinet reshuffle was brought back to the cabinet in the powerful position of Minister of State in the Office of the President (*Daily Nation*, January 15 1997). This indeed shows how informal operations between Moi and Biwott have eventually become formal with his legitimized appointment as a cabinet member.

Delegations to the Head of State

In Kenya, other sources of the informal (unwritten) bureaucracy are the numerous delegations from different groups within the society that pay visits to the President, either in the official residence in Nairobi or his private home. Usually, the so-called goodwill delegations, follow the African tradition of subjects taking gifts to the king or the leader of their society. They will usually bring along a problem that they expect to be solved during the visit or immediately thereafter. These delegations have been one source of policies running the government. Whatever is granted to the delegation (informally) may later find its way in a parliamentary debate for it to be formalized.

In October 1992, for instance, a delegation of *Jua Kali* operators went to visit the President at the State House in Nairobi. The delegation pledged, like all other delegations, their loyalty to the President and declared publicly (on live television and radio coverage) their support to the President. After the delegation leader narrated how all the *Jua Kalis* adore the President and think of him as "a fatherly gift from God," he pulled from his pocket a manuscript addressing some of the problems facing the *Jua Kali*. The manuscript read as follows:

> Mzee, (Swahili for "respectable elderly person," like father), we in the *Jua Kali* are working hard to build the nation as you have asked all of us to do but we have a few problems that we think you and your government can help us solve. Mzee, we have no plots of land in the cities we work in, and we need some so as to ensure permanence of location which in

turn will give us more customers. Mzee, we also need improved credit facilities from the banks, especially the public banks, like Kenya Commercial Bank or the National Bank of Kenya. Mzee, we also need funds to put up sheds in our places of work . . . Mzee, we present these problems to you, knowing that within your powers and understanding of the low income groups like us, you will solve our problems. (field notes)

The President authoritatively inquired: "where is my Minister of Lands?" and as soon as he stood on attention, the president ordered him to look into the plot issue for the *Jua Kali* and grant them their request. From this example, note how the president is addressed with traditional respectability where an able elder man was treated as the sole leader, second only "to godliness—the giver of all," a position the president gets due to his position. Also note that the *Jua Kali* leader is also provoking such humility because he is well aware that the informal request if granted will only take a short while before it is formalized. The interplay of the speech exchange is therefore deliberate—informal as it is to grant what will later be a formal official policy—as was the case in issuance of plots for the *Jua Kali* members to operate their business in Nairobi and in all other Kenyan towns where the groups organized themselves and made the request through the local administrators—the President's officers who were now busy transforming the informal to formal following the President's pronouncement. This happens frequently, hence the need to view it in the analysis of the State as complementary to the formal bureaucratic decision-making process.

Delegations have involved teachers, women's organizations, religious groups and businessmen. All of them pledge loyalty to the President in the African way. They request state favors informally. Once they are granted, they gradually become formal through constant appeals and delegations to the head of state. Even when they may not become formal *per se*, they are tolerated by formal agencies, and previous harassment by state officials, for example, may be put on hold for some time.

Presidential Decrees

Presidential decrees are announcements made by the President that become law even without debate for the bill in the legislature, and the whole administration structure of the State reinforces it by simply qualifying that "this is what the President said." These decrees have often been used in cities, especially where informal housing in the squatter settlements may have been targeted for demolition. The squatters, knowing that the City Council of Nairobi plans to demolish their makeshift houses, on the day the President is passing near the settlement going on official business elsewhere, organize themselves and wait for the President in his long motorcade in a strategic location. The women and the school children dress colorfully and have some songs and dances prepared to entertain the president and, as with the delegations discussed above, they will have a leader who will appeal to the president: "Mzee, we are told the City Council is planning to demolish our houses and, as you can see, we have nowhere to go. We kindly and respectively ask you to intervene for us."

Depending on his mood and maybe on how much he was touched by the entertainment, he may declare on the spot that the City Council should leave those squatters where they are. A recent example (January 1997) was the closing of the schools in the slum area bordering the Nairobi industrial area. An appeal by residents who walked for about twelve miles to the Statehouse received a positive directive from the President, who decreed that the schools be left alone. This was a humiliation to the junior administrators. These are some of the consequences of such decrees—the slum residents were jubilant about this "formal" recognition of their schools (*Daily Nation*, January 10 1997). The first *Jua Kali* sheds in 1986-87 were built up as a result of a decree that took place in Kamukunji when the President stopped near the workplaces of metal artisans.

The informal economy may be supported by such decrees but can also be hurt by them. The latter is likely to happen when an Asian businessmen delegation goes to the president and complains about the informal sector. Then, a decree in disfavor of the informal sector may be issued as was done in the late 1980s when most of the food sellers in Nairobi's industrial area had their premises demolished as a result of Asian business owners' complaint that food sellers were an eyesore and a nuisance to the customers—a request favored by such a presidential decree. Influential land owners have been known to go to the president and complain that the squatters are occupying their land. In light of certain reasons, a decree to demolish houses is issued immediately and is backed by the city and state police. The system obviously fosters inconsistency in decision-making, for the president tends to issue decrees with very partial information on his hands. In an attempt to please all, some get hurt in the process. Frequently, those hurt most are also the lowest socially-economically ranked members of the society.

Inconsistent behavior of the State does not only occur toward the informal economy. Lengthy negotiations with the International Monetary Fund and the World Bank may be dismissed in one public meeting because the president wishes to boost his popularity by deciding to do things the *Kikwetu* (our) way, despite the consequences or implications for the negotiations. In 1991, the International Monetary Fund (IMF) and World Bank representatives were shocked when a deal they had sealed that required the government of Kenya to introduce cost-sharing of fees in public hospitals was one day dismissed by the president who said the Wananchi (people of Kenya—usually referring to common man) cannot afford the newly introduced system. The project was described as foreign and unappealing. Not surprisingly, after two years, the cost-sharing system is back, but its stability remains in question.

In my analysis of informality in Kenya, I have focused on the presidency because in almost all African countries the other arms of the government/state—the judiciary and the legislature—heavily depend on the president. The ideal expectation in the Western state of the horizontal power sharing among the executive, the legislature and the judiciary are replaced by the vertical power holding of the executive, mainly the presidency. This continues to produce the informal unwritten bureaucracy that is so characteristic of the Kenyan state as well as the African state in general. The president's home and those of other leaders of stature have been turned into informal administrative centers where the informal (unwritten) bureaucracy goes on during meetings of different sections of the Kenyan society. Meetings and requests take place in those realms.

The informality of the Kenyan state has equivalents in other parts of the world where it exists albeit with variations. Informality there, however, can exist in sections of the society other than the Presidency. In all instances, informality contributes much to the functioning mode of a government and needs to be fully understood for carrying out a complete analysis of state policies and implementation. Putnam's work on the Italian state, for instance, considers vertical associations in the Southern Italy and horizontal associations in the North to explain both the structure of government and divergent economic development. Going back to Italy's medieval times, Putnam (1993) underlines the significance of informal social process through communal associations. Cappechi (1989) offered a parallel analysis of Emilia-Romagna. This region, because it was controlled by the former Communist Party (PCI), has advanced in its informal sector activities through the Party's promotion of small sector and informal activities. The Party leaders understood the strength of these activities, mainly, artisan, and have exchanged policies for votes. As in Kenya, the Italian state exhibits informality emerging from traditional roots and counteracting official and modern political processes. The next chapter examines informality in the socioeconomic realms of society.

7

Social Networks and the Dynamism of the Informal Sector

In this chapter, I discuss ethnicity, friendship and kinship as the major basis of the social networks that characterize Nairobi's informal sector. I identified the same basis of social networks among the informal economy operators in Harare. I argue that ethnicity is significant in understanding how the informal sector operates in Nairobi. I hypothesize that ethnicity has been instrumental in establishing occupation of specific subsectors in the informal sector, thus complicating, and sometimes determining, entry. Diagnosing ethnic identification in this sector is not only important for understanding how it operates but also for policy formulation, particularly at a period when the government and international donor agencies are targeting the informal economy as the cornerstone for the future economic development of Kenya and other Third World countries (Republic of Kenya 1986).

ETHNICITY

At least 40 different ethnic groups exist in Kenya (see Map 1). Most of them are represented in Nairobi. This is because of the rural-urban migration process that continued to increase, especially after independence when anti-urban migration laws for the Africans were lifted. During the colonial period, ethnic identification was exploited by the administrators to facilitate their divide-and-rule policy. Thus an antagonistic atmosphere was created between different ethnic groups, or tribes, as they were referred to by the colonialists. Just before Kenya's independence, for example, small tribes like the Kalenjin, Mijikenda, Maasai and others, with the support of the minority European settlers, advocated regional autonomy (*majimbo*) instead of a united nation. They feared lack of representation in a national government predicted to be led by the two major ethnic groups in Kenya—the Kikuyu and the Luo. The two political parties just before independence were based on ethnic lines of affiliation. Kenya African Democratic Union (KADU) was the party of the smaller ethnic groups and minority European settlers while Kenya African National Union (KANU) was the party of the larger ethnic groups, mainly a Kikuyu-Luo coalition. Ethnic identity and antagonism at the national level dates back to the colonial period. After independence in 1963, the KADU party folded, and in 1964 all the former KADU political leaders crossed over to KANU, advocating national unity and abandoning their earlier call for regional autonomy. It would appear at face value that the ethnic problem at the national level was over, but political events in the few years that followed proved otherwise.

As O'Connor (1983, 110) correctly observes in his study of the African city, ethnic identity is not something consciously and keenly felt by most people living in the rural communities where all members are of the same ethnic group and engage in few direct contacts with people of other groups. However, moving into a city and into close contact with people of other groups, speaking other languages and so on, one becomes much more explicitly conscious of ethnic identity. This was what was happening in Nairobi, particularly in the late 1960s and in the 1970s. Referring to this period, O'Connor gives the example of Nairobi and Harare (formerly Salisbury) as two cities in tropical Africa that were so ethnically divided that they perhaps did not form "societies" at all (O'Connor 1983, 99).

Studies of ethnicity at a macro level, its effects on state formation in Africa, have been done (Rothchild and Oluonsola 1982; Rothchild 1984). Authors in the edited volume by Rothchild show the kind of problem ethnicity has posed for national unity in various parts of Africa such as the Sudan, Ethiopia and South Africa, and how it is a continuous political problem in several other countries. In this chapter, I am more concerned with ethnicity at a micro level, specifically, urban ethnicity and how it is manifested in the lowest level of economic production. I also discuss the potential problems (social and political) of such kinds of ethnic manifestations.

Ethnicity is always a sensitive subject, and scholars, as well as politicians and census-takers, are sometimes reluctant to give explicit attention to it. Yet any discussion of cities in tropical Africa cannot avoid it. For good or ill, ethnic identity matters greatly to most people (O'Connor 1983, 99). It is the sensitivity of this subject that has probably deterred most indigenous Africans from writing about it, leaving the subject to Western social scientists such as Mitchell (1969), Gluckman (1961), Southhall (1973), Shack (1973) and Rothchild (1973). I agree with O'Connor that a discussion of cities in tropical Africa cannot avoid the subject of ethnicity. This is regardless of whether the study is by a foreign or an indigenous scholar. Because, more often than not, ethnicity as a social phenomenon is defined in terms of strife (Cohen 1969, 4), a local scholar may be concerned with biases in the analysis of ethnic behavior of those being studied. At times, oversimplification of the impact of ethnic identity is given to avoid the sensitivity of the subject. I will limit the analysis and interpretation to the observations and findings during the research period.

Before rural-urban migration in search of employment, further education and better income opportunities, most of Kenya's ethnic groups lived in their respective rural regions such as the Luos in Nyanza, the Maasai in the Rift Valley and the Kikuyus in Central Province. The rural areas inhabited by specific ethnic groups were characterized by homogeneity in cultural traditions and, more important, in language. Tribal rituals like circumcision and harvest dances strengthened the bond of belonging to one ethnic group which usually claimed the same ancestry.

Rural-urban migration in the 1950s, with increasing numbers in the following decades, brought together different ethnic groups who shared very little in common. They had different cultural traditions and different languages. The new phenomenon of Africans in the urban areas first attracted anthropologists from the Manchester school, notably Gluckman (1961) and Mitchell (1969). They were intrigued with the adaptation of urban life in the cities of Central Africa, especially in Zambia's copper belt. They were influenced in their analysis by Wirth's ([1938] 1969) classic essay, "Urbanism as a Way of Life." Not surprisingly, Gluckman argued that the urban life was leading to "detribalization" in African cities and therefore the African city was a melting pot for the African tribal traditions. This thesis was later proven wrong.

Instead, other scholars such as Epstein (1969) argued, with support from field observations in Zambia's copper belt, that when people of diverse origins have only recently come together and most retain close ties with their home areas, "tribal" feelings tend to be more intense than within the more homogeneous rural societies. Shack (1973), in a study conducted among the Gurage in Addis Ababa, argued that African towns are not melting pots for the rural Africans with diverse tribal backgrounds. Even after living in an urban environment for periods of up to a generation or more, Africans in town retain their tribal identity and membership in the rural society.

As O'Connor argues, this "tribal identification" of Africans in towns is one area in which tropical Africa differs markedly from most of Asia and Latin America. Even in the latter places, "tribes" are recognized, but only a very small portion of the urban population is regarded as "tribal." Tropical Africa is exceptional because in each city nearly all those who are not members of racial minorities, (i.e., whites and Asians), can say without hesitation to which "tribe" they belong. This is true of Nairobi where virtually everyone except the Asians and Europeans will quickly identify themselves as Luo, Kikuyu, Luhya or Kamba. This becomes a problem especially when there is scarcity of resources to be distributed (e.g., jobs in the formal sector or food kiosks in the informal sector in any city).

Studies of rural-urban migration in Africa and other Third World countries have identified its selective characteristic. The process "selects" young adults (primarily aged 20-30), the educated who are in search of white collar jobs in the towns, and usually more men than women. There is one category that has not been emphasized in previous studies which is identifiable with early migration of Africans into Nairobi. This selectivity is based on *ethnicity* or different "tribes." Among the first ethnic groups to migrate to Nairobi were the Kikuyus, mainly because of their proximity to the city. Deciding to travel an average of 60 miles to Nairobi is easier for a jobless Kikuyu in the rural areas than for other groups. It would be a difficult decision for a jobless Luhya or Luo who would need to travel an average of 180 miles to get there. In 1969, for example, the Kikuyu comprised 38% of Nairobi's total population, followed by the Luhya with 13%, the Luo and the

Kamba with 12% each of the total population (Republic of Kenya 1971). In 1979, the Kikuyu population had declined to 33% of total population in Nairobi. They were, however, still the largest ethnic group in Nairobi, and Parkin (1975, 152) suggests that most inhabitants then regarded it as an essentially Kikuyu city. The same may be said in 1996 despite the increase in proportions of the other major groups. The other major tribes increased their numbers in 1979 with the Luo attaining 18%, Luhya 16% and the Kamba 12% of the total population in Nairobi (Republic of Kenya 1980).

The Luos clearly did not migrate to Nairobi because of their proximity. Luo land is more than 200 miles away from Nairobi. Instead, most of them were initially hired as clerks in the government corporations, like the railways and the post office, which have headquarters in Nairobi. The British colonial administration policy of divide-and-rule encouraged employment of the Luo in such corporations and discouraged employment of the Kikuyu who were suspected of sympathizing with the anti-colonial Mau Mau movement. The Luhya migrants, who like the Luos are a far distance from Nairobi, were first hired as house servants for the European community in Nairobi, a job few Kikuyus would have been given because of the mistrust toward them by the colonial establishment. Kambas, like the Kikuyus, come from near Nairobi. This partly explains their early migration there. They also have certain skills, mainly wood carving and stone carving, not shared by many other ethnic groups. Since their settlement in Nairobi, they have advanced these skills and are known to make beautiful art craft and carvings which they sell to the tourists and affluent Kenyans. The early Kikuyu migrants were involved in various kinds of trade in Nairobi and between Nairobi and their adjacent rural homes.

The extent to which ethnic ties have helped with the initial settlement of new migrants is a subject studied widely in Africa and in Latin America. Studies of urbanization in Africa dating back to the 1960s (e.g., Epstein 1969; Gluckman 1961; Southhall 1973; Gugler and Gilbert 1982) have supported the argument that rural ties are significant in settling new urban migrants. In other areas like Latin America, studies by Lomnitz (1977) and Roberts (1978) have also shown that rural ties are useful in settling new urban migrants. My study confirms this finding. It also shows how such rural ties have become a backbone for establishing an economic activity in the urban informal economy.

Theoretical Perspectives

Sociologically, "urban ethnicity" suggests that ethnicity has a social function in the urban areas. The separation from tribal life and entry into urban life, far from weakening the bonds between tribal members, actually strengthens them (Shack 1973). It is the strength of such bonds and how they have been articulated by Nairobi migrants to acquire economic opportunities in the 1980s that is sociologically intriguing. Earlier anthropologists who studied Central and East African urban areas—Mitchell, Gluckman and Southhall—all insisted that ethnicity in towns is primarily a means of classifying the multitude of Africans of heterogeneous origins who live together in urban areas. Ethnic classification is the basis of urban life. Shack (1973) found that urban ethnicity in Addis Ababa manifests itself in ways unlike what had been observed in other parts of African towns.

Besides the classification of heterogeneous African groups (which is not considered significant now), urban ethnicity has become a useful political and economic asset in Africa in the 1980s. Ethnic ties are certainly of profound importance in most cities as a source of social security in providing for the few elderly who remain there, for the sick and for the many unemployed and underemployed (O'Connor 1983). In the absence of social welfare systems in Kenya and Zimbabwe, as in most Third World countries, ethnic ties play almost an equivalent role to the social welfare system found in most Western countries.

Kinship and friendship ties cannot be underestimated, as I argue in the next section. Ethnicity provides the context of more intimate ties. The new migrant, for example, will depend on kinsmen for shelter but will turn to a wider group of co-ethnics in seeking a job. Those who do not have many kinsmen in the city must rely on others of their own tribe or ethnic group as a substitute. O'Connor (1983) observes, as I did during my study, that "social distance" is such that friendship patterns are strongly influenced by ethnic affiliation. Even in most ethnically diverse cities in tropical Africa, nine out of ten people specify a co-ethnic as their best friend (O'Connor 1983)! In a study in Indonesia, Bruner (1973, 181) found the same thing about the Batak—"that every individual interaction in the city of Medan occurs within a larger framework of ethnic group relations". Brunner focused on a theme that my study in Nairobi also raised, that is, "positive identification is not just a matter of convenience or politeness in Medan, but it is rather an economic and political necessity" (Brunner 1973, 182). The extent to which this was found in Nairobi is discussed below. Brunner (1973, 182), more specifically on this point, noted that "no Tapanuli Batak enters the city as such. He enters along a network, through a system, occupies a particular social structure slot, and there is invariably someone else, most frequently a relative, to help interpret the urban experience in terms he can understand. No man has to recapitulate the experience of his group and learn about the city on his own."

Ethnic identification in Nairobi, then, fulfills the commonly accepted role of settling migrants; furthermore, it is well entrenched in the urban informal sector. Such statements by ILO (1972) that the informal sector is characterized by ease of entry should be recast with the theme of social networks and their role in this sector. No one enters the informal sector as such. He or she has to move along a network. Ethnicity helps new migrants settle and find an economic activity. I argue that in understanding the social dynamics of the informal sector in Nairobi (specifically ethnicity), one may unearth part of the secret of its success in job creation when compared with the formal sector.

I found that certain ethnic groups predominate in some informal subsectors. Ethnic categories may be imprecise, and in part even fictional, and they may be played down by governments, but they are very real to most citizens. Nairobi's inhabitants, for instance, almost invariably perceive their neighbors not only as old or young (age), as rich or poor (class), as men or women (gender), but also as African, Asian or European, as Kikuyu, Kamba, Luo, Kalenjin or Luhya, and this greatly influences their attitudes toward each other. Such social identities also form the basis of social interaction which has extended to economic interaction as with the informal economy. The relevance becomes clearer when some subsectors are targeted for government support (loans or permanent work spaces) while others, possibly dominated by a different ethnic group, are not supported and continue to be harassed by government officials. Such a situation may be of concern mainly in capital cities since most of the provincial cities are basically run by local ethnic groups which tend to be more homogeneous. Capital cities in most Third World countries are the financial centers and the seats of governments. What happens there, for example, in Nairobi, is likely to have an impact on the rest of the country. As mentioned earlier, such tensions are likely to occur when there is scarcity of resources to be distributed.

Research Findings

Looking at the general distribution of the sample (Nairobi's), I found that there were three ethnic groups that were significantly represented in the subsectors of the informal economy I studied. These were the Kikuyu, the Luo and the Luhya. These are also among the largest ethnic groups in the country and in Nairobi (Republic of Kenya Census 1979). Other smaller ethnic groups like the Kamba, Kalenjin, the Maasai and others were scantily represented. The general distribution of my sample was as follows: Kikuyu 48%, Luo 36%, Luhya 7% and others, 12%. This fact by itself is not surprising as it confirms the national trend and distribution of Nairobi's population by ethnic groups.

Various subsectors were operated by specific ethnic groups. They also perpetuated the entry of the same ethnic group members to any open space for running a business or allocation of new food kiosks. This was mainly through passing to each other timely information, specifically to co-ethnics. This finding applied mainly to the drum sellers and the food sellers. I also found that customers, especially in the food-selling business, patronized certain sellers based on their ethnic identity. This sometimes boosted the sellers' business. The opposite was true in the case of two Luo women who lost their customers to a Luhya woman. *Trust* is a very important concept in the world view of the informal sector operators. It forms an important basis of *social capital* among these entrepreneurs. They rely on trust to decide whether to give credit to their customers. There was strong evidence from the fieldwork showing that sellers trusted members of their ethnic groups more than customers from other groups and credit was usually advanced to co-ethnics.

Seventy-seven percent of the food sellers were Kikuyu, mainly women who sold food from kiosks. No Luo or Luhya had a food kiosk in Nairobi's industrial area where this study was conducted. On the other hand, 70% of the women who sold food in the streets' adjacent gates of major factories were Luo. Twenty-five percent of this category was Luhya and only 5% was Kikuyu. The significance of this distinction is understood better when one realizes that the kiosks are more advantageous in many ways than the open street locations. The kiosk is a semi-permanent structure usually allocated by the City Council. It usually has clean, running water and therefore meets basic sanitation requirements compared with the street food selling locations. Operators in kiosks do pay a license fee to the City Council. This has not, however, saved them from indiscriminate demolition ordered by the City Council on various occasions. Most kiosk owners live in perpetual fear that one day they will lose all their belongings in a demolition. This is not unfounded fear if compared with results from elsewhere. Irene Tinker (1987) in her monograph on street foods gives the example of the devastating effects demolition had on food sellers in Ile-Ife, Nigeria. Her study found that before demolition, 75% of the enterprises that moved had employed assistants; after the move, only 25% did. They also found that more than 90% of the street food sellers were making less than half the income they made before they were forcibly moved.

The kiosk owners do not pay taxes for their business; in this way they operate similarly to the food sellers outside the street. The food kiosk operators tend to make more money mainly because they operate longer hours (12 hours) compared with outside food sellers who are at their selling locations during the lunch hours only (approximately two hours). The kiosks, in theory, could appeal to more customers since they were open for longer hours, and various people, besides working in the factories, could patronize them anytime. In practice, only a few women food sellers that operated outside did better business than some kiosk owners. This was, however, the exception and not the rule. The food kiosk has kitchen facilities. The food sellers operating from outside locations had no choice but to cook food in their homes, commute or walk to their selling locations before noon and vacate their locations after the lunch hour. They also had to rely on more specific customers than the food kiosk owners.

Whichever way one looks at it, owning a kiosk was more advantageous and prestigious than having a location outside a factory gate. This observation was confirmed by the respondents. It was intriguing therefore to find that there was such a distinct distribution on ethnicity in these two subcategories. This became more of an intriguing research issue for me when the food sellers operating outside reported that they would prefer a kiosk to "their outside locations" if there were any available. They were also aware and conscious of the fact that the kiosks were owned predominantly by the Kikuyu.

One key respondent, Mary, whom I asked to explain why there was a disproportionate distribution of these two major ethnic groups in the two categories of food selling places, said the following:

> I think the Kikuyu dominate ownership of the food kiosks for the following reasons. The Kikuyu had experienced a lot of poverty during the colonial administration period and especially during the Mau Mau movement up to the time of independence. Many of them were jobless and landless and were therefore ready to undertake any business or job opportunities that arose. After independence when colonial rules were relaxed, many were ready to put up kiosks, look for licenses and they therefore overtook most of the other ethnic groups. Most of the other ethnic groups at that time (in the 1960s and 1970s) appeared satisfied with their economic welfare and stayed at home with their families. Those who were in need and in search of small scale business opportunities were allocated kiosks then and they happened to have been Kikuyus. (field notes)

This respondent's explanation about why there has been a mushrooming of food sellers operating outside the major factory gates is that they (mostly Luhya, Luo and other minority ethnic groups) had started experiencing the economic pressure and hardships that the Kikuyus experienced almost two decades earlier. Having no alternative, they have ended up cooking food and selling it outside the factories. They do not have much choice, mainly because the kiosks are already occupied by the Kikuyu, and very rarely are new ones being allocated. The turnover rate of the kiosk owners is almost nonexistent. They are valued assets. Even when there was a change of ownership, it was usually among family members and rarely to outsiders.

This respondent, Mary, did not think (as I did) that the City Commission's relaxation of the bylaws, characterized by infrequent harassment of outside food sellers, contributed to the rapid increase of this category—"It may be a coincidence." While Mary's explanation was echoed by most respondents who owned kiosks and by a minority of those selling food outside, at least 60% of the food sellers reported that the relaxation of the city bylaws had encouraged them to start selling food outside the main factory gates in Nairobi's Industrial Area. Mary's argument was based on the economic history of the Kikuyu and was indirectly supported by those selling food outside. Ninety percent of the respondents reported hard economic situations (e.g., their spouse's salary not being enough for school fees or being recently divorced or widowed) that inevitably led to their needing a supplemental income to buy clothes and food for the family. The hardship has been more of a reality to most Kenyans and particularly Nairobi residents in the early 1980s.

I argue that both explanations, that is, the economic history of the

Kikuyu and the relaxed bylaws of the City Commission, are plausible. I also add that history favored the Kikuyus in the 1960s and 1970s. The patron-client relationship so characteristic of African governments (Young 1982, 1994)—as discussed above—may have been operational during these allocations. Because most outside food sellers came after the kiosk owners were already established, it was difficult to prove this point from the respondents—none reported to have been allocated a kiosk based on ethnicity. What is clear and indisputable is that at the time of my study the Kikuyu dominated the food kiosks and the Luo dominated food selling outside factory gates.

A policy implication is that if more favorable policies directed toward the food kiosk owners by the city or the central government were to arise at the expense of the outside food selling locations, an interpretation based on ethnic identity would be inevitable. The Luos would argue rightly that the Kikuyu were being favored and would not simply sit and say the government is supporting the informal economy. This happened in May 1990 when the Muoroto village was demolished. The outcry was that the Kikuyu who predominated Muoroto were being annihilated by the Kenya government. The slum was identified with an ethnic group and the government action interpreted as an action against the Kikuyu and not the slum *per se*.

My hypothesis, that ethnicity may determine entry, was overwhelmingly supported by the data in the case of the food sellers (both in kiosks and outside). All the food kiosks reported that they had been informed about allocation of kiosks by a co-ethnic. Without such information and facilitation "entry" would have been very difficult as well as outright impossible in some cases. From a sociological perspective, it should be clear by now that "there is no ease of entry into the informal economy." It is complex and difficult, and one has to know how to navigate the social hurdles especially those imposed by ethnicity. However, the ease would be achieved if one's co-ethnics are involved in allocation of available opportunities, like in the case of food kiosks on which I have focused.

Timely information is a very crucial element in the informal economy because it is because of such information that a potential operator would go to City Hall to seek an application. This is what took place in the case of the food kiosks. It clearly shows that "the ease of entry" as suggested by earlier studies based on an economic perspective (e.g., ILO 1972; House 1984) is not easy at all. To get the food kiosk license was more important than to have the capital to start it. If one did not come from the group that had the information and passed it among themselves, then chances of getting the kiosk were very remote. Thus, even in what finally appears as "formal" allocation of kiosks, a high degree of "informality" had taken place earlier. The behind-the-scenes operations which may later be formalized are the most critical here.

Outside food selling appears, at face value, informal and haphazard. A casual observer may also think that anyone can bring cooked food, lay it outside any given factory and be instantly in business! In fact, entering the business of selling food is very complicated. In the Nairobi study, I found that ethnic identity was very important at a general level to determine who gets space outside which industries and along which streets. Spaces were therefore ethnically allocated in an "informal" way from an outsider's view but had become quite "formalized" among the women food sellers. More than 90% of the women reported that a friend told them about the space appropriate for food selling. I found that in 90% of the cases, this friend was a co-ethnic. When studying this subsector, the only Kikuyu woman I identified selling food outside one factory reported that she was told about the space by her friend who was a Luo and a member of her Christian church—both were born-again Christians. This was the only case among the women respondents. In the other cases, co-ethnics told each other about available spaces and supported each other in first settlement, thereby "colonizing" most of the outside food selling spaces. Despite the fact that outside food selling was less prestigious and usually had lower returns than kiosks, for 80% of the women in the sample, this was their only way to contribute to the family budget. Ethnic identity is informally a prerequisite for entry into the available spaces. This may explain why the Luo women continue to dominate the outside food selling of the major streets in Nairobi's industrial area, especially along Addis Ababa Road, Kampala Road and Likoni Road.

Ethnic distinctions among the other subsectors were substantial but not as vast as among the food sellers. The metal artisans were ethnically distributed as follows: Kikuyu, 47%; Luo, 28%; Luhya, 3%; others (mainly Kamba), 22%. Like the food sellers, ethnic identity was very strong among the metal artisans. Metal artisanry is one subsector in the informal sector that requires technical skills to make such items as farm tools, cooking pots, metal boxes, frying pans, woks, water buckets, lanterns and much else. Previous studies of the artisans (King 1977; Ndua and Ngethe 1984) show that training to acquire the relevant skills is mainly done informally through apprenticeship and not in a formal institution.   The apprentices get their sponsors through social networks—friends and kin—but all from co-ethnics.   Thus ethnic identification among the metal artisans is not only important for the acquisition of space from which to operate, but also for getting the skills necessary to start operating.   Some skills were safeguarded by those who knew them and were only passed along in a selective manner.   Here, the criterion of selection was ethnicity.   Understanding this "informal" criterion of selection and training among the metal artisans is important especially to non-governmental organizations (NGOs) that have been planning to introduce skill training workshops for the metal artisans.

A simple observation of the metal artisans shows ethnic distribution by activity as follows: the Kikuyus mainly make metal boxes and cooking stoves, especially the improved "energy saving stoves" (*jiko*), and they make and repair aluminum cooking pots; the Luos are over-represented in making frying pans, wash basins (popularly known as *karai* in Kiswahili) and woks; and the Kambas primarily make the decorated metal boxes that are mainly bought by high school students in lieu of vinyl or leather suitcases, which are too expensive and unaffordable to most of them.

To elaborate on this point, and especially to show how safeguarded some skills are, I will now discuss the case study of lantern making.   The tin lamp, which uses kerosene and a regular wick, appears as if it is so simple that anybody can make one without any technical skills or shortage of the relevant parts.   However, lantern making is not that simple, and it requires intensive training.   There are some raw materials, for example, a special kind of wax, that must be used to complete the desired tin lamp.   Those who know where it can be bought are unwilling to share this information with others who are not their friends, relatives or co-ethnics.   The tin lamp is an important source of light for thousands of city homes without electricity.   It is the main source of light for most low income earners and the poor in Nairobi who live in the major slums of Mathare and Kibera.   Most rural homes also rely on the tin lamp for their lighting.   It is convenient and, above all, affordable.

The chief tin lamp maker among the metal artisan (*Jua Kali* operators) I studied is Mr. John Ngumba, a Kikuyu who comes from Gaichanjiru in Muranga district.   Of the ten tin lamp makers in the "house" they occupy, eight are from the same village, Gaichanjiru, and two are from Embu, a district that borders the Central Province of Kenya where Muranga is located.   I was interested in finding out why there was what appeared to be such a "coincidence."   Ngumba explained that there was an old man in Gaichanjiru who had the skills of making tin lamps. He taught the people in Ngumba's village starting with Ngumba. "When I learned the skills, I continued to teach other people in my home area, mainly friends and relatives—for example, my younger brother, who is right here in this 'house' with me but who is now producing his own tin lamps."

The significance of social networks in the transfer of skills surpasses the possession of money. Ngumba insisted on teaching skills to friends and relatives who were all co-ethnics, and not those who simply showed up with money. He would rather forfeit money and teach the skills only to those from his village. This was quite surprising to me. The strength of social networks in the transfer of skills is evidenced here: the logic of the national market forces is surpassed by that of social networks.

The Luos, on the other hand, predominantly make the frying pans, wash basins (*karais*) and woks. Although a few Kikuyus and other ethnic groups also made some, it was clear from the observations that the Luos were far superior in making these items and their products sold faster. They had a better finish and were of a better quality, hence customers preferred them to those made by the other ethnic groups. The apprenticeship for learning how to make those items was also based on ethnicity.

Ethnic biases were also evident in allocation of spaces, particularly in the roof-shed sanctioned to be built by President Moi when he visited the metal artisans in April 1986. The metal artisans who operate under this roof-shed have a loose organization called "Kamukunji Metal Workers and Blacksmiths" Organization. The chair of this organization who is a Kikuyu had the final say on who got a space, which is referred to as "house," in the roof-shed complex. Each "house" measures ten by twenty feet and accommodates eight to ten people. Artisans are expected to work there, store their tools and sell their finished products in front of the "house." There were more Kikuyus in these "houses," followed numerically by Luos. Some Luo artisans (10%) reported biases in the allocation in favor of the Kikuyus by the Kikuyu chair. Regardless of the reporting of this matter which was considered sensitive, especially because the chair was influential, my observations confirm that there were more Kikuyus than any other ethnic group in the "houses." Seventy percent of those occupying the houses were Kikuyus. Other affairs of the organization also had ethnically bias overtones—for example, the selection of artisans who may have qualified to apply for loans from the Kenya Commercial Bank. This selection may have led to an attempt to have ethnic balance at the organization's leadership level. At the time of the study, the chair was a Kikuyu and the secretary, a Luo, holding the two important offices of the organization. It was evident, however, that the chair controlled the affairs of the organization. He was more educated and knowledgeable than the secretary which may have tilted the balance of power control in his favor. Besides, he had the support of the Kikuyu artisans who were the majority in the roof-shed.

The metal artisans are seen as future indigenous manufacturers who may save the country some foreign currency as they continue using locally available materials to produce their products. They also produce goods that are competitive in the market with those produced by big corporations but at lower prices. Their labor intensity and ability to recruit new employees have made them a darling of government spokesmen who support the development and growth of the informal economy. This may also explain why the President visited them more than once in 1986-87. Within this context of state support, ethnic composition may be a potential problem for policy implementation. A policy of supporting the metal artisans may need to consider the ethnic composition of those it is supporting. A potential problem based on the ethnic imbalance could be avoided.

The impact of ethnicity is evident among the metal artisans. It has essentially facilitated entry through the transfer of skills and allocation of spaces in the "houses" from where they operate. The practice of ethnicity determining entry in the informal sector was more evident among those artisans operating outside the roof-shed. My findings show that customers were more likely to purchase from fellow co-ethnics. They usually thought that a co-ethnic would sell the same item cheaper than an artisan from a different ethnic group. Some artisans actually did that on days when business was very low. This was, however, not always true, as the artisans informed us. They try to set uniform prices for the general good of their business. They preferred the competition to be based on the quality and the finish of the products rather than on the hiking and lowering of prices. The latter, according to the respondents, would be interpreted as betrayal of the solidarity the artisans wanted to portray to the outsiders.

Another subsector which also showed a strong ethnic identity is the drum seller. These are the most enterprising among all those in the subsectors I studied in Nairobi. They have more capital because to be a good drum seller one needs to have substantive starting capital, preferably not less than Ksh. 2,000 (about $115). Because the drum sellers have many customers, such as the metal artisans in Nairobi and many others who come from all over the country, a good supply of materials is required. The drum sellers reported more income than any of the operators in the other subsectors I studied.

The ethnic distribution of the drum sellers is comparable to that of the food sellers discussed earlier. The distribution was as follows: Kikuyu, 80%; Luhya, 13%; Luo, none; others, 7%. Note the significant absence of Luos in the drum-selling subsector and the predominance of the Kikuyu. The Kikuyu have literally "colonized" the drum-selling spaces in Shauri Moyo and along Jogoo Road which are the main areas where this subsector is located in Nairobi. This has been maintained mainly through transfer of information of an open available space to co-ethnics. One Kikuyu woman respondent explained how she used to sell drums wholesale until one of her co-ethnics who was an employee of one of her customers told her of an available space that she could occupy. With the collaboration of the neighbors who sold their drums adjacent to the available space, she occupied it and started selling drums. The neighbors were also her co-ethnics.

One of the few Luhya drum sellers explained that his other co-ethnic had learned of the space through a Kikuyu man who was her friend and had been a pioneer in the drum-selling business. Like in the case of food sellers, passing relevant information about available space to operate business is more important than possession of capital. The drum sellers confirmed this to be the case, particularly because they had capital to start a business but did not do so until co-ethnics showed them the way to enter the available spaces. A study done in Nairobi on passenger taxis (popularly called *matatus*) by Sunita, Manudu and Lamba (1982) showed how difficult it was for a new *matatu* owner to get a parking space at the terminus to load and off-load passengers. Collaborating with those who already had the "right" of occupying the parking spaces was the only way to acquire one. This finding again disputes the "ease of entry" characterization of the informal sector as long as it ignores the social dynamics involved in ensuring entry.

The drum sellers portrayed another dimension facilitating entry besides ethnicity. This was regionalism. Not only were most of them Kikuyus, but they were predominantly from specific regions, mainly Nyeri (Othaya Division) and Muranga (Kangema Division). These were the two regions that were overly represented among the drum sellers. The two regions are also neighbors and have had a long history of social interaction through marriage. Thus a pattern of social ties that facilitated entry in the drum-selling subsector may be perceived following the direction of the arrows as shown in Figure 7.1 below.

Figure 7.1. Entry into the drum selling subsector

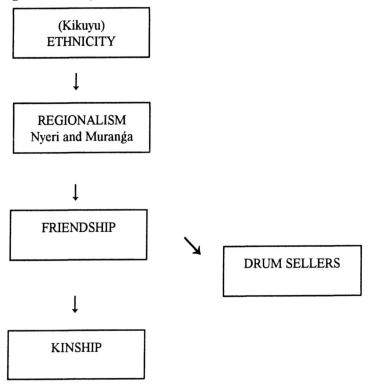

Figure 7.1 shows that the social dynamics at various levels were at play to facilitate entry in the drum-selling subsector. Such dynamics, I argue, should not be taken for granted as they may actually have adverse implications on policy toward such a subsector. For example, during fieldwork, the drum sellers reported the possibility that the government might relocate them to a more permanent place, more spacious than their present location and allegedly with a better infrastructure. They also hoped it would be a location where they could store and lock up their materials, where they could put up simple office space and install telephone and electricity. These facilities were not available in their present location. Such a possibility was being discussed with the local

chief who was reportedly looking for an alternative favorable location. While I consider such support a positive contribution toward the informal economy by some state agents, the extent that this will be supporting a specific ethnic group in Nairobi is evident. I argue that such cases of support are guided not only by economic concerns but social ones should be considered as well. The latter have the potential of leading to ethnic tensions which could in turn lead to political unrest and possibly poor economic performance of these drum sellers. In other words, I am suggesting a long-term policy consideration of all factors at play and not a short-term one concerned with immediate economic gains.

The last subsector under consideration is the garment maker. Garment making was mainly done in the city markets. There were also those who made garments in their homes. The ethnic distribution among the garment makers was as follows: Luo, 63%; Kikuyu, 26%; Luhya, 6%; others, 5%. In my sample, the Luo were over-represented. This may be due to the sampling in various city markets, some of which were predominantly Luo. "Burma" market is a good example. I was interested in finding out why this market was predominantly Luo. As I had done in the case of food kiosks discussed above, I interviewed a key respondent, a Luo man who had been in "Burma" market long enough to be able to explain why it was largely Luo.

My key respondent was in his mid-fifties and a resident of Nairobi for twenty-five years. He gave four reasons for the predominance of the Luos in Burma market, mainly in garment making and other trades. His first reason was that before and immediately after independence (1963) the Luos who were in Nairobi started settling in Shauri Moyo and Kaloleni. This market was in a neighborhood that they had already occupied. Through the process of transfer of information discussed above and their proximity to the market, most stalls were allocated to them. The second reason he gave was that most of the Luo gained employment with the East African Railways and so they were allocated staff houses in Makongeni which is adjacent to this market. This again helped them in getting first-hand information about the establishment of the new market, and so they applied and obtained the stalls. Third, as "Burma" market came up in a neighborhood that was predominantly occupied by the Luos, most of the customers were also Luos. This brought problems of low sales for the other few ethnic groups who had obtained stalls because the Luo customers patronized Luo businesses. The members of the other ethnic groups who had businesses here decided to abandon their stalls and look for places elsewhere due to lack of customers. Fourth, he concluded that when the Luo who originally procured the stalls began going out of business or retiring, they passed the stalls on to their relatives (cf. with the food kiosks above). Ownership of stalls through "inheritance" has promoted the Luo's predominance in this market. In 1996, 90% of the garment makers in this market were Luo.

As in other subsectors discussed earlier, ethnic identity facilitated entry in garment making. It was also important in the transfer of skills through apprenticeship, although the chance of a garment maker going to a formal institution to acquire the skills was much higher compared with any of the other subsectors that I studied. I found that ethnic identity among the garment makers was not as important as in the other subsectors in the transfer of necessary skills. This may be explained by the fact that there are many inexpensive formal institutions that teach tailoring and the art of making clothes in general. It was also evident that those who learned the skills through apprenticeship depended on ethnic identity to get a sponsor.

Analysis and Conclusions on Ethnic Dynamics

The discussion on the role of ethnicity in Nairobi's informal sector could be summarized in the following five points:

1.   Ethnicity has influenced allocation of premises on which to do business. This was evidenced by the food kiosks in Nairobi's industrial area.

2.   Ethnic identity influenced, and to some extent determined, the transfer of skills and technology. This made it difficult for others from different ethnic groups to enter certain trades of subsectors. The example of the Kikuyu from Gaichanjiru in Muranġa dominating the skills of tin lamp making clarifies this point.

3.   I found ethnicity to be significant in establishing market and customers, hence ensuring survival and growth of a given economic activity. Two examples from the findings can clarify this point further. The first one is the case of the Luhya woman who established her food selling outside the glass factory on Addis Ababa Road whose employees were

predominantly Luhya. Despite violent objections of the Luo women who were already established adjacent to this factory, the Luhya workers patronized their co-ethnic, and her food selling became popular and overshadowed that of the Luo women. The second example can be extracted from the case of the Luo's continued dominance of the garment making and other trades in the stalls of "Burma" market. The Luo who surrounded the market's neighborhood were loyal customers to Luo traders, hence the other traders from the different ethnic groups had to leave as their sales dropped drastically. I also noted in this example the continuous dominance by the Luo of the stalls in this market through "inheritance" which is based on ethnic identity.

4.   Ethnicity actually determines entry in the informal economy as was evidenced by the various examples among the four subsectors. This practice may be closer to what Goran Hyden (1982) describes as the economy of affection. As noted in the discussion above, the transfer of information is very important, especially when space to be allocated formally or informally is scarce. The examples of the Luo in "Burma" market, the Kikuyu in drum selling and in food kiosks and the Luo women selling food outside all clarify further the significance of ethnicity in necessitating entry into the informal economy.

5.   I found the concept of *trust* to be very important among all the informal sector operators. I also established that ethnicity and trust building were closely linked. Ethnic identity, especially in food selling, determined whether one would be served food on credit to pay at the end of the month or in two weeks depending on when one was paid. I observed that it was more common for a Luo to serve food on credit to a Luo, a Luhya to a Luhya and a Kikuyu to a Kikuyu. The few instances where this was not so ended in problems. This was evidenced in the case where the Luhya woman served on credit to a man from a different ethnic group, a Kisii. The Kisii man did not honor the payment when he had promised. He gave the Luhya woman various excuses and avoided coming to work on pay day. According

to the food seller, he did that deliberately to avoid her. He
could come to work on other days when he suspected he
would not face the food seller. The Luhya woman lamented
and regretted giving credit to this man. Her main concern
was that he was from a different ethnic group and she swore
not to repeat the mistake ever again.

One ethnic group that was under-represented among the food sellers
did not seem to follow the above pattern, that is, ethnicity giving the
basis for trust, and therefore, consideration to give credit. This ethnic
group was the Kamba. According to one of the Kamba food sellers (who
was also a key respondent) she would rather give credit to people from
other ethnic groups than to her co-ethnics. Her explanation was that the
Kamba are jealous and envious of each other's success and may never
pay back a credit to run down the business of their co-ethnic. She also
added that, in fact, they do not patronize her food, especially when they
had money. They only came to her when they were without money and
were looking for food service on credit. She usually declined to show
them that she knows they do not buy from her when they have cash
money. My observations confirmed her story as I found that very few
Kambas patronized her food especially during the beginning and the end
of the month, when they were loaded with cash from their salary
payments. This case of one ethnic group is unique as the opposite is true
of other ethnic groups. They build more trust with their co-ethnics who
also patronized their businesses and were therefore likely to be given
small credits on services they could not afford to pay promptly.

I have gone beyond showing the significance of ethnicity in settling
new migrants in African cities like Nairobi during the urbanization
process as was noted by earlier researchers like Gluckman (1960) and
Mitchell (1969). I have shown, using selected case studies, the
significance of ethnicity and ethnic dynamics in establishing and
developing economic activities, even those that may be regarded as
simple and easy to enter (e.g., food selling in Nairobi's industrial area
outside the factory gates).

In rejecting the "ease of entry" characterization of the informal
economy, I have advanced the need to evaluate the social composition of
those in the informal sector. I have also shown how relevant the
understanding of social dynamics, like those based on ethnic identity, is
for the informal economy operators themselves and those charged with
policy formulation and implementation.

Finally, I underline the significance of ethnicity in both social and economic spheres even in the modern urban centers in Africa like Nairobi and Harare. Ethnicity did not melt away with urbanization and modernization as had earlier been predicted. Indeed, it has re-emerged as urban ethnicity which as I have argued is more evident where scarcity of resources is prevalent. This happens to be the case in Nairobi and Harare as well as in most other cities in Africa and the rest of the Third World. I will now turn to friendship and kinship, showing their dynamics toward the informal economy.

FRIENDSHIP AND KINSHIP AS IMPORTANT SOCIAL RESOURCES FOR THE INFORMAL ECONOMY

Kinship in the African sense is synonymous with family. The African "family" usually refers to persons outside one's immediate family as the extended family. The nuclear family is mainly a Western idea and only a few Western-educated Africans can think of their families as the "nuclear family." The family, or in this case kinship, extends to distant relatives related through birth or marriage. Knowing who one's relatives are is sometimes hard, especially as migration from rural homes has taken relatives to various towns or other rural districts. When someone is established as a member of the family, African culture expects every member to respond with all the hospitality accorded to a close kin. Kinship in my discussion is defined as any recognized member of the family, however distant. Sometimes it could be one's brother; other times, it could be the son of one's uncle's estranged wife.

Friendship in the context of this study refers to any person that the respondent feels close to and could share his/her problems. For men and, to a lesser degree, for women, it also refers to someone with whom one spends after-work hours drinking beer (as in Harare) or sharing roast meat (*nyama choma*), a popular pastime of all social classes in Nairobi.

The African family has many dependents beyond those who may be considered part of the immediate family. They especially depend on those with jobs in towns for assistance in the form of money, advice, food and clothing. Newly arrived immigrants count on their relatives and sometimes friends to accommodate them in their first months as they try to find ways of being on their own. Because those in the informal economy receive little or no support from the State, reliance on relatives and friends becomes a continuous preoccupation.

In my Nairobi sample of 200 respondents, 89% had dependents other than a spouse and children, and 60% reported that they usually gave cash to those dependents. Of those 123 who answered the question whether they received training through the formal training or through apprenticeship, 86% learned their skills through apprenticeship. Apprenticeship was mainly organized around families or kinship networks. Without such networks, it was difficult to acquire skills. Affording training in formal training institutions was too expensive for most of them. For example, tailoring schools in downtown Nairobi would usually charge almost four times what one would pay as an apprentice attached to a friend or relative. Paying a friend or kinsman was usually in token form, sometimes a gift without attaching a monetary value.

As an answer to the question of how important it was to live next to relatives, 84% reported that it was "very important." They valued the presence of their relatives for various reasons, including advice and cash assistance in case of financial difficulties. Only 16% of the respondents indicated that it was "not important" to live close to relatives.

The importance of relatives in reference to working in the informal sector is reinforced by the response to the question of whom they knew in the city of Nairobi before migrating there. Table 7.1 represents the results of this question. Seventy-nine percent of the respondents knew a relative in Nairobi before they arrived there. Only 9% of the respondents knew a friend, and another 9% knew no one. The findings from the data show that 91% of the respondents knew somebody in the city prior to their arrival. They did not migrate blindly to the city. Ninety-seven percent of the respondents reported that their social contacts were very useful in assisting them to settle in the city. They reported getting initial accommodation and later hints and advice on how to make money.

In a more specific attempt to find out the usefulness of social contacts (mainly friends and relatives) in finding jobs or starting off a business, I asked the question: "How useful were social contacts in finding a job or starting a small-scale business?"   Sixty-eight percent of the respondents reported that it was very useful. A minority, 28%, reported that they had not found contacts useful in helping them start. In another related question in which I asked them to rate the usefulness of social contacts in starting an occupation, 80% reported that the social contacts were "very useful" in helping them start their current occupation.

I wanted to find out from the respondents which of the two, relatives or friends, were particularly helpful in entering their occupation. Fifty-eight percent had been helped by relatives, while 38% reported having received assistance from friends. As I noted above, 79% of the respondents knew a relative in Nairobi who helped them in their initial settling. There is then a consistency in the importance of relatives, both in terms of work as well as living arrangements.

Table 7.1
Persons in Nairobi Known by the Respondents Prior to Arrival

	No.	Percent
Friend	17	9
Relative	153	79
Neighbor from rural home	6	3
Nobody	17	9
Other	1	.5
N=194		

How Different Social Contacts Helped Respondents

It is not enough to say that friends and relatives helped the respondents in the informal economy. Finding out the contribution of different social contacts is also necessary. Forty-seven percent of the respondents reported that their families helped by training through apprenticeships and by offering advice. This was especially the case among metal artisans and garment makers. Twenty-six percent of the respondents reported that they received financial assistance from friends. Friends were less likely to give financial help.

Relatives, then, helped mainly by giving money in the form of small loans and by giving materials like tools, drums, sewing machines, cloth and cooking utensils. In fact, 68% of informal economy operators depended on such loans. Commercial banks rarely supported the respondents. Such an arrangement has advantages. The biggest is that an informal loan does not require collateral. A second is that informal loans are normally interest-free.

Any economist will see the financial value of such social ties. As Lomnitz (1977) argued, "the secret of survival of huge marginal populations in Latin American cities lies in the efficient use of their social resources." In the same way, I contend that the success of the informal sector in Nairobi and its ability to create employment, even where the formal sector has failed, is a result of social networks and the type of financial arrangements that these can offer, and indeed have offered, as evidenced among the respondents.

The concept of trust is, of course, fundamental for understanding transactions and relationships among informal sector operators. It is trust that facilitates financial assistance when government agencies have failed. The evidence from the findings is that kinship ensures more trust, hence more financial support comes from relatives. Trust enhances social capital which becomes real capital especially for the informal economy operators who are limited especially in borrowing from the formal financiers.

A few cases of abuse of trust were reported by some respondents. In one case, two drum sellers who were relatives were no longer on speaking terms because one advanced a loan to the other and, according to the lender, was never paid back in full. Such instances, however, were rare. Most loans were honored, and this "system of loaning" is present throughout the sector. In a sense, it is "formal" to insiders, and "informal" to outsiders such as banks and government agencies.

I also asked which, among friends, relatives and personal capital, was, in their opinion, the most important help in developing their business. The respondents' answers are presented in Table 7.2. As with the other findings, relatives were clearly reported to be the most important network in developing one's business in the informal economy. Friends and capital (which refers mainly to personal savings prior to the economic activity they were involved at the time of the interview) were reported second in order of importance by 23% of the respondents in each case.

The findings also showed that most respondents had more confidence in their relatives. In a question that asked them whom they would go to for help of any kind and particularly help related to their informal sector activities, 43% reported that they would first approach their relatives. Twenty-six percent reported that they would go to their friends, while 23% reported that they would just try to solve their problem on their own. Those who responded in the latter were also more likely to be more entrepreneurial and had slightly higher incomes than the average respondent. Not surprisingly, only 2% of the respondents reported that they could seek help from their government or any formal organization. The disregard that most of the respondents had toward the State is evidenced here. The 2% who reported that they would seek help from the State were among those metal artisans in the government-constructed shed. Generally, these artisans were more receptive to government initiatives because of the assistance of the roof shed that they had gotten nine months before my study.

Table 7.2 Most Important Resource in Developing Business		
	No.	Percent
Friend	45	23
Relative	97	50
Capital	45	23
Other	6	4
N=193		

I wanted to find out how often the respondents contacted friends or relatives for "advice." Advice in this context was defined as helpful information regarding sources of materials, location of sales and tips to improve the business. The findings show that most respondents contact friends for advice more than any other group of social networks. Fifty-three percent reported that they contact friends "very often" for advice. Answering the same question, only 30% reported contacting relatives for advice "very often." This agrees with the trend that the data has so far established, that is, when it comes to money, the favorable contact was toward kinsmen and, when it comes to advice, it was toward friends. I should note here that 99% of respondents reported to have relatives and friends.

While I want to emphasize the importance of friends and relatives for the informal economy, I do not intend to downplay the importance of capital, especially in the initial stages of starting a small-scale business. Indeed, despite the fact that the small scale business activities in the informal sector require little capital to start, it was difficult for many respondents to find that amount. Seventy-eight percent of them reported that insufficient capital was a major problem encountered when they were establishing their present occupation. Entry is indeed difficult on financial terms, despite arguments to the contrary (ILO 1972; House 1984).

I finally asked the respondents to tell me which of the two, capital or social contacts in general, had been more valuable in their business experience. Forty-five percent of the respondents reported that social contacts (friends and relatives) were more important to them than money. Yet 41% of the respondents indicated that having some capital was also important. They preferred having both money and contacts, but on a scale of one to two, social contacts were still ranked 1 by 75% of the respondents.

The role of kinship networks in the informal sector was usually reciprocal. In one case, a respondent, Mary, explained how social contacts, specifically her own brother, contributed to the advancement of her drum-selling business. She started by narrating her brother's wedding, which had taken place three months prior to my interview. She lamented that her brother's wedding was a liability to her business. She reported huge expenses from her drum selling which she incurred when trying to help her brother during the wedding. For example, she had to pay for the bus fare ticket to bring their mother and immediate relatives from the rural areas to Nairobi. She also had to buy the mother expensive clothes befitting the occasion. She then had to pay for new clothes for her daughters, who were to be flower girls in the wedding as well as for herself. Despite all these expenses on behalf of her brother's wedding, Mary still looked at the bright side of things and was counting on her brother to help her boost her business, which was shrinking after the wedding. At the time of the study, her brother, who was a company executive, was arranging for Mary to buy a truck that would be used for transporting drums from Nairobi's industrial area to the selling site where she operated. Owning one's truck is a goal for most drum sellers. It reduces transportation costs.

Other situations evidenced the role of friendship networks in the informal sector. Friendship ties were crucial in getting tenders from factories that sold drums. Knowing people as friends in the factory management ensured one of getting a tender and having exclusive rights to buy drums from that particular factory. In another case, knowing someone in a factory that made bottle corks from metal sheets permitted under-counting of the sheets they bought, reducing the price of supplies purchased. Those doing the under-counting received kickbacks, which was not uncommon in this business. Most "friends" of this type are Africans employed by Asians. While this practice may appear to be a simple case of corruption, I argue that without established friendships, it could not take place. I witnessed the under-counting on several occasions. It was usually done with such genius that the owners could be standing right there when the counting was taking place and not notice it.

Friendship ties are also important in the transfer of skills, especially among the metal artisans. One of my respondents, Njuguna, was a metalsmith who made farm tools like hoes, chisels and other scrap metal tools used for sharpening construction tools. He explained how he learned his skills from his father's friend who was from neighboring Uganda. Njuguna's father asked his Ugandan friend to teach his son the metalsmith skills. Njuguna then benefitted from his father's friendship with the Ugandan expert to become a metalsmith which was the basis of his economic operation. Friendship, however, in some cases goes beyond ethnic ties. The case of Kikwao, who is a Kamba employed by Mary, a Kikuyu, is a good example. Mary is a close friend of Kikwao's sister. On the recommendation of the sister, Mary employed Kikwao as a sales assistant in her drum selling business. The friendship between the employer and the employee's sister reinforced the trust that Mary bestowed to her employee.

Analysis of Social Networks (Friendship and Kinship) by Subsectors

Table 7.3 presents the results from the question that asked respondents how important it was for them to live close to their relatives. It appears that the more secure the operators felt in their occupation, the less they wanted to live close to their relatives. I noted that the garment makers and the food sellers reported a greater need to live close to their relatives, 95% and 85% respectively. The drum sellers, who are the most stable and with more income than any other subsector I studied, were the lowest in reporting the need to live close to their relatives. Though 59% is not low by itself, it is relatively low when compared with operators in the other categories.

Table 7.3 Importance of Living Close to Relatives			
Sub-category	No.	%	N for each category
Metal Artisans (shed)	28	72	39
Metal Artisans (outside)	16	70	23
Drum Sellers	17	59	29
Food Sellers (in kiosks)	16	62	26
Food Sellers (outside)	17	85	20
Garment Makers (in stalls)	32	74	43
Garment Makers (outside)	19	95	20
N=200			

All the respondents in the different subsectors reported that they knew more relatives than friends in the city prior to their arrival. In fact, respondents from food sellers and garment makers reported that they knew no friends but only relatives. The latter reported the highest knowledge of relatives before their arrival in Nairobi. Ninety percent of them reported that they knew a relative before arriving. Among the food sellers in kiosks, on the other hand, only 56% reported knowing somebody.

The results from the data suggest that some subsectors may require more collaboration with other relatives or friends than others. In the case just reviewed, food sellers in kiosks need not have known relatives. The reason might be that the garment makers arrived into Nairobi in the 1970s, while the food sellers migrated in the 1960s. Most garment makers migrated for the specific purpose of reaching a relative to learn the skills. In the 1960s, on the other hand, no one could have preceded the food sellers as most of them were the pioneers in migrating to the city.

Table 7.4 presents findings from a question that asked respondents to indicate whether it was "very useful" or "not useful" at all to have had social contacts when they started their occupations. I only report those

who answered positively. The missing ones are those who answered
negatively.

Table 7.4
Rating Social Contacts in Starting Present Occupation: Percentage
Saying "Very Useful"

Sub-category	No.	%	N for each category
Metal Artisans (shed)	27	73	37
Metal Artisans (outside)	20	87	23
Drum Sellers	20	87	23
Food Sellers (in kiosks)	17	74	23
Food Sellers (outside)	14	74	19
Garment Makers (in stalls)	40	94	43
Garment Makers (outside)	16	80	20
N=192			

Most of the respondents, regardless of the subcategory, rated social
contacts highly in starting their present occupations. More garment
makers (stall and outside) and metal artisans (outside) relied more on
their social contacts to establish their present occupation. I wanted to be
more specific and find out which social contacts these were. Table 7.5
presents the outcome of a question that asked the respondents which
social contacts helped them most in starting their business occupations.

Except for the metal artisans (outside) and the food sellers (outside),
all the other subcategories were helped more substantially by relatives to
start their occupations than by friends. These two subcategories are also
the lowest in terms of income generation compared with other subsectors
that I studied. This finding conforms with the earlier one which showed
that relatives were more likely to give money while friends give advice.
Given that in these two subcategories the initial capital is not as high as
in the other subcategories, the need for a relative to give money did not
arise. The need for a friend to give advice on space availability did arise,

and this explains why they reported more friends than relatives helping them in starting their occupation.

Table 7.5
Social Contacts Helping to Start Occupations

Sub-category	Relative			Friend		
	No.	%	N*	No.	%	N*
Metal Artisans (shed)	19	62	31	10	32	31
Metal Artisans (outside)	6	38	16	9	56	16
Drum Sellers	16	50	32	8	40	20
Food Sellers (in kiosks)	8	53	15	6	40	15
Food Sellers (outside)	7	47	15	8	53	15
Garment Makers (in stalls)	22	67	33	11	33	33
Garment Makers (outside)	12	75	16	4	25	16

N=192
*=Number of respondents who answered the question: "Which social contacts, relatives or friends, helped you start your occupation?"

CONCLUSION

In this chapter I have discussed and shown the significance of social resources in economic situations, particularly among the operators of Nairobi's informal economy. The social dynamics depicted here by kinship and friendship are one of the "secrets" of the continuous development of the informal economy in Third World cities, even when the governments of those countries may not be supporting it. The social networks have for a long time been the mortar behind the growth of the informal economy. The informal contributions to this sector of these networks include facilitating entry, giving money for starting a business or dealing with a crisis and giving advice. The data have clearly shown the reliance of those operating in the informal economy on specific social networks. Weak ties, which, according to Granovetter (1974), are important in securing a career position, are not present or effective among those in the informal economy. The strong ties tend to be more effective for these entrepreneurs.

8
Gender and the Informal Economy

Women in Africa have traditionally been responsible for raising children. In various cases, their duties have extended beyond clothing, feeding and educating children, to being responsible for the financial well being of the family. In this chapter, I argue that gender categorization plays an important role in the establishment and growth of the informal economy. Women who work in the urban informal economy tend to be in less lucrative sectors. They have less access to valuable information, have little or no start-up capital, and work longer hours than their male counterparts. They have unique relationships with customers, suppliers, the state and the local police, as shown previously (see Chapter 7). Like men, they depend on social networks, but I found that their networks are different from those of men. Women's social networks generally offer emotional support, consolation, hope and a sense of community, all of which are valuable assets in starting and managing an informal economic activity. Because traditionally they have had no access to capital, women to this day cannot offer each other the same financial support to start a business as men do. This chapter, then, discusses the impact of gender on the dynamics of the informal economy. It identifies the subsectors more likely controlled by the women of Nairobi and the unique role that networks have played in those illegal activities.

SUBSECTORS OCCUPIED BY WOMEN

Women's participation in the labor force has increased since women became primary income earners. Faced with increasing economic needs and unable to find employment in the modern sector firms or in the civil service, women have sought and found jobs in the informal sector. Thus, half the women in low and middle income residential areas like Uhuru, Eastleigh, Buruburu and Madaraka work in the garment-making sub-sector. Gender segregation in the labor market is an important dimension of the Kenyan informal economy. Two main classifications comprise the activities in the informal sector:

1.   Industrial, which involves "manufacturing," metal fabrication, welding, auto mechanics, carpentry, etc. These are activities that demand a fair amount of technical skill earned from formal institutions or through apprenticeship.

2.   Retail trade services, which include street hawkers, street food selling, market selling and hair dressing. The hair dressers, especially those operating high technology modern salons, tend to make more money than the other women retailers.

The Central Bureau of Statistics (CBS) in Kenya distinguishes between five classifications, all of which could be subsumed in the two main ones that I have just discussed. These include manufacturing, construction, wholesale and retail trade, hotels and restaurants, transport and communication and community, social and personal services.

Whatever classification one uses, women are clearly likely to be engaged in trade and service. I found that most women do not have the funds for an activity that requires high initial capital. In a recent study (Macharia 1993), I found that welding required the most funding (Ksh. 31,824), with auto mechanics' open-air garaging following (Ksh. 29,750). Tailoring required the least funding (Ksh. 7,902). Tinsmithing (Ksh. 9,321) and carpentry (Ksh. 9,881) were closer to tailoring. Confirming my hypothesis (that women are likely to be engaged in less capital-intensive economic activities), most women active in these subsectors were working in tailoring (which is a technically-oriented subsector); almost none were in the others. The women who were engaged in tailoring, which, when compared with food selling and other services, still required substantial initial capital, were generally married. Women engaged in tailoring who were not married had either worked before in a public or a private firm.

Two of the largest labor markets for women are street food selling, already discussed in greater detail in Chapter 5, and garment making. Both require very small initial investment. The bulk of food selling takes place along the streets of Nairobi's industrial area or outside specific factory gates. Construction sites around the city are other prime areas for women food sellers. Women cook food at home and bring it on the sites by carrying it on their backs, pushing it on wheelbarrows or by taking public transport. Factory gates are usually "colonized" by women based on the length of time they have been on the site.

Street Food Selling

Street food selling is a very uncertain and time-consuming business. City police randomly come to confiscate food and appliances. Women generally cannot corrupt police officers as often as men involved in other "illegal" activities can. This is mainly because they do not have as much money as the men; also, they are unlikely to have instantaneous intimacy, which is essential for a corrupt deal to take place. The men are more likely to meet the police at beer-drinking places in the evenings where they settle deals over a drink—an opportunity most women especially mothers (single or married) are denied by their home chores. Thus, there is continuous conflict between women food sellers who occupy the "outside" sites and kiosk owners. From the interviews, it became clear that the latter felt that they were losing customers to those women, because they sold maize, beans and porridge, all much cheaper than food at the kiosk. Kiosk owners, in addition, had legitimate licenses from the City Council, which permitted them to operate in assigned locations and put pressure on police officers to take action against their competitors. The description of street traders in Jakarta, who must continuously shift the location of their food stands to avoid police harassment, closely resembles that of Nairobi's women (Jellinek 1988). The case of women food sellers in Harare (Horn 1994) was very similar to that of Nairobi.

Besides food selling in the streets of Nairobi's industrial area, women also make earnings by selling cooked food in construction sites to workers, office messengers, cleaners, drivers and low-paid clerks. In 1992-94, for example, the site adjacent to the main entrance of the

University of Nairobi was a haven for women food sellers. Four new tall buildings, with no less than twenty-five floors, were being built at the time. Like the women in the industrial area, however, those selling in construction sites are also uncertain about their future. They confessed to us that their livelihood depended on the construction of new buildings.

Cooked food is just one area of specialization for women. There is also the raw food division, specializing in fruits and vegetables. This too takes place on the streets, especially on busy ones in the central business district of Nairobi. For those selling fruits, vegetables and dry raw foods (e.g., rice, beans and corn), wit and fastness to dodge the ever-harassing city police are almost as important as having start-up capital. These women depend on their eight- to ten-year-old children to spy for encroaching police and send warning signals. The speed at which products already laid down on a street pavement are put back into bags and a "market scene" is turned into a normal street path is amazing. The best times for selling fruits and vegetables are the lunch hour and after five o'clock, when people leave offices for home. The constant surveillance by the police makes this group of women difficult to interview. Some of these women were willing to talk, especially on an evening that they have made a profit by selling all that they brought to the streets without crossing paths with the police. As with kiosk owners in the industrial area of Nairobi, some owners of grocery stores and food supermarkets on these streets vehemently expressed their wrath against the women fruit and vegetable sellers. The customers, however, mainly middle and lower-income earners working in Nairobi, relied on these women for cheap products.

Garment Making and Selling

Tailoring in some major markets is comparable to the sweatshops of New York and Los Angeles (Sassen 1994). Most of the garment makers have licenses. Yet, they are harassed, especially because they operate on illegal sites. Others may not have the licenses and, like the food sellers above, they have to keep dodging the city police. The garment makers are more stable in location of operation than the garment sellers who have no fixed locations of operation and are constantly on the run to get away from the city police. The garment sellers who did not form part of the original study usually sell second-hand clothes bought from middlemen who may have imported them from the United States or

Europe. These could be clothes bought cheaply from America's Salvation Army Stores or given free by church organizations. They have become almost the daily wear for most urban and rural low and middle-income groups. These clothes are referred to as *mitumba*, Swahili for second-hand clothes. In Nairobi, *mitumba* selling is not a very respected occupation, but from the sellers' point of view, they make good profits and they have a wide market. The owners of established formal shops in Nairobi's central business district are permanently complaining to the city officials to get rid of the *mitumba* sellers, who are out-competing the owners, especially among the low income groups and the lower middle classes.

In Nairobi, garment making is concentrated in the markets of Shauri Moyo (popularly known as Burma) Jogoo Market, Gikomba and in the women's residential homes in the squatter settlement of Mathare and in neighboring Pumwani, Pangani and Eastleigh. Those working at home, who usually subcontract from established Asian firms, complained of being exploited. This form of exploitation seems common in Third World cities. It compares with gender discrimination in wages reported from India, where women's incomes decline from Rs. 300-500 a month in factories to Rs. 200-300 in workshops to less than Rs. 100 in home production (Gugler 1988).

Hairdressing

Hairdressing is another sub-sector dominated by women. Depending on the modern equipment a hairdresser has, this can be a very lucrative business. Most of the women, however, did not have modern equipment like electric hair dryers and, therefore, did not make much money. The majority did not have the modern skills of perfecting hairdressing. Most of them worked on street corners in residential areas or outside their houses. It is a completely different business for those who run high-tech hair salons in Nairobi's downtown. These women make more money and run their salons like any modern formal business activity.

Beer Sellers

There are illicit beer sellers in most squatter settlements (Nelson 1979). I did not concentrate on this group which, as Nelson noted, usually combine beer selling with prostitution. Although many women are in this occupation, it falls outside the scope of this study. It is, however, important to mention it as a major economic activity especially for the majority of women in the slum and squatter areas of Nairobi as well as in the low density townships surrounding Harare. My focus in this study is on legitimate (in the eyes of the society) and not illegitimate occupations.

WOMEN'S NETWORKS

I have already discussed the importance of various kinds of social networks that have kept the informal sector growing despite lack of any government support. These are mainly ethnicity, friendship, kinship and rural place of origin. The women engaged in the informal sector, just like the men, relied on the same networks. The findings show that different social networks fulfilled different functions for women than men. Some kinds of networks are also more significant to one gender than the other.

Ethnicity, for example, established close co-ethnic support groups for women as well as for the men. Among the women in some sub-sectors, like street food selling, the ethnic divide was so clear that not only did women from the same ethnic group sell from adjacent sites, but their customers from the factories were also their co-ethnics. They also prepared ethnic foods: for example, the Luo way of making maize and beans was different from the Kikuyu's or the Luhya's which may have led to ethnic specificity from the customers. Ethnic solidarity, especially among the street food sellers and the drum sellers, in my study, was conspicuous and fully acknowledged. The case in this study of the successful Luhya woman, who was physically assaulted by two Luo women for establishing her selling site in what they considered their site, is a good example of the ethnic solidarity as it was expressed by these women. I also found that the rotation credit, ideally an affair involving contribution of Ksh. 10 per day, which was given to one of the women each day to supplement her sales for the day, went along ethnic lines. In a street which had, for example, all Kikuyu women, the contribution was done by all of them. If there were ten women, with each contributing Ksh. 10, one of them on a daily rotational basis got Ksh. 100 every ten days. The same principle was applied by the other main ethnic groups in food selling, the Luo and the Luhya. These monies became handy especially on a day of bad sales or on a day that one was arrested by the police and needed to be bailed out of jail. It also became part of the women's saving plans. Indeed some formalized non-governmental organizations (NGOs) like the Kenya Women's Trust Fund have initiated this kind of savings plan for women in areas that do not have it already. When it becomes an established form of savings plan, women are given a group loan which they pay back weekly from their daily savings. Many financial agencies are now using the system described here, which was first popularized in Bangladesh by the Grameen Bank as collateral to necessitate them to give loans to low income women involved in the informal economy.

Trust among the women food sellers, and between them and their customers, who were mainly men, was also along ethnic lines. Trust for this group was an integral part of their daily business because often a customer would show up hungry and with no money for various reasons. He would either say he will pay the following day, at mid-month, or at the end of the month. The women food sellers had to decide quickly, based on their judgment, whether to trust the customer and risk serving him, or whether to stand firm on the principle of "no cash, no lunch." Usually, with an exception of one ethnic group, the Akamba, the ethnic factor was a major influence on whether a customer was served on credit or not. Those from an ethnic group different from the woman food seller's were not advanced credit. The Akamba women food sellers, on the other hand, would rather give credit to someone from another ethnic group than their own. They argued that they could not trust their men mainly because they would like to eat for free and are not anxious to see them (the women) prosper in business. Comments like, "they are jealous and envious," which implied a carry-over in the city of the male chauvinism characteristic of the traditional rural areas, gave men the right not to pay the women. The Akamba women were an exception in this regard, whereas others, like the Luhya woman mentioned above, benefitted and enlarged her business mainly because of having loyal and trusted male customers from her own ethnic group. For the other main sub-sector I studied, the garment makers, trust between the women and the customers and cooperation among the women also went along ethnic lines.

One area where there were clear differences between men and women and the social network dynamics was that of friendship. I found that women, more likely than men, had long-lasting friendships between different ethnic lines. Two women food sellers from different ethnic groups could, for example, be friends and support each other even though they belonged to a different credit rotation group. This was understood as part of business where ties could go along ethnic lines in public, but the private realm had a different basis of attraction and, clearly, friendship lines did not always follow ethnic lines. I found a number of Luo women who were friends with the Kikuyu or the Luhya, although they could have never been colleagues. One conclusion I drew from the friendship networks among the women was that, more so than among men, friendship among women gave emotional and caring support. The support, however, was usually non-material. Indeed, I found that while men could borrow money from friends to start a business or to improve an ongoing one, women could not give any cases where they borrowed money from a friend to start or to improve their business—but the friends were always there to ask about a sick child at home, a quarrel with in-laws or an assault from the husband. I consider this support (despite being non-monetary) equally important in the overall contribution to the business activities the women were involved in and single it out as a difference in the use of networks between men and women. In a study in a Mexico city shanty town, Cerranda del Condor, Lomntiz (1974) identified different friendship patterns between men and women, with the men's being reinforced by what she referred to as *cuatismo*. The functions in the Mexico case were not as distinct as I have described here, but do compare well and emphasize that social networks may have different functions between genders.

Kinship as a support network was not as important for the women as it was for the men in my study. I found that more women would rely on friends for emotional support and caring for each other's sick child more than they did with kinsmen. They also relied more on their rotational-credit associations which were founded along ethnic lines. Part of the relative decreasing significance of kinship as a support network for the women may be explained by the fact that 80% of them were single parents (divorced, widowed or never married). Typically, the women in the city (which was usually seen as a place for men to migrate to while women stayed in the rural areas) may not receive much support from their own relatives, especially male relatives who may believe the women are in the wrong place. Other women relatives in the city may be in hardship situations just like those in the informal economy and may not have as much time for each other to develop supportive networks. Those relatives in the rural areas may be in more hardship than those in the city and may only "wish their relatives well" from the distant and not necessarily offer any meaningful support.

THE DISADVANTAGED POSITION OF WOMEN

Women in the modern work situation, both in the formal and informal economy, have started from a disadvantaged position all over the world mainly due to the traditional sex division of labor which did not encourage women to work outside the home. That disadvantaged position for women in Nairobi and Harare continues particularly in the informal economy. Some disadvantages women face which have yet to be addressed seriously by existing policies or programs include the following:

1.   Legal discrimination, especially in property ownership rights, which in most countries, and especially Kenya, favor the men over the women—Women's lack of possession of title deeds for family land works against them when they want to borrow money from formal institutions, like banks, that usually recognize the title deed in the borrower's name as enough collateral. The logic for men having been the registered owners of family property has been overtaken by modern social processes which have led to urbanization, high rates of divorce and the continuing number of single mothers who would have benefitted from the modern system had property been registered in their names. Until recently, in many banks, a man had to co-sign a loan agreement even in situations where a business, for example, garment-making or drum-selling, may be solely owned by the woman.

2.   Engagement in unpaid domestic work, especially in modern cities where the women do not have their traditional small farms (shambas) to cultivate food crops—In the cities, like Nairobi, such situations have led to family problems especially among the low- and middle-class families when the single salary from the man is barely enough to meet daily

needs. Although Freeman (1991) suggests that many women are involved in urban agriculture to supplement the family income, this is far from being adequate. Indeed, the traditional expectation of women as homemakers is not so in the city.

3.   Education bias from early years of school—First, there is the bias for many parents in the past not working to educate girls in favor of boys, the results of which continue to show today in the low-paying labor markets occupied by women. The second form of bias was in the school system itself where boys were encouraged to take scientific and technically-oriented subjects. Many boys got early training in technical subjects. In Kenya, for example, there were Technical Secondary Schools teaching mechanics and woodwork to the boys while there were none for girls. The equivalent for girls was home economic subjects, something that only helped to reinforce the traditional sex-division of labor. Its impact is visible today: women end up working in low-paying economic activities, more service- than production-oriented. The technical production-oriented activities in both Nairobi and Harare generate more income. These activities tend to be predominated by men while the women predominate the less income-generating activities, mainly the service-oriented ones.

4.   Continuous bias against women's occupations in the city from the State—The City Hall is especially run by men who, generally, have little patience with women food sellers on the streets. The sub-sectors operated by women were the most harassed by the city police, and the same thing continues to date where state policy is generally not as sympathetic to women-occupied sub-sectors, like food selling or *mitumba* selling, as it is with men-occupied sub-sectors like metal-artisans.

The disadvantages outlined above against women in the informal economy that are mainly due to unfavorable policy and lack of specific programs to improve the women's welfare have meant more cut-throat competition among women entrepreneurs whether in food selling or garment-making. The competition was more conspicuous among women than men. This may support and explain further the finding that women's friendships were more emotional-supporting than economic-(financial) supporting.

The state policy supposedly aimed at creating an enabling environment for future successful development of the informal sector has not said much about women's occupations, and it generally supports the growth of the technically-oriented sub-sectors dominated by men. Women in the informal sector are more subjected to police harassment on a daily basis than their male counterparts.

A number of programs in support of women in the informal economy have come from NGOs internationally funded. The leading one in Kenya, whose priority is the welfare of women in the low-income category, is the Kenya Women Finance Trust (KWFT), which is an affiliate of the International Women's Bank (headquartered in Washington, D.C.). This organization has established low lending for women in the informal economy without asking for formal requirements such as collateral. KWFT has its headquarters in Nairobi, but most of its operations are in rural towns of Eldoret, Karatina and Kilifi. It is only recently (1993) that they have started lending programs in Nairobi's squatter settlement of Kibera. The organization works closely with the women who are to become their potential borrowers. They educate them on simple financial management, making investment decisions, simple balancing of accounts and basic bookkeeping. They also work closely with them to build trust (both for the women and KWFT). They advise them to form groups of five women (Watano) who are engaged in a similar business, know each other and eventually develop friendship and trust. Each group of five women then forms one large group of thirty women (Kikundi Cha Wanawake) who meet regularly every week to discuss their business progress and to pay part of their loan back to KWFT, whose officer is always present at these meetings. The loan could be as low as Ksh. 5,000 and is increased after the first payment of the full amount, including the low interest charged. This form of lending money to women is based solely on the idea of *trust* which is gradually built as people get to know each other more, and this is why the meetings of five and then thirty women are required for any women who borrow money from KWFT. It is a modification of the Grameen Bank first developed in Bangladesh to lend money to the poor in slum areas.

There are a few other NGOs using similar methods to help improve women's informal economic ventures like the Kenya Rural Enterprise

Program (K-REP) whose Juhudi program is very similar to KWFT's. The National Council of Churches in Kenya (NCCK) has similar programs in Nairobi and other major towns. All these organizations reported 100% loan repayment from the women, who are primarily their clients, and the women also reported that they were happy with the program. One criticism I have regarding this otherwise successful program from the NGOs is that the loan levels for the women are still very low compared with what men in welding or auto mechanics get from other organizations. The loan levels should be raised beyond mere survival to levels that they can generate a viable business activity. Whereas the lenders should be cautionary about increasing the loan amounts, the need to ensure that the loan will also boost to a higher level the women's businesses should be paramount and the guide to the relationship between the agent lender and the women clients. Otherwise, the poor women may end up working for the lending institutions. Although the interest rates are lower than on money borrowed from conventional banks, there is interest to be paid all the same. The loan really should be aimed at ensuring a gradual move from survival to a profit-making enterprise for the women clients.

The State should emulate the work of the few NGOs dedicated to improvement of the women's welfare in the informal economy. The policy, especially the current one showing bias against women's activities, should be eradicated and encouragement on equal basis be given just like what is happening for the men's activities. *Jua Kali* should encompass women's activities, and they should benefit from programs being introduced by the World Bank through the government in the same way as the men in the technical skills subsectors. Given that most technical schools previously encouraged men, the policy should be changed to encourage young women to be involved in the technical subjects. This will eventually provide women who are versatile in both service and production sectors of the informal economy. When women are given the same opportunities as men, they are equally capable, and they manage their businesses well. Most women in the informal economy are the sole bread winners as a result of being widowed, separated or divorced. Women, therefore, take their occupations as seriously as the men do!

9

Small Enterprise Development and the Alleviation of Poverty in Kenya

Unlike the previous chapters that have examined the social and political dynamics of the informal economy, I will in this chapter examine the effects of small scale enterprises on the alleviation of poverty in Kenya. In other words, can small enterprise development nationwide eradicate or at least alleviate poverty? While this was a constant question I had during my original research and thereafter, the need to answer this question was heightened in early 1994 by the interest that the United Nations Development Program (UNDP) had on the small scale enterprises. Like other development agencies operating in Kenya (ODA, USAID, CIDA, etc.), UNDP was particularly interested in developing a program that would support small enterprise development to alleviate poverty in Africa, starting with Kenya where the *Jua Kali* sector was already doing well as I have shown in earlier chapters.

Several ways of alleviating poverty exist once the causes are identified. The concern of this chapter is to discuss the increased participation of Kenyans in the small scale enterprises ranging from hawking to vegetable selling to garment making, *Jua Kali* activities as one possible solution to the poverty problem. Other possibilities include ensuring formal education for all citizens with the hope that jobs will be created either in the private or public sector. This unfortunately appears not to have worked well in most developing countries in Africa (e.g., Nigeria) or in Asia (e.g., India) where the number of unemployed university graduates has been on the rise. Kenya has not been spared from this phenomenon and a notable increase of unemployed university graduates has been growing especially in the last six years (1990-1996). Besides education for all, improvement of agriculture, especially small scale rural farming, has been advocated widely by leading advisers in public policy as a way to alleviate poverty in Kenya. It goes back to a few years after independence in 1963 when President Kenyatta popularized the call of *Turudi Mashambani,* Swahili for "Let Us Go Back to the Land." Some people heeded the call, but due to landlessness (especially in the heavily populated parts of Central Province, Western Province or the dry lands of Eastern Province) rural-urban migration increased every year. That call generally did not alleviate poverty either in the rural or in the urban areas; neither did it halt the urbanization process. The urban population has risen to more than 25 percent in the 1990s compared with 15 percent in the 1970s and only 8 percent in the 1960s when the call of "going back to the land" was at its climax.

There may not be a singular solution to the alleviation of poverty. I must however make the point that the growth of small enterprises and the development of an entrepreneurial culture both in the rural and urban areas is a key answer to the problem. Entrepreneurship has its advantages. For example, it requires little physical space to operate from, when compared with engagement in improved agriculture or "returning to the land" that may not be there. Entrepreneurship, which calls for innovation and risk-taking, may not require one to be employed in a white collar job, which has been the expectation of most university graduates. The fact that entrepreneurs will be self employed in most cases and will also create jobs for others through sub-contracting makes this solution for the poverty problem worth more attention as different agencies and the government seek ways to promote entrepreneurship. This is not novel by itself as small scale enterprises have existed since and even before 1963 when Kenya became independent. What is important and critical is the degree of involvement by more people: improving the quality of the existing small scale enterprises and encouraging start-ups that will continue in the struggle to alleviate poverty in Kenya.

Poverty has not been an easy idea to understand and to explain in Kenya or in other countries. It is worth making the point that most of us as a society can identify poverty. Like one of my respondent's put it, "you know poverty when you see it." Both quantitative and qualitative descriptions of poverty abound in the literature (Danziger and Weinberg 1986; Wilson 1987). Poverty exists at the micro level (individual families) and at the macro level (national) as compared with other nations. Measuring poverty at the micro level remains a complicated matter. This is so mainly because getting exact figures for all individual incomes is problematic. People are not always honest in reporting their incomes. There is a tendency to report only one source of income, ordinarily that from their regular employment, while other possible income sources may remain unreported. Different lifestyles and personal choices (e.g., a rich person choosing to live in a slum or a squatter settlement) also make measuring poverty at the micro level more difficult. At the macro-economic level, there is no doubt that Kenya is a poor country. Indeed a recent report by the United Nations International Children's and Educational Fund (UNICEF) ranked Kenya as the twenty-third poorest country in the world with a per capita income of US $360 (UNICEF 1990).

Poverty at the individual or household level is still difficult to quantify and to ascertain. We also do not have all the answers about whom the poor really are, and whether they themselves think they are poor or why. What this suggests are more in-depth studies of poverty that hopefully would bring out its multiple causes. This would help in hopefully avoiding a quick fix to a problem that seems recurrent and increasing every other year. A sustainable solution is worth investigating. It is a concern even in small scale enterprise development that I am supporting here. One aspect of these enterprises that I am critical about is in the many mushrooming credit agents. Most of them have been reporting high repayment, no default from the small scale entrepreneurs, but one wonders whether the small credit that was advanced and was to be repaid with interest was actually beneficial in boosting a vertical social mobility to the recipient. This is an area that has to be looked at critically and with genuine concern for those that need to be moved out of poverty. Another area of concern is whether small scale enterprises may work well for all communities in Kenya given that some are more predisposed to farming, fishing and raising livestock and not necessarily in small scale business enterprises. Such concern may lead to identifying various kinds of small scale enterprises that may work in certain communities and those that may not work before applying a homogeneous small enterprise program for all.

POVERTY AND THE POOR IN KENYA

The poor are those people who are living below the poverty line. The poverty line is defined by the UNDP Human Development Report as income below which one cannot afford a minimum nutritionally adequate diet plus essential non-food requirements. In Kenya, all those who are either unemployed or underemployed (making less than Ksh. 1000) and are composed of a family of five, assuming they have no other support, are according to this definition, poor. I will also, for the sake of further clarity, distinguish between the *rural poor* and the *urban poor*.

The *rural poor* include the following:
  a) The smallholder farmers—This group consists of those growing subsistence crops like maize, beans, and potatoes in acreage of up to two acres in the high density population areas and in four acres or more in low density population areas that also tend to be poor agriculturally.

  b) The landless—These are people in the rural areas who do not have any land of their own. They have to live as squatters in other people's land or in the local shopping centers as tenants. Most of these form the bulk of rural manual workers who tend to be underemployed and rarely make the Ksh. 1000 mark I have adopted for this definition. Some of the landless may be engaged in simple trade like selling bananas or greens; they may also have some skills like artisans or cobblers, but they still make too little money to move them above the poverty line.

  c) Nomadic pastoralists—This group tends to be poor mainly because of the harsh climatic conditions in which they are involved. They may have livestock that sometimes die en masse in case of drought. They tend to have very little money to live above the poverty line. This is characteristic of some parts of Samburu and Turkana areas of North Eastern Kenya.

The *urban poor* include the following:
  a)   Families   with   both   parents,   unemployed   or underemployed—These tend to be mostly in the slums and squatter settlements of most Kenyan towns (e.g., Mathare, Dandora, Korogocho or Kibera in Nairobi; Chaani in Mombasa; Pandipieri

in Kisumu; Kiandutu in Thika). Indeed, every town in Kenya has its share of such settlements, which is by itself a sign of poverty even without the fine measurements that are still being developed by various organizations.

b) Female headed households—These tend to be more in the urban areas than in the rural areas. Due to the social stigma attached to a female heading a household in the rural areas (either because of divorce, being widowed or never married), such women will migrate to an urban area where there is more anonymity and generally more tolerance. This group, especially those jobless and with children, are poor and most of them live in the squatter settlements discussed above.

c) Street children—This is really a new phenomenon in Kenya's urban areas, especially the major ones like Nairobi, where there is an exploding number of poor children. They will continue to be poor in their adulthood if the situation is not controlled early enough.

Why Are They Poor?

There are various reasons that may explain why the above groups are poor. Some of these reasons are individualistic and cannot be applied wholesale to the groups outlined above. Individualistic causes of poverty, like being orphaned, sickness (physical or mental) being a victim of theft, etc., will not concern us here because no institutionalized program can fully address them. The communal reasons are as follows: landlessness; drought; high fertility rates; poor performance of the national economy; high rates of inflation that have driven many businesses to go under and have diminished the buying power of most Kenyans, driving them below the poverty line; dropping out in school, hence unpreparedness for any worthwhile career that would push one above the poverty line. There are also occasional political upheavals that have led to ethnic clashes in various parts of Kenya leaving the victims below the poverty line due to the losses of livestock or crop harvests that they encountered. Lack of jobs, especially in the urban areas that have witnessed much rural urban migration in the last thirty years of Kenya's political independence has also contributed to growing numbers of the poor.

Where Are the Poor?

The poor are everywhere in Kenya but the majority, approx. 13 million (an estimate by IFAD) live in the rural areas as either smallholder farmers, landless or nomadic pastoralists (IFAD 1992). Those in the urban areas mostly live in the squatter and slum areas of the towns and some in the streets like the street children and some elderly homeless that one encounters in most of the towns in Kenya. Others (2-4 million) live in makeshift shanty towns like the ones in Mathare and parts of Korogocho in Nairobi.

How Can the Poor Be Assisted to a Survival Level?

The various groups I have identified as poor may require different ways to be helped out of their poverty situation. The poor are not homogenous. They are heterogeneous and therefore will call for different approaches to bring them to a level of survival.

The smallholder farmers may require a betterment of their producer prices especially those in cash crop growing areas—be it sugar, tea, cotton or coffee. They also may require that the government "keep off" from controlling prices and instead leave it to the market forces. They may want all restrictions of movements of their farm products to be eliminated to be able to sell what they produce anywhere and to be able to sell at the highest price offered. In 1995, the restrictions on maize movement were lifted by the Kenya government. This was a good sign, but it was long overdue. They may also need subsidy for fertilizer products to increase their yield; this may enable them to reach a level that is above subsistence and possibly above the poverty line. Th rural access roads and the main roads in their localities should be improved, and all-weather roads should be constructed. This will ensure the possibility of their products reaching the markets on time especially if they are perishable vegetables like tomatoes.

The landless, on the other hand, need to be supplied with land or with capital to start a viable small business that can bring an income that will put them above the poverty line. The government may still have land in various parts of the country where such landless could be resettled. A policy of equal distribution of land should be devised and those who acquired land in dubious circumstances should be required to surrender it for fair redistribution to the landless Kenyans. Such heinous acts like the ethnic clashes which rendered more Kenyans landless should be stopped by the government to avoid pushing more Kenyans below survival levels.

The nomadic pastoralists may require huge programs to irrigate their land to make it more productive. They may also require better access to the markets where they could sell their livestock at least before the drought wipes them out.

In the urban areas, more jobs should be created both in the formal and the informal sector. More emphasis should be given to the latter because it appears more promising in creating employment that is decent enough to move people into and beyond survival levels. At least the engagement in some of the *Jua Kali* activities like welding, metal artisans and hair dressing has moved many Kenyans in the last eight years into survival levels. For the female-headed households, I suggest finding ways for them to diversify their trade interests to go beyond selling groundnuts or just vegetables. The women should be made to understand that they could try other entrepreneurial activities, like garment selling, alongside whatever trade they have been involved in. Through training or other kinds of guidance, they should be geared to more lucrative trades like stylish hair dressing, garment making and technical activities like metal artisanry or various mechanics that are today dominated by men. For the street children, a more accommodating school system should be established and special homes and schools for such children should be started. The government and concerned donor agencies would have to put money into such a program that would pay off once responsible youth are brought up off the streets, preparing for a future like other children living at home with their families.

SOME FACTS ABOUT POVERTY IN KENYA

The economy started to decline in the late 1970s and 1980s, and the government became increasingly unable to provide basic services to its citizens, leading large numbers to fall below the poverty line. UNICEF, which has been a leading organization producing research reports on poverty in Kenya in a study on Nairobi found that the government expenditure on water and sewage, basic necessities for most people, decreased by 28 percent per year in the 1980s (UNICEF 1991). In another study, UNICEF has classified the main groups of the poor in Kenya as follows: the pastoralist, small scale farmers, landless rural workers, the urban poor (usually referring to those who live in slums), the homeless and the disabled (UNICEF 1989). The study by the International Fund for Agricultural Development (IFAD) entitled *The State of Rural Poverty: An Inquiry into Causes and Consequences* provides recent comprehensive data on the rural poor in Kenya. This study found that in 1988 there were approximately 18 million people living in the rural area (about 78 percent of the population of Kenya). Of these, 55 per cent are listed as poor, that is living below the poverty line. The absolute numbers of people vulnerable to falling below the poverty line included 10,263,000 smallholder farmers, 2,341,000 landless people and 954,000 nomadic pastoralist (IFAD 1992). Some communities (e.g., the poor nomads) will require other forms of intervention besides small enterprise development programs that are still alien to their lifestyles.

The IFAD study in its profile of the rural poor from a previous study in 1988 found that the poor consisted of 57 percent smallholder farmers, 13 percent landless, 5.3 percent nomadic pastoralist and 3.9 percent small artisans and fishermen. The study also found that households headed by women were 30 percent of the total rural households. During the mid 1980s, 6,302,000 women were living in poverty (IFAD 1992). In terms of maternal mortality according to the same study, an average of 170 women out 100,000 died of childbirth related causes every year from 1980 to 1987. From 1983 to 1987, only 28 percent of women on average gave birth while attended by a trained health worker. It is clear from these facts that women, especially in the rural areas are in deeper levels of poverty, and that poverty programs may have to address more specifically their problems as being unique from those of the men. Besides the statistical information from IFAD, the Food Agricultural Organization (FAO) has classified Kenya as "one of the low income, food-deficit countries" which means that she must often import food (IFAD 1992). This has already been happening in the last few years with the government acknowledging widespread famine and hunger in the country at the beginning of 1997, a famine that still looms wide.

In an attempt to explain what has kept the levels of poverty growing in Kenya, some researchers have turned to the overwhelming inequality in land distribution and the lack of good arable land as part of the answer to the question of continued low agricultural production that may partially explain persistent poverty especially in the rural areas (Mukui, 1990). In the years between 1992-1994, the ethnic clashes in most rural areas (especially the most arable Rift Valley Province in such areas as Molo, Burnt Forest, Pokot, Enosupukia) contributed to a loss of agricultural production and lives. The clashes mainly between the Kalenjin ethnic groups and Non-Kalenjin like the Kikuyu, Luo and Abaluhya incapacitated the resident productivity resulting to an increase among the poor from the affected areas. It is right to conceive that small scale enterprises in those areas were also negatively affected, derailing their potential capability to alleviate poverty. It is very important therefore that even when different researchers or development agencies may be promoting a program like the Small Enterprise Development (SED), the overall political atmosphere in the country should be assessed. Obviously government support would be a bonus to a successful program as it would protect destruction within the affected ethnic clash areas.

Despite efforts to redistribute land after independence, inequality in land ownership in Kenya has continued to be a major factor in rural (and increasingly urban) poverty. Inequality in land and income distribution is in itself a major contributor to the persisting growth of poverty in Kenya. With a Gini coefficient of 0.72, Kenya has one of the highest rates of inequality in the world (UNICEF/GOK 1990). It has also been established that the richest 20 percent of the population in Kenya earns 25 times what the poorest 20 percent earns. The equivalent for Japan, the world's richest country is four times (UNICEF/GOK 1990). The most recent figures on land distribution available from IFAD (for the years 1976 to 1979) show that in terms of income, the lowest 20 percent of the Kenyan population owned 0.2 percent, and the third and fourth quarter owned 4.6 and 11.2 percent of the land, respectively, while the highest 20 percent of the income population owned 84 percent of the land (IFAD 1992). The Human Development Index (HDI) ranks Kenya as a low human development country with an HDI of 0.366 (the highest being one) with a life expectancy of 59.7 years, an adult literacy rate of 69 percent and a real per capita income of US $1,010 (UNDP 1994). The figures and fact discussed here highlighting the systematic inequality in the distribution of available resources explains mainly why the poor in Kenya are yet to move out of poverty. This is particularly the case in the rural areas, but the same can be said of the urban areas, discussed in the next section.

Urban Poverty in Kenya

Large studies on urban poverty in Kenya like the one on rural poverty by IFAD and a few others by UNICEF are lacking. There have been a number of disconnected studies focusing on the informal sector dating back to the internationally renowned International Labor Organization study in Kenya published in 1972 (ILO 1972). More recent studies have focused on small manufacturing and especially women garment makers (King 1996; McCormick 1994); the social networks and the State's role in the informal sector, which I have discussed in earlier chapters; the informal sector in smaller towns like Nakuru (Ngethe and Wahome 1988). These studies, though alluding to the significance of the informal sector in the country's economic welfare, do not directly address themselves to the alleviation of poverty *per se*. Their interest is primarily on low income earners in the urban areas. UNICEF (1991), as was the case above with the rural poor, did an urban study and identified three groups as the urban poor:

a) the poor families with both parents underemployed or unemployed;
b) female headed households; and
c) gangs of street children.

A number of push factors can explain the continuous rural-urban migration, which itself is directly related to the increase of poverty in the urban areas: lack of favorable government pricing policies for agricultural products (farmers are the poorest paid despite hard work and long hours); gender bias in land inheritance forcing many divorced and widowed women to come to the towns; and lack of employment opportunities in the rural areas. Economic reasons mainly account for the ever increasing rural-urban migration in Kenya. This may be explained partly by the assumed expectation that the towns have better economic opportunities than the rural areas. What this assumption suggests is that were there ample economic opportunities in the rural areas, for example, improved farming and an increase in small and micro enterprises, rural-urban migration could be reduced and eventually this would also reduce urban poverty. More women in Kenya are being affected by poor economic conditions and therefore more are migrating to the urban areas than the men. Indeed, according to UNICEF, in recent years, more women than men have been migrating into the towns. The ratio of men to women has been steadily declining and in the near future women could outnumber men in Kenya's big towns (UNICEF 1993). Most of these women have come to the city because they have been divorced, widowed or are young single mothers without any means of support. What this means is that the number of female-headed or -managed households in the urban areas have been steadily increasing. UNICEF estimates that almost one-third of the households in Kenya are headed by women. [Note: "women-managed households" refers to those families where the woman is the primary provider because she is unmarried, widowed or her husband is absent for any period]. In certain slum and squatter settlements in Nairobi such as Mathare, Kibera, Korogocho and sections of Dandora, women-headed households make up 60 to 80 percent. Their households apparently are among the poorest in Nairobi.

UNDP AND GOVERNMENT INVOLVEMENT IN SMALL ENTERPRISE DEVELOPMENT POLICY

In this section, I will examine the involvement of one Development Agencies, particularly UNDP and the government of Kenya in the Small Enterprise Development (SED) nationwide. As a United Nations body, the UNDP can only be involved in any country through the government of the day unlike non-governmental organizations that can go directly to the people. In the last ten years (1986-1996) the Government of Kenya (GOK) has shown more interest in the promotion of small and micro enterprises as evidenced in its Policy Papers like the Sessional Paper No. 1 of 1986, the Sessional paper No. 2 of 1992 and the Development Plan of 1989-1993. All these papers have emphasized the importance of small scale enterprises in the country's economy. There are also a number of government ministries directly involved in implementing assistance programs for the SED programs: the Ministry of Planning and National Development; the Ministry of Technical Training and Technology, particularly the Department of Applied Technology; and the Ministry of Culture and Social Services. The latter has been active in trying to reach women's groups.

Despite the presence of the policy papers I have mentioned and the various ministries, critics like myself find a lack of coordination of the government policy that has usually been very poorly implemented. The same small enterprises as I discussed earlier have suffered at the hands of government security officers who have bulldozed the homes of the entrepreneurs like was the case of Muoroto (Macharia 1992b). Due to a lengthy and inefficient red-tape bureaucracy, small-scale entrepreneurs have had to face many months before acquiring licenses for their operations. They also have to deal with a poor infrastructure, despite the government's rhetoric that it is in their support. This is a perfect illustration of the gap between policy on paper and implementation on the ground. If the small and micro enterprises will be seen to work toward alleviation of poverty as widely perceived, the UNDP in particular because of its favorable leverage with the government will have to request the elimination of some bylaws that perpetually continue to impoverish the poor despite their high entrepreneurial spirit. Examples of such bylaws are those inhibiting trade or different forms of commercial activities in residential areas. Such inhibition effects women, in particular, who make up the largest number of the poor. Without such a bylaw exposing them to irritable arrests, they would be operating small enterprises outside their homes without facing the wrath of the city police, who currently have to arrest them, accusing them of breaking the bylaw. As noted earlier, the harassment toward the street hawkers, garment sellers, etc. that is still common in Nairobi underlines yet another contradiction with the government's commitment to its prolific Sessional papers in support of promoting small and micro-enterprises. Certainly, the impact of the government's promotion of the small enterprise development is not impressive. The government through the various relevant departments should specialize more in taking up a facilitating role, especially by eliminating all the blocking bylaws, some of which date back to colonial days, cleaning up corrupt officers from the system especially in local councils where most of the small scale enterprises start facing problems. Such problems include getting a premise to operate, getting a license where one is required and getting advice on what commodity to sell when and where. These are but a few of the bottlenecks that may hamper the growth of small enterprises and in the end it will slow efforts to alleviate poverty. Positive engagement by the UNDP and the government would be necessary in the overall successful development of the small enterprises.

Specific Role of the Small Enterprise in Poverty Alleviation

As I suggested in the introduction to this chapter, small and micro enterprise development along with further promotion of small scale farming holds the major part of the solution toward alleviating poverty in Kenya. Small enterprises are still doing well economically, even during times of recession. The advantage they have over other activities like farming should be nurtured and promoted further to create business sub-groups, which will eventually create employment as the market sales increase. Small enterprise development as a means to alleviate poverty in Kenya will be *essential* for the following reasons:

a) Due to continued unemployment in both public and private sectors, most people, either educated or uneducated, will turn to small enterprises. *Necessity* will draw people into this direction and, given the lack of starting capital for most people, the majority will inevitably start small! One positive minor contribution with this trend is that the kind of necessity leading families or individuals into small scale enterprises is also indirectly creating a generation of entrepreneurs and creating an entrepreneurial culture where none existed in some communities. The development of such a culture will not only be significant in helping to alleviate poverty now and in the immediate future but, much more, this will be important for the overall economic development of Kenya into the 21st century. Indeed, there are entrepreneurial values that are being formed among Kenyans engaging in small enterprises. Such values include saving, identifying business opportunities and deferring money use for something else considered important in promoting overall development. These values are being acquired by some of the small scale entrepreneurs but will eventually be useful for developing Kenya's economic future and alleviating poverty.

b) More capital could be flowing into the informal markets than in the formal ones and indeed one should not be surprised to learn that the bulk of the credit in the future will be found in the small enterprise development program.

c) Seventy-five percent of all new jobs in Kenya will be in the informal economy (small and micro-enterprises). About 40 percent of the current jobs in Kenya are in the informal economy and at least 14,000 businesses are registered as small enterprises. This goes further to show the inevitability of practically supporting small and micro enterprises development. It is one way of targeting the poor and one with a dynamic promise to alleviate their poverty.

Benefactors of UNDP Intervention

In this section, I examine specific areas of intervention that the UNDP office in Kenya, which was planning to get more involved in the small enterprise development beginning 1994, could contribute.

For the poor in the rural areas, the UNDP through its SED program could intervene as follows:

a) The smallholder farmers who are keen businessmen and women should be supported by arranging for affordable loans. The UNDP either through NGOs or a relevant government department could prepare some of those entrepreneurially-oriented smallholders in deciding which small scale enterprise they would be involved in especially helping with starting capital that most of them lack. The starting capital may be a grant or a loan with a low interest and with a realistic grace period to allow the small business to "take off." The UNDP could also in collaboration with the Kenya government identify certain regions with high potential (but hindered to achieve it due to a poor infrastructure, like roads) improve them to allow quicker access to the markets, which is important for the smallholder farmer.

b) The landless should be a special target for the UNDP's SED program. In the event there is no land available and since the land issue can get to be too politically uncomfortable for UNDP, then giving start-up soft loans for the landless to be engaged in small scale business would be a very germane contribution. The UNDP should identify the landless using local elders or local administrators. They should also interest these landless by being able to give them some technical skills in the local youth polytechnic or such workshops that could be established aimed at reaching the landless and deliberately giving them an alternative lifestyle that could push them to the survival level.

c) The nomadic pastoralist may be a difficult group for the UNDP to introduce any of the SED programs. The government of Kenya should consult with the leaders of the pastoralist groups and know where to put up irrigation schemes as suggested earlier. If the UNDP or other sister agencies, like United Nations Environment Program (UNEP), have the funds to support such programs, then they should do so.

d) The urban unemployed and the underemployed could be assisted through the UNDP's SED program. This would be by giving these people either grants or loans with low interest to start businesses. Most of these people do not have any businesses because they do not have starting capital and do not therefore qualify to receive loans from some of the existing NGOs that usually give loans to those already with a business. The UNDP should consider starting an NGO or funding an existing one to cater to the interests of the poor who need "start-ups" and in most cases those without any collateral. Some training that the UNDP could fund should be given to those who will start the new NGO or to those in the existing ones who will now be required to focus more on the poor who have no existing business yet have the potential.

The UNDP should also continue their discussions with relevant government Ministries to eradicate most of the impediments that hinder the free development of growth of small scale enterprises especially in the urban areas due to existing unfavorable bylaws, for example, no trade activity in a residential area that affects women with small children a lot because they are not able to be mobile due to their home chores to go to the designated trade areas. The UNDP in collaboration with the Directorate of Applied Technology should boost some of the technical training programs, especially at the village and youth polytechnic levels, to give some technical skills because it is apparent that those engaged in small scale enterprises that apply technical skills make more money and are therefore likely to move out of poverty faster than, for example, a hawker or a vegetable seller. The self-reliance an organization like UNDP would want to see among those who come out of poverty may be better achieved through a technical skill. Helping to fund such a program would be a big contribution to the alleviation of poverty within this group and eventually to the rest of the country.

e) The female heads of household need special attention because as women they are generally discriminated by the social-economic structure as it is today in Kenya making it harder for the women to get credit, and therefore to compete fairly with their men counterparts. I suggest the UNDP's SED program design either through training or through occasional workshops ways of deliberately orienting women to more viable business activities depending on the locality identified. These could be hair dressing, garment making, welding, selling hardware goods, etc. which will go beyond the simple trade of vegetables and cooked food that many women in this category are involved in. The UNDP should also establish a grant or a credit scheme special to women in these categories and experts either in existing NGOS or a new one should be trained to be particularly concerned with raising the survival levels of such women. Start-up loans or capital should be established for such women.

f) The street children in the urban areas may not benefit directly from the UNDP's SED program. However, the UNDP could suggest to their sister agency UNICEF to support special school programs and homes for these children as suggested above. Business education and technical education could be introduced in such schools to prepare the children to be self-reliant and to live above survival levels in the future.

Who Will Do What?

To be able to assist the segment of the poor discussed in the above section, the UNDP will need to collaborate closely with the relevant government Ministries: specifically, the Office of the President, especially to reach the local administrators who may be able to identify the landless and the truly needy; the Ministry of Planning and Development, who may have profiles of the poor; and the Ministry of Research, Technical Training and Technology, particularly the Directorate of Applied Technology, which has been in the forefront from the government side "supporting" *Jua Kali* development. I realize UNDP is already funding some of the activities of this Ministry—more funding, especially that requiring more emphasis on those below the poverty line, should be given.

Besides the relevant government Ministries, UNDP should identify existing NGOs like K-REP, PRIDE, NCCK and the Dandora Catholic

Church, with its unique revolving loan for the poor in the slums. The UNDP should re-orient its attention not to those already in business but to those below survival levels. Funding for such training should be given by the UNDP or other interested donors.

The UNDP should seek collaboration with some of the donors that are currently involved in various ways in alleviating poverty in Kenya. It should appeal to those other donors to give grants and low-interest credits and train in the technical areas that are still lacking. Such donors may include the Netherlands Embassy Program on Poverty and Urban Development, GTZ's informal sector program, ODA's program on small scale entrepreneurs and the Ford Foundation's program on community development, to mention but a few.

The UNDP should also approach UN agencies: UNICEF, with its concern for poor street children; HABITAT, to help the poor get better housing in the squatter settlements; and UNEP, to assist those poor nomadic pastoralists that may not fit quite well with UNDP's small SED program. UNDP should also contact the World Bank for possible collaboration, especially given its recent interest in poverty in developing countries.

If the UNDP got seriously involved in the above suggested ways of alleviating poverty and focused on the suggested segments, a positive impact would be forthcoming. We could see many of those Kenyans below the poverty line moving to survival levels and later in progression to comfortable living levels!

CONCLUSIONS AND RECOMMENDATIONS

The small and micro enterprises are already in place in most Kenyan towns and most rural trading centers. Further support and promotion in the recommended ways I suggest below will improve the alleviation of poverty in Kenya. The UNDP and the Government of Kenya as well other interested foreign donors like the Ford Foundation, the Netherlands government through their Nairobi Embassy, the Overseas development Agency (ODA), the United States Aid for International Development (USAID), NGOs like the Kenya Rural Enterprise Programme (K-REP), Promotion of Rural Initiatives and Development Enterprises (PRIDE), Kenya Women Finance Trust (KWFT), Kenya Assistance management programme (K-MAP) and private organizations like the commercial banks, will all have to make their interventions in what I refer to as external inputs toward this sector. These will include the following:

a) Encouraging proper coordination between the government, non-governmental organizations the private sector and the donors in the varied efforts to support the small enterprise development.

b) Supplying the needed infrastructure, especially sheds which are usually the work sites, especially for the *Jua Kali* artisans. The entrepreneurs should be involved in choosing the location, the design and the material used for the shed construction. Modifications relevant to specific areas should be adopted instead of having a uniform shed for the whole country that may not be desirable; for example, a shed on the coast, which is hotter, should be more open and with better ventilation than one in Nairobi or other highland locations.

c) Communication patterns, especially the poor roads that lead to the *Jua Kali* shed locations in most towns—impassable during the rainy season and unbearably dusty during the hot season—make the location unattractive to customers almost all year long. All weather roads need to be constructed in the short distances between the main roads and the sheds. In some sheds like Nairobi's Shauri Moyo, the distance may be as short as half a mile but in rainy, muddy days, this is a disaster and it is not the usual routine for those operating in the sheds. Trucks delivering raw materials cannot reach there and customers are discouraged to go there. This is bad for the business and is in contradiction with a policy that explicitly claims to be in support of small enterprise development.

d) A Business Advisory Center possibly in a local university where research, consulting, hands-on teaching and various design projects could be tried would be an additional external intervention offered by the government with support from the UNDP and other Agencies (foreign or local) interested in poverty alleviation using the small enterprises as the vehicle to achieve that goal.

e) Electrical power, particularly in rural trading centers, which should also be promoted especially to curb the rapid rural-urban migration. There are many welders, carpenters and auto mechanics who would benefit from the presence of electrical power in the rural areas as it would give them new heights in their business endeavors.

f) Ensuring access to credit facilities even to the poor entrepreneurs, some who are seeking start-up capital and not funds for further development of an already existing enterprise. This is very important if programs to alleviate poverty will indeed reach the very needy. Interviews I held with formerly poor people in Dandora, Nairobi, showed that they were able to move from shacks in Mathare to at least a two-bedroom stone house in Dandora due to a loan that was initially given by the City Council of Nairobi and a follow-up one given by the Catholic Church of Dandora. Although credit facilities through social networks have been the norm among small scale entrepreneurs as discussed earlier, an institutionalized system with accessibility for all would be a desirable external intervention.

With the above positive interventions and the internal individualistic motivation of the small scale entrepreneurs, which have not been in question for many Kenyans, small enterprise development would clearly make a major contribution in alleviating poverty nationwide.

10

Conclusion and Policy Recommendations

In this chapter, I summarize the main themes of this book and offer policy recommendations with the emphasis on the first one mainly: the significance of the informal economy in African cities. Migration to these cities and over-urbanization continue to be on the rise partly because the informal economy offers the rural people the prospect of a higher standard of living. This is in comparison to the impoverished rural lifestyles with unemployment, landlessness, famine or drought depending, on the place of origin of the migrants.

The second major theme is that the African city, from its administration to the operation of sections of its economy, runs on social connections/networks. Ethnicity, friendship and kinship networks explain the dynamics of the informal economy (entry, success, labor markets, etc.) and the channels through which the State supports or harasses it. Indeed, a major point of the book has been to argue that the State is responsible for the success of the informal economy even though it started as an unwilling partner and is still shy to show full support across the board for all the sub-sectors of this economy.

The significance of the role of social networks in the informal economy as I have discussed in this book is that it challenges the

argument made by the International Labour Organization (ILO) that
entering the informal economy is easy. According to the ILO, one needs
a minimum amount of capital to start an informal activity. I found that
networks and the support of the State are at least as important as capital
(networks, one can argue, often provide sources of capital). Social
networks assist in three ways:

1. The locations where the informal businesses operate are
   often illegal. Social connections reveal which areas can be
   illegally occupied. The case of the drum sellers showed this.
   All of them reported having been informed of a free space for
   their business by a relative, a co-ethnic or a friend.

2. There are few places to get raw materials. Connections will
   reveal those places. Metal artisans, I saw, rely heavily on
   various kinds of scrap metal and other special materials that
   are found and traded only with the help of co-ethnics and
   friends.

3. Some locations were already "colonized" by some members
   of a specific ethnic group or people from the same rural place
   of origin. This meant that the growth of an activity was not
   as free as one may have expected. Instead, social
   interconnections made things happen. This fact has been
   ignored by students of the informal economy (ILO 1972;
   House 1984). Economists have been mainly concerned with
   the economic gains that the informal sector offers and not
   with the process that led to the "success" of the informal
   economy.

The informal economies in Nairobi and Harare are, therefore,
essentially social. A major contribution of this book is documenting how
the informal economy is network-based. This conclusion holds up well
for the rest of Third World countries where the informal economy has
been reported as thriving in the last decade, especially in Africa (Portes
1986), Latin America (Roberts 1989) and Asia (McGee 1985).

Different social networks contributed in different ways to the
dynamics of the informal economy. Social networks based on kinship
contributed money to establish a small business. Respondents went to
seek financial help from relatives, who were usually willing to give them

small interest-free loans. Establishing credit among the informal economy operators is difficult, especially from formal institutions that require some collateral or at least proof of economic stability and constant income. Informal economy operators usually have irregular incomes and nothing substantive to qualify as collateral.

The financial support of relatives explains part of the growth of the informal economy. Drum sellers, for example, need constant cash because the materials they sell may be available sporadically. Being able to get instant cash to buy the available materials is important. The only source of immediate financial support is relatives. Relatives are the "*informal banks*" of the informal economy operators. The collateral here is usually the blood relations and the trust that may already be established before any financial transaction takes place.

Friends, on the other hand, are not particularly helpful in contributing money to the informal economy operators. They are more helpful in passing on information that is relevant for establishing and developing the business. Friends also offer sound business advice. Most respondents, for example, reported learning of their current sites of operation from a friend. This was the case among all the four sub-sectors I studied, although it was more common among the women food sellers and the metal artisans operating outside the roof shed. Knowledge of where to operate and guidance about where to get raw materials, as well as which customers to attract and the related selling gimmicks, is a significant part of the development of the informal economy. Social networks based on friendship were, then, also crucial and critical to the development of the urban informal economy.

Friendship contributed to the informal economy in another important way. Operators tried to minimize harassment from the police or other law enforcement agencies by establishing friendships with those in the administration, particularly those charged with maintaining law and order in areas that the informal economy was predominant. Several drum sellers, for example, told me of how they made sure that the local chief was their friend. They invited the chief to occasional lunch meetings to foster their ties. The chief himself would approach the drum sellers for donations for a development project. If the latter contributed generously to the chief's request, he would defend their tenure in the places they occupied, pleading and lobbying with his superiors that these people had nowhere else to go and that they had too much property at stake to be evacuated.

In trying to understand types of helpful social networks, I have identified ethnicity as an important variable in itself. Ethnicity may be the basis of kinship networks, if one assumes that all relatives are co-ethnics. I, however, found it necessary to discuss the two, kinship and ethnicity separately, because ethnicity is a sensitive variable (O'Connor 1983) in most African countries. Political leaders, for example, have come to realize that ethnic loyalty has been far stronger than national party loyalties. In some countries like Nigeria, Zimbabwe and Uganda, national political parties are inherently ethnic in composition and character. Zimbabwe's African National Union (ZANU), led by Robert Mugabe, the current president, is predominantly Shona, whereas the Zimbabwe African Peoples Union (ZAPU) led by the ailing Joshua Nkomo is predominantly Ndebele. Indeed, the three major opposition parties that emerged in Kenya in 1992, when multiparty elections were held for the first time since 1963, were ethnic in their composition. These are Ford Kenya (Luo), Democratic Party of Kenya (Kikuyu) and Ford Asili (Kikuyu). Regional composition was a major factor among the Kikuyus, which explains the presence of two Kikuyu parties. It is interesting to note the almost universal acceptance at the macro level that the national parties will be heavily ethnically segregated, but at the micro level when one looks at the informal economy operators, the ethnic segregation is not taken as obvious and indeed there are many who would like to think the contrary (e.g., that there are no ethnic concerns among the metal artisans or the women food sellers). I have made the case here showing how even at the micro level, the ethnic dynamics going on at the macro level have guided entry and survival within chosen informal economy operations.

Ethnic consciousness is still significant in modern African cities, and it is perhaps the strongest force organizing the informal economy in African cities. In Nairobi, I found the metal artisans were not just metal artisans, but they were Kikuyus, Luos or Kambas in their conscience and character of operation. Various skills are dominated by specific ethnic groups. For example, the Luo mainly made wash basins while the Kikuyu mainly made cooking stoves and metal boxes. The space allocation in the roofed shed was also ethnically-oriented: different ethnic groups occupied specific sections of the roof sheds.

My research has shown that there has been informal interaction between state officials and informal sector operators, even when there has been absolutely no official recognition of their work sector. Indeed, social networks alone are not enough to establish and develop informal economic activities. For their continuous growth, the State has to be involved. Except for the illegal or criminal activities, which I did not include in this study, the kinds of activities I studied (drum selling, food selling, garment making and metal artisanry) were all operating in the open. There has been some collaboration between the informal economy operators and some officials usually done in two ways:

1.   Patron-client relationships—This occurs when state officials assist informal sector operators with certain expectations of reciprocation, such as political support during local campaigns for public offices.

2.   Social networks—Ethnicity, kinship or friendship can tie actors in the State and the informal economy. Friendship, for the drum sellers, ensured that government officials allowed drum sellers to continue occupying their present location even though the site was initially illegally occupied. Ethnicity strongly influenced the allocation of food kiosks in the industrial area of Nairobi.

The State, then, is a major actor in the development and growth of the informal economy. As Castells (1986) argues, "the informal sector has little to do with capital but has more to do with the state!" I have shown however, that the State can both support and harass the informal economy and have suggested that social networks in themselves provide the clue for the apparently erratic behavior of the State. The State has fluctuated in its support of the informal economy. As a result, there is much suspicion among informal economy operators concerning the actual motives of the government in its wake of a sudden positive attitude toward them. The garment makers were reluctant to report their incomes because they were in constant fear that the City Council was going to hike their license fees. The respondents I interviewed from the four sub-sectors had their own expectations from the government. I sum them up by giving the expectations of one metal artisan that are fairly representative of the respondents in the different sub-sectors. He had the following four points to make:

1.   The State should leave us alone to conduct our daily business.

2.   The government should pressure banks to lend without

asking for tangible property as collateral.

3.   The government should be more direct in consulting us, especially on loan matters and other problems, instead of being indirect.

4.   The directive by the State that the government bank, Kenya Commercial Bank, ought to devise ways of easing loan programs for the informal economy operators appears to have benefitted other small-scale businessmen who may not have been the ones the president had in mind when he gave the directive.

During the time of my original research (1987-1988), no metal artisan had benefitted from such loans. A year later when I went back to the field, this had not changed. The metal artisans that I talked to about this matter believed there was some corruption going on between the bank officials and the middle-class businessmen who were benefitting from the loan system.   I found a similar pattern in housing programs for low-income groups.   Housing programs, like the site and service schemes, meant to benefit the low-income groups ended up benefitting the middle and upper income groups (Macharia 1985).

I note clearly that the relationship between the State and the informal economy is still a delicate one. It is characterized by suspicion. The weakness of the state organization in Africa and its lack of legitimacy, characterized by both covert and overt corruption and favoritism (e.g., in Mobutu's Zaire (Young 1985; Shatzberg 1988)), may explain the basis of such distrust by the citizens and especially those in the informal sector. Although Kenya's state machinery is more stable than in most other African countries, it is not without corruption and nepotism. Considering these facts, I will now suggest some policy recommendations.

The informal economy in Kenya and Zimbabwe, as well as other Third World nations, must be recognized as an important part of the general economy of those countries.   The complexity, productivity, organization and dynamism of the informal economy have often been ignored by researchers, who have categorized it as a low-income yielding field for unqualified workers.   Sound policies can only be designed once the informal economy is defined on more realistic terms.   That would mean the acknowledgment of its powerful economic potential especially in the cities as well as in the smaller rural towns.

Policymakers in governments and international organizations should recognize the role that the State has had in fostering the informal economy. Knowledge of social networks and their role both in the informal economy, its relationship with the State and the State itself must guide planning. The perception that networks, especially ethnicity, are harmful to overall economic development must be corrected. For once, the positive contribution of ethnicity especially in the informal economic founding and growth ought to be appreciated. My study shows, for instance, how ethnicity helps sectors of the informal economy to navigate and prosper to growth.

Although in this study, I emphasized the importance of the informal economy in Third World economies, I do not see the informal economy as the ultimate alternative to unemployment and underemployment. Governments and private companies should not rely on the existence of the informal economy as a solution to problems. The informal economy is *not* an alternative to destitution for those deprived of access to modern employment (i.e., the formal economy). If the government relaxed its efforts to ensure employment in the country, it would be disastrous for the informal economy, since the latter depends on the market in the formal economy. Clear interdependence and exchange between the two economies form one overall economy for the city and the country. Weakening one should not be the solution. Both should be strengthened, hence, my repeated call for more State support for all the sub-sectors in this economy.

Appendix

INSTITUTE FOR DEVELOPMENT STUDIES
UNIVERSITY OF NAIROBI

THE ROLE OF SOCIAL NETWORKS AND THE STATE IN THE URBAN INFORMAL SECTOR IN NAIROBI

QUESTIONNAIRE NO._____

ENUMERATOR

SUBSECTOR

SURVEY AREA

CONFIDENTIAL

Good Morning/Afternoon,

My name is _____. I am from the Institute for Development Studies, University of Nairobi. We are visiting people in this area and asking them questions about their social networks and how they have assisted them in the informal economic activities in Nairobi. The information will be very useful in understanding how the informal sector operates. Recommendations based on the information you give may be of great assistance to the future of the urban informal sector in Nairobi and other Kenya towns.

I would be grateful if you could help me answering the questions.

Thank you very much.

GENERAL

1. Name of respondent (optional) _____

2. Home district _____

3. When did you come to Nairobi? _____

4. Why did you come to Nairobi? _____

5. Your position in this economic activity?
   Owner   _____
   Employee   _____
   Relative of owner   _____
   Friend of owner   _____
   Other (specify)   _____

6. What kind of economic activity?
   Metal Artisans (specify goods produced)
   Drum Seller
   Food Seller (kiosk)
   Food Seller (outside)
   Garment Maker

7. Describe in more details the main activity in your business.

8. For kiosk owners and government workers only:
   a. Who owns the space that your enterprise is located?
       i.   City Commission
       ii.   Private Owner
       iii.   Other (specify)
   b. If rented, how much money is the rent per month?
       Kshs._____

SOCIAL BACKGROUND

9. Age _____ years

10. Sex: a. Male
             b. Female

11. Marital Status: a. Single
                       b. Married

12. Occupation of spouse   _____

13. Number of children   _____

14. Any other dependents: a. Yes
                             b. No

15. What kind of assistance do you give to your dependents?
     Cash   _____
     Other (specify) _____

16. What did your parents do for their living?
   a. Employed in the civil service
   b. Employed in the private sector
   c. Self-employed in a trade (specify) _____
   d. Peasant/farmer

17.   What level of education did you attain?
  a.   None
  b.   Part primary
  c.   Primary (C.P.E./K.A.P.E.)
  d.   Part secondary

18.   Explain any kind of training that you have had to prepare you for the present occupation.

  _____

19.   How long was the training, if any? _____years/months

20.   Explain whether is was an apprentice or in a formal training school.

  _____

SOCIAL NETWORKS

21.   Some people feel it is important to live close to their relatives and see a lot of them; for others it is not that important. How important is it to you as an individual?
  a.   Very important
  b.   Somewhat important
  c.   Not important at all
  d.   Any other   _____

22.   Who did you know in this city before you arrived?
  a.   Friend(s)
  b.   Relative
  c.   Neighbor in rural home
  d.   Member of some religious group
  e.   Nobody
  f.   Other (specify)   _____

23.   How useful in your opinion were the contacts you had when you
        came to this city?
  a.   Very useful
  b.   Useful
  c.   Somewhat useful
  d.   Not useful at all
        N.A.

24.   How useful were those contacts in helping you find your first job
        or business in Nairobi?
  a.   Very useful
  b.   Useful
  c.   Somewhat useful
  d.   Not useful at all

25.   List about three of your previous occupations before you started
        this one.

        _____

        Explain why you left the last two, or at least the last one.

        _____

  a.   Recall and tell us briefly how you started your present
        occupation.

        _____

  b.   How would rate the social contacts you had in starting your
        present occupation?
        i.   Very useful
        ii.   Useful
        iii.   Somewhat useful
        iv.   Not useful at all

  c.   Which were these social contacts (be specific)?

        _____

26.   In what ways have your friends, relatives, rural neighbors, urban
        neighbors, members of some religious group helped you in
        developing your present business, in the last one year. (Be
        specific).
   a.   Friends   _____
   b.   Relatives   _____
   c.   Rural neighbors   _____
   d.   Urban neighbors _____
   e.   People from some religious group _____
   f.   Other   _____

27.   Which of the following has been of great importance to the
        development of your business? Rank in order of importance.
   a.   Friends
   b.   Relatives
   c.   Capital (personal resources)
   d.   Local politicians
   e.   Other (specify)

28.   If you had a small problem, say you wanted to borrow some
        money for this business or other use, who would you first go to?
        Please be specific. (Note: if respondent gives name, ask
        relationship involved.)

        _____

29.   If the problem is connected with the government, for example,
        harassment by Local Administration or city police, etc. who do
        you go to remedy the problem?

        _____

30.   Do you have friends and relatives in this city?
   a.   Yes
   b.   No

31.   If yes, how often do you contact them for advice or solutions to a problem related to your occupation?

    a.   Friends
- i.   Very often
- ii.   Often
- iii. Rarely
- iv. Never

    b.   Relatives
- i.   Very often
- ii.   Often
- iii. Rarely
- iv. Never

    c.   Others (specify) _____
- i.   Very often
- ii.   Often
- iii. Rarely
- iv. Never

32.   If you had problem establishing your business, how did you overcome them?

    a.   Assistance from friends
    b.   Assistance from relatives
    c.   Assistance from people of the same origin
    d.   Government authorities (specify)

33.   It has been said that to start and develop a business like the one you are now doing, the social contacts you have, e.g., friends, relatives, members of some ethnic group, etc. are more important than the actual money (capital) you have. Do you:

    a.   Strongly agree
    b.   Agree
    c.   Strongly disagree
    d.   Disagree

34.   Explain which of the above was more important in your case.

_____

_____

35.   Do you belong to any social organization?
        a.   Yes
        b.   No

36.   If yes, what is its name?   _____

37.   Was it of any assistance to you when establishing this business
        or any previous one? Give details.

        _____

STATE

38.   Have you had any interaction with any of the following?
        a.   Local chief
        b.   Local district officer
        c.   Police
        d.   Local politicians, e.g., councillor, M.P.
        e.   National politicians
        f.   Any other (specify)

39.   For each of those you have had interaction, specify what form
        the interaction took.

        _____

40.   If you had no interaction with any of the above officials, say
        why this was so.

        _____

41.   Would you say any of the above officials have been of help
        towards your starting and developing this business. Explain
        briefly.

        _____
        _____

42.   Have you received some assistance from the government in
        general that has led to your starting and developing this
        business?
        a.   Yes
        b.   No

43.   If yes, explain what kind.

_____

44.   Have you ever experienced any kind of harassment in your business?
   a.   Yes
   b.   No

45.   If yes, what kind and from where. Please explain.

_____

46.   Has there been any government official that has visited you work place recently? (In the last two years?)
   a.   Yes
   b.   No

47.   If yes, who was it?   _____

48.   What benefits would you say this has given to your business?

_____

49.   If you had problems in starting your business and developing it to what it is now, how did you overcome them?
   a.   Assistance from friends
   b.   Assistance from relatives
   c.   Assistance from people of the same rural origin
   d.   Government authorities (specify)

50.   What three things would you like to see done by the State (Government)?
   a.   To help your business expand
   b.   To help the informal sector in Nairobi to expand

INCOME AND LABOR

51.   What do you consider as your monthly income from this business?
      _____ Kshs.

      (Note: if a respondent responds for the daily or weekly income, compute it for a month.)

52.   How much do you pay yourself as salary per month?
      _____ Kshs.

53.   Supposing you were employed doing the same kind of work that you are now doing, how much money (salary) would you demand per month?
      _____ Kshs.

54.   What is your total monthly expenditure on the following items?
    a.   House
    b.   Fees (education)
    c.   Food
    d.   Clothes
    e.   Salaries to employees
    f.   Transport
    g.   Any other (specify)
       i.   Do you have any other source of income?
         Yes   No

       ii.   Do you own any land, and if so how big is it?

55.   How many people work regularly in this place counting yourself but not counting casual laborers?
      Full time workers   _____
      Part time workers   _____
      Trainees or apprentices   _____
      Total   _____

56.   Do you ever employ casual labor?   Yes   No

57.   If yes, how many casual laborers did you employ last week?

        _____

58.   Are any of the workers members of your family?
        Yes   No

59.   If yes, how many family members are full time employees, part
        time workers, trainees or apprentices?
        Full time workers   _____
        Part time workers   _____
        Trainees or apprentices   _____
        Total   _____

60.   If not family members, is there any other you would consider
        being related to them; for example, friends, people from some
        rural area living in the same residential area here in Nairobi,
        etc. Please specify.

        _____

        _____

61.   What major factors determine the number of persons working
        in this business?
    a. Capital equipment
    b. Good business
    c. Relatives looking for jobs
    d. Friends looking for jobs
    e. Due to limited space
    f. Any other (specify)   _____

                                     _____

References

Anderson, Perry. 1979. *Lineages of the Absolutist State*. London: Verso Editions.

Baker, Charles M., Andrew M. Hamer and Andrew R. Morrison. 1994. *Beyond Urban Bias in Africa: Urbanization in the Era of Structural Adjustment*. Portsmouth, NH: Heinemann.

Barnett, Donald C. and Karari Njama. 1966. *Mau Mau from Within: Autobiography and Analysis of Kenya's Peasant Revolt*. New York: Monthly Review Press.

Blomley, Ray and Chris Gerry, eds. 1979. *Casual Work and Poverty in Third World Cities*. New York: John Wiley and Sons Publishers.

Bloomberg, L. N. and C. Abrams. 1965. *United Nations Mission to Kenya on Housing*. New York: United Nations.

Breese, Gerald (ed.). 1969. *The City In Newly Developing Countries*. Englewood Cliffs, NJ: Prentice Hall.

Bruner, E.M. 1973. Kin and non-kin. Pp. 373-392 in *Urban*

Anthropology, ed. A. Southhall. New York: Oxford.

Calzavazra, Liviana M. 1983. Social network and access to jobs: A study of five ethnic groups in Toronto, Research Paper no.145. Toronto, Center for Urban and Community Studies, University of Toronto.

Capecchi, Vittorio. 1978. *La Piccola Impresa nell'Economia Italiana: Politica del Lavoro e Proposte per il Mezzogiorno nell'Iniziativa del Sindacato*. Bari: De Donato.

_____. 1989. The informal economy and the development of flexible specialization in Emilia-Romagna. Pp. 189-215 in *The Informal economy: Studies in Advanced and Less Developed Countries*, eds. A. Portes, M. Castells and L. Benton. Baltimore, MD: Johns Hopkins University.

Cardoso, Fernardo H. and E. Falletto. 1979. *Dependency and Development in Latin America*. Berkeley: University of California Press.

Castells, Manuel. 1977. *The Urban Question: A Marxist Approach*. London: E. Arnold.

Castells, M. and Portes A. 1986. World underneath: The origins, dynamics and effects of the informal economy. Paper presented at the Informal Economy Conference, October 14, Harper's Ferry, West Virginia.

Clapham, C. 1985. *Third World Politics: An Introduction*. Madison: University of Wisconsin Press.

Cohen, Abner. 1988. The politics of ethnicity in African towns. Pp. 328-337 in *The Urbanization of the Third World*, ed. J. Gugler. Oxford: Oxford University Press.

Daily Nation. 1987. Demolition of food kiosks, 27 December.

_____. 1988. All African games and the need to keep Nairobi clean, 22 July.

_____. 1997. Major cabinet reshuffle in Kenya, 15 January.

Danziger, Sheldon H., Gary D. Sandefur and Daniel H. Weinberg, eds. 1994. *Confronting Poverty: Prescriptions for Change*. Cambridge: Harvard University Press.

Davies, R. 1992. Urban developments. Pp. 149-175 in *Zimbabwe in Transition*, ed. S. Baynham. Stockholm: Almqvist and Wiksell.

De Soto, Hernando. 1987. *The Other Path: The Invisible Revolution in the Third World*. New York: Harper and Row Publishers.

Dinesen, Isak (Karen Blixen). 1937. *Out of Africa*. London: Putnam Press.

Drakakis-Smith, David. 1987. *The Third World City*. London: Methuen.

_____, ed. 1990. *Economic Growth and Urbanization in Developing Areas*. London: Routledge.

Due Jean, M. and Gladwin H. Christina. 1991. Impacts of Structural Adjustment Programs on African women farmers and female-headed households. *American Journal of Agricultural Economics* 93:30-61.

Epstein, A. L. 1969. The network and urban social organization. Pp. 77-113 in *Social Networks in Urban Situations*, ed. J. C. Mitchell. Manchester: University Press.

Faruque, Rashid. 1983. *Population and Development*. Washington D.C.: Development Economics Department, East African Country Programs Department, World Bank.

Fischer, Claude S, ed. 1977. *Networks and Places*. New York: Free Press.

_____. 1984. *The Urban Experience*. New York: Harcourt Brace Jovanovich.

Frank, Andre G. 1967. *Capitalism and Underdevelopment in America:*

Historical Studies of Chile and Brazil. New York: Monthly Review Press.

Freeman, Donald B. 1991. A City of Farmers: Informal Urban Agriculture in the Open Spaces of Nairobi, Kenya. Montreal: McGill-Queen's University Press.

Geertz, Clifford. 1973. *The Interpretation of Culture: Selected Essays.* New York: Basic Books.

Gluckman, M. 1960. *Custom and Conflict in Africa.* Oxford: Blackwell.

Granovetter, Mark S. 1974. *Getting a Job: A Study of Contacts and Careers.* Cambridge, MA: Harvard University Press.

Greiner, Guillermo and Alex Stepick, ed. 1992. *Miami Now: Immigration, Ethnicity, and Social Change.* Gainesville: University Press of Florida.

Grosh, Barbara and R. Mukandara. 1994. *State Owned Enterprises in Africa.* Boulder, CO: L. Rienner Publishers.

Gugler, Josef. 1988. Overurbanization reconsidered. Pp. 74-92 in *The Urbanization of the Third World*, ed. J. Gugler. Oxford: Oxford University Press.

Gugler, Josef and W. Gilbert. 1982. *Urbanization in Developing Countries.* New York: Academic Press.

Hake, Andrew. 1977. *African Metropolis: Nairobi's Self Help City.* New York: St. Martin's Press.

Hart, Keith. 1973. Informal income opportunities and urban employment in Ghana. *Journal of Modern African Studies* 11:61-89.

House, J. W. 1984. Nairobi's informal sector: Dynamic entrepreneurs or surplus labor. *Economic Development and Cultural Change* 32(2):277-302.

Hyden, G. 1983. *No Shortcut to Progress.* Berkeley: University of California Press.

International Fund for Agricultural Development. 1992. *The State of the World Poverty: An Inquiry into Its Causes and Consequences.* New York: New York University Press.

International Labor Organization. 1972. *Employment. Incomes and Employment: A Strategy for Increasing Productive Employment in Kenya.* Geneva: International Labor Organization.

_____. 1991. *The Dilemma of the Informal Sector, 1991. Report of the Organization Director-General (Part 1).* Geneva: International Labor Office.

Jellinek, Lea. 1988. The changing fortunes of a Jakarta street trader. Pp. 204-224 in the Urbanization of the Third World, ed. J. Gugler. Oxford: Oxford University Press.

Khundker, Nasreen. 1988. The fuzziness of the informal sector: Can we afford to throw away the baby with the bath water? *World Development* 16:1253-1265.

King, Kenneth. 1977. *The African Artisan: Education and the Informal Sector in Kenya.* London: Teachers College Press.

_____. 1979. Skill acquisition in the informal sector of an African economy: The Kenya case. *Journal of Development Studies* 11(2):1975.

_____. 1996. *Jua Kali Kenya: Change and Development in an Informal Economy 1970-1995.* London: James Currey.

Kinyanjui, M. N. 1996. Entrepreneurial characteristics, motives and small and medium sized enterprises formation and development in Central Kenya. *Small Enterprises: Flexibility and Networking in an African Context,* eds. D. McCormick and P. Pedersen. Nairobi, Kenya: Longhorn.

Kitching, Gavin. 1980. *Class and Economic Change in Kenya: The Making of an African Petite-Bourgeoisie.* New Haven: Yale University

Press.

Landel-Mills Pierre.   1992.   Governance, cultural change, and employment. *Journal of Modern African Studies* 30(4):543-568.

Langdon, Steven. 1981. *Multinational Corporations in the Political Economy of Kenya.* New York: St. Martin's Press.

Lauguerre, Michel. 1994. *The Informal City.* New York: St. Martin's Press.

Leys, Colin.   1975.   *Underdevelopment in Kenya: The Political Economy of Neo-Colonialism, 1964-1971.* Berkeley: University of California Press.

Light, Ivan. 1972. *Ethnic Enterprise in America: Business and Welfare Among Chinese, Japanese, and Blacks.* Berkeley: University of California Press.

Light, Ivan and Edna Bonacich.   1988.   *Immigrant Entrepreneurs: Koreans in Los Angeles, 1965-1982.* Berkeley: University of California Press.

Lomnitz, L. 1974. The social and economic organization of a Mexican shanty town. Pp. 242-263 in *The Urbanization of the Third World*, ed. J. Gugler. Oxford: Oxford University Press.

_____. 1977. *Networks and Marginality: Life in a Mexican Shanty Town.* New York: Academic Press.

Lubell, Harold. 1990. Resilience amid crisis: The informal sector of Dakar. *International Labor Review* 129(3):387-396.

_____. 1991. *The Informal Sector in the 1980s and 1990s.* Washington D.C.: OECD Publications and Information Centre.

Lugalla, Joe.   1995.   *Crisis Urbanization and Urban Poverty in Tanzania.* Lanham, MD: University Press of America.

Mabogunje, Akin. 1972. *Regional Mobility and Resource Development in West Africa.* Montreal: McGill-Queen's University Press.

Macharia, Kinuthia. 1985. Housing Policy in Kenya—the view from the bottom: A survey of low-income residents in Nairobi and Thika. *International Journal of Urban and Regional Research* 9(3):405-420.

_____. 1989. The role of social networks and the state in the urban informal sector: The case of Nairobi, Kenya. Ph.D. diss., Department of Sociology, University of California, Berkeley.

_____. 1991. On slum clearance and its relevance to the informal economy in Nairobi, Kenya. Paper presented at the Symposium on Technology, Culture and Development in the Third World: Examples and Lessons from Africa, May, Ohio State University, Columbus, Ohio.

_____. 1992a. Occupational health risks among *Jua Kali* operators: A Plan of action by the year 2000. Paper presented at the Third *Jua Kali* Exhibition Symposium, November, Golf Hotel, Kakamega.

_____. 1992b. Slum clearance and the informal economy in Nairobi. *Journal of Modern African Studies* 30(2):221-236.

Mattera, Philip. 1985. *Off the Books: The Rise of the Underground Economy.* New York: St. Martin's Press.

Mazumdar, D. 1976. The urban informal sector. *World Development* 4:655-79.

McClelland, David. 1961. *The Achieving Society.* Princeton, NJ: Van Nostrand.

McCormick, Dorothy. 1994. Women in business: Class and Nairobi's small and medium-sized producers. *Courtyards, Markets, City Streets: Urban Women in Africa,* ed. K. Sheldon. Boulder, CO: Westview Press.

McGee, Terry G. 1985. Mass markets, little markets. Some preliminary thoughts on the growth of consumption and its relationship to urbanization: A case study of Malaysia. Pp. 205-234 in *Markets and Marketing. Monographs in Economic Anthropology, no. 4.* New York: University Press of America.

Medard, J. F. 1982. The underdeveloped state in tropical Africa: Political clientelism or neo-patrimonialism? Pp.162-192 in *Private Patronage and Public Power: Political Clientelism in the Modern State.*, ed. C. Clapham. New York: St. Martin's Press.

Miller, Norman N. 1984. *Kenya: The Quest for Prosperity.* Boulder, CO: Westview Press.

Mingione, Enzo. 1991. *Fragmented Societies: A Sociology of Economic Life Beyond the Market Paradigm.* Cambridge, MA.: Blackwell.

Mitchell, J. C. 1969. *Social Networks in Urban Situations.* Manchester: Manchester.

Moser, C. O. 1984. The informal sector reworked: Viability and vulnerability in urban development. *Regional Development Dialogue* 5(2):135-178.

Mukui, J. T., ed. 1979. *Price and Marketing Controls in Kenya: Papers Presented at a Workshop Held at the Institute for Development Studies of the University of Nairobi, 26-29 March, 1979.* Nairobi: IDS, University of Nairobi.

_____. 1990. Income distribution in Kenya: A preliminary analysis. Report prepared for the USAID, USAID, Nairobi.

Nan, Lin and Peter Marsden. 1982. *Social Structure and Network Analysis.* Beverly Hills: Sage.

Ndua, G. and N. Ngethe. 1984. Education, training and welfare in the informal sector: A study of carpentry and metal work in the Eastlands of Nairobi, Kenya (Report for Undugu Society of Kenya). Working paper, Institute for Development Studies, University of Nairobi, Nairobi.

Nelson, Nici. 1979. How women and men get by: The sexual division of labour in the informal sector of a Nairobi squatter settlement. Pp. 183-203 in *Casual Work and Poverty in Third World Cities*, eds. R. Blomley and C. Gerry. New York: John Wiley and Sons Publishers.

Ngethe, N. and J. Wahome. 1989. The rural informal sector in Kenya: A study of micro-enterprises in Nyeri, Meru, Uasin Gishu and Siaya districts, IDS Occasional Paper No. 54. Working paper, University of Nairobi, Nairobi.

Nientied, Peter and Jan Van der Linden. 1985. Approaches to housing in the Third World. *International Journal of Urban and Regional Research* 9(3):311-329.

O'Connor, A. M. 1983. *The African City.* London: Hutchinson University Library.

Park, Robert E. 1952. *Human Communities: The City and Human Ecology.* Glencoe, IL: Free Press.

Parker, J. and C. Aleke-Dondo. 1991. Kibera's small enterprise sector: Baseline survey report, Gemini working paper no.17. Working paper, Gemini, Bethesda, MD.

Parsons, Talcott. 1966. *Societies: Evolutionary and Comparative Perspective.* Englewood Cliffs, NJ: Prentice-Hall.

Peattie, Lisa Redfield. 1987a. An idea in good currency and how it grew: The informal sector. *World Development* 15:851-860.

_____. 1987b. *Planning, Rethinking Ciudad Guayana.* Ann Arbor: University of Michigan Press.

Perlman, Janice. 1976. *The Myth of Marginality: Urban Poverty and Politics in Rio de Janeiro.* Berkeley: University of California Press.

Portes, A., S. Blitzen and J. Curtis. 1986. The urban informal sector in Uruguay: Its internal structure, characteristics and effects. *World Development* 14:727-741.

Portes, Alejandro, Manuel Castells and Lauren Benton, eds. 1989. *The Informal Economy: Studies in Advanced and Less Developed Countries.* Baltimore, MD: Johns Hopkins University Press.

Portes, Alejandro and Saskia Sassen-Koob. 1987. Making it

underground: Comparative material on the informal sector in Western market economies. *American Journal of Sociology* 93:30-61.

Portes, A. and J. Walton. 1983. *Labor, Class and the International System*. New York: Academic Press.

PREALC. 1976. *The Employment Problem in Latin America*. Santiago: Economic Commission for Latin America.

Preston-Whyte , Eleanor and Christian Rogerson, eds. 1991. *South Africa's Informal Economy*. Cape Town: Oxford University Press.

Putnam, Robert D., Robert Leonardi and Raffaello Nanaetti. 1993. *Making Democracy Work: Civic Tradition in Modern Italy*. Princeton, NJ: Princeton University Press.

Republic of Kenya. 1974. *The Development Plan 1974-1977*. Nairobi: Government Printer.

_____. 1978. *The Development Plan 1978-1983*. Nairobi: Government Printer.

_____. 1979. *Kenya Population Census*. Nairobi: Government Printer.

_____. 1984. *The Development Plan 1984-1988*. Nairobi: Government Printer.

_____. 1986a. *Economic Management for Renewed Growth, Sessional Paper No. 1*. Nairobi: Government Printer.

_____. 1986b. *Central Bureau of Statistics (CBS) 1986*. Nairobi: Government Printer.

_____. 1987. *The Economic Survey*. Nairobi: Government Printer.

_____. 1988. *Economic Survey*. Nairobi: Government Printer.

_____. 1991. *Development and Employment in Kenya, Sessional Paper No. 1*. Nairobi: Government Printer.

_____. 1992a. *Economic Survey*. Nairobi: Government Printer.

_____. 1992b. *Small Enterprise and Jua Kali Development in Kenya, Sessional Paper No. 2*. Nairobi: Government Printer.

_____. 1995. *Kenya Statistical Abstract 1995*. Nairobi: Government Printer.

_____. 1996. *Economic Survey*. Nairobi: Government Printer.

Richardson, Harry. 1984. The role of the urban informal sector: An overview. *Regional Development Dialogue* 5(3):3-40.

Roberts, Bryan. 1978. *Cities of Peasants*. London: Sage.

_____. 1989. Employment structure, life cycle, and life chances: Formal and informal sectors in Guadalajara. Pp. 41-59 in *The Informal Economy. Studies in Advanced and Less Developed Countries*, ed. A. Portes, M Castells and L. A. Benton. Baltimore, MD: The Johns Hopkins University Press.

Rostow, Walt W. 1960. *The Stages of Economic Growth: A Non-Communist Manifesto*. Cambridge, England: University Press.

Rothchild, Donald. 1973. *Racial Bargaining in Independent Kenya: A Study of Minorities and Decolonization*. London: Oxford University Press.

_____. 1984. Social incoherence and the mediatory role of the State. Pp. 99-125 in *African Security Issues: Sovereignty, Stability, and Solidarity.*, ed. Bruce E. Arlinghaus. Boulder: Westview Press.

Rothchild, Donald and Victor Oluonsola. 1983. *The State Versus Ethnic Claims: African Policy Dilemmas*. Boulder, CO: Westview Press.

Saito, Katrine. 1990. *The Informal Sector in Zimbabwe: The Role of Women. Report no.9006-ZIM*. Washington, D.C.: World Bank.

_____. 1991. Women and microenterprise development in Zimbabwe: Constraints to development. Paper presented at the Annual Meeting of the African Studies Association, November, St. Louis, MO.

Sandbrook, Richard. 1982. *The Politics of Basic Needs: Urban Aspects of Assaulting Poverty in Africa*. London: Heinemann.

Saskia, Sassen-Koob. 1989. New York's informal economy. Pp. 60-77 in *The Informal Economy. Studies in Advanced and Less Developed Countries*, ed. A. Portes, M Castells and L. A. Benton. Baltimore, MD: The Johns Hopkins University Press.

Sennett, Richard. 1969. *Classic Essays on the Culture of Cities*. Englewood Cliffs, NJ: Prentice Hall.

Sethruman, S. V. 1981. *The Urban Informal Sector in Developing Countries*. Geneva: International Labor Office.

Shack, W. A. 1973. Urban ethnicity and the cultural process of urbanization in Ethiopia. Pp.251-286 in *Urban Anthropology*, ed. A. Southhall. New York: Oxford University Press.

Shartzberg, Michael. 1988. *The Dialectics of Oppression in Zaire*. Bloomington: Indiana University Press.

Simmel, G. [1905] 1969. The metropolis and mental life. Reprint, pp. 47-60 in *Classic Essays on the Culture of Cities*, ed. R. Sennett, Englewood Cliffs. NJ: Prentice-Hall (page citations are to the reprint edition).

Sjoberg, Gideon. 1960. *The Preindustrial City, Past and Present*. Glencoe, IL: Free Press.

Skocpol, Theda. 1985. Bringing the state back in: Strategies of analysis in current research. Pp. 3-43 in *Bringing the State Back In*, ed. P. Evans, D. Rueschemeyer and T. Skocpol. Cambridge: Harvard University City Press.

Smelser, Neil J. 1971. Stability, instability and the analysis of political corruption. Pp. 7-29 in *Stability and Social Change.*, eds. Barber Bernard and Alex Inkeles. Boston: Little, Brown and Company.

Smelser, Neil J. 1991. Conversation with the author. Berkeley, CA, 12 June.

Soja, Edward W. 1970. *The African Experience.* Evanston: Northwestern University Press.

Southhall, A. 1973. *Urban Anthropology: Cross-cultural Studies of Urbanization.* New York: Oxford University Press.

The Standard. 1982. Dissolution of city council, 19 October.

Standing, Guy. 1989. The "British Experiment": Structural adjustment or accelerated decline? Pp. 279-297 in *The Informal Economy. Studies in Advances and Less Developed Countries,* eds. A. Portes, M. Castells and L. A. Benton. Baltimore: Johns Hopkins University Press.

Stren, Richard E. 1978. *Housing the Urban Poor in Africa.* Berkeley, CA: Institute of International Studies, University of California.

_____. 1994. Urban research in Africa, 1960-92. *Urban Studies* 31(415):729-743.

Stren, Richard E. and Rodney White. 1989. African Cities in a Crisis: Managing Rapid Urban Growth. Boulder, CO: Westview Press.

Sunita, K., M. Manudu and D. Lamba. 1982. *The Matatu Mode of Public Transport in Metropolitan Nairobi.* Nairobi: Mazingira Institute.

Tinker, Irene. 1982. *Gender Equity in Development: A Policy Perspective.* Washington, D.C.: Equity Policy Center.

Tomecko, J. and C. Aleke-Dodo. 1992. Improving the growth potential of the small scale and informal sectors. Report prepared for the World Bank Economic Memo, Nairobi.

United Nation's Children's Fund (UNICEF). 1984. *Situation Analysis of Children and Women in Kenya: Section 1. Some determinants of Well Being.* Nairobi: Central Bureau of Statistics, Ministry of Finance and Planning.

_____. 1991. *Challenges of Children and Women in the 1990s: Eastern and Southern Africa Profile*. Nairobi: Eastern and South African Regional Office.

United Nation's Children's Fund (UNICEF) and Government of Kenya. 1992. *Children and Women in Kenya: Situational Analysis*. Nairobi: UNICEF.

Wallerstein, Immanuel M. 1974. *The Modern World System*. New York: Academic Press.

_____. 1984. *The Politics of the World; The Movements and the Civilization: Essays*. New York: Cambridge University Press.

Weber, Max. 1905 (1958). *The City*. Glencoe, IL: Free Press.

_____. 1968. *Economy and Society*. New York: Bedminster Press.

Weekly Review. 1983. The new city commission, 5 June.

_____. 1995. Third international airport, 17 June.

Weingrod, Alex. 1968. Patrons, patronage and political parties. *Comparative Studies in Society and History* 10:376-400.

Weiss, Linda. 1988. *Creating Capitalism: The State and Small Business Since 1945*. Oxford: Basil Blackwell.

Werlin, Herbert H. 1965. The Nairobi city council: A study in comparative local government. *Comparative Studies in Society and History* 8:192.

White, Luise. 1990. *The Comforts of Home: Prostitution in Colonial Nairobi*. Chicago: University of Chicago Press.

Wilson , Julius W. 1987. *The Truly Disadvantaged*. Chicago: University of Chicago Press.

Wirth, L. 1938. Urbanism as a way of life. Reprinted in *Classic Essays on the Culture of Cities*, ed. R. Sennett. Englewood Cliffs, NJ: Prentice-

Hall, 1969, 143-164. First published in *American Journal of Sociology* 44:3-24, 1938.

World Bank. 1983. *Kenya. A Country Study.* Washington, D.C.: The World Bank.

Young, Crawford, ed. 1985. *The Rise and Decline of the Zairean State.* Madison: University of Wisconsin Press.

_____. 1982. *Ideology and Development in Africa.* New Haven: Yale University Press.

Zimbabwe. 1986. First Five-Year Development Plan 1986-1990, Vol. 1 Harare: Government Printer.

Index

ABOUT THE AUTHOR

Kinuthia Macharia is currently a professor in the Sociology Department at American University, Washington, D.C. Before arriving at American University in the Fall of 1995, he was a professor in the Sociology Department at Harvard University, Cambridge, MA, between 1990 and 1995. He came to study in the United States on a Fulbright scholarship and earned his Masters and Ph.D. degrees from the University of California at Berkeley in 1989. Prior to that he had earned his BA (First Class Honors) from the University of Nairobi, Kenya, where he received the Ghandi Smarak Prize and the Shell Prize as the top student in the Faculty of Arts in 1980. His research on urban problems and development in Africa has been published in renowned refereed journals like the *International Journal of Urban and Regional Research* and the *Journal of Modern African Studies*. He has been a consultant for the UNDP, the Ford Foundation, the Government of Kenya, the World Bank and the Population Council.